1/98

D0025394

Civil War
Generalship

CIVIL WAR GENERALSHIP

The Art of Command

W. J. Wood

PRAEGER

Westport, Connecticut
London

Library of Congress Cataloging-in-Publication Data

Wood, W. J. (William J.), 1917–
    Civil War generalship : the art of command / W. J. Wood.
      p. cm.
    Includes bibliographical references and index.
    ISBN 0–275–95054–9 (alk. paper)
    1. United States—History—Civil War, 1861–1865—Campaigns.
2. Command of troops—History—19th century. 3. United States.
Army—History—Civil War, 1861–1865. 4. Confederate States of
America. Army—History. 5. Military art and science—United
States—History—19th century. I. Title.
  E470.W877 1997
  973.7'3—dc20   96–28548

British Library Cataloguing in Publication Data is available.

Library of Congress Catalog Card Number: 96–28548
ISBN: 0–275–95054–9

First published in 1997

Praeger Publishers, 88 Post Road West, Westport, CT 06881
An imprint of Greenwood Publishing Group, Inc.

Printed in the United States of America

The paper used in this book complies with the
Permanent Paper Standard issued by the National
Information Standards Organization (Z39.48–1984).

10 9 8 7 6 5 4 3 2 1

for Barbara

Contents

Illustrations

FIGURES

DRAWINGS AND PHOTOGRAPHS

Preface

At a time when American military leaders are confronting the problem of developing global strategies that were inconceivable less than a decade ago, it may seem less than useful to look back to our Civil War for direction in guiding military thought for the future. Yet it may prove instructive to recall that *two* American nations were engaged in the greatest war, in terms of both manpower and human sacrifice, that Americans have ever had to fight—including the two World Wars. With that recollection it is also useful to recognize that, for the first time in our history, massed armies, made up of hundreds of thousands of civilian soldiers, had to be organized and trained to fight a war in which both sides were determined to settle for nothing less than total military victory. And when those armies were led to battle, the leaders on both sides were confronted with problems of strategy and tactics that were as inconceivable as had been their war less than a decade before. How those leaders dealt with those problems became the subject and the substance of this writing. To describe the legacy that their military thought leaves for future leaders then became the goal of this book; whether that goal has been attained is left to the judgement of the reader.

The journey toward the goal takes the form of an exploration through five progressive parts. Part One defines the underlying problem that the commanders of both Union and Confederate forces had to come to grips with and maps the ground for the exploration of an art of command which the commanders in question had to create for themselves. Parts Two, Three, and Four present the campaigns and battles wherein the reader can observe the commanders as each confronted his opponent and used his art to conduct his campaign and fight its climactic battle. Part Five reviews the character of each of the six commanders as it affected his development of an art of command, and ends by presenting conclusions regarding the legacy left by the founders of a pragmatic art.

Acknowledgments

In expressing gratitude for the help I've gotten throughout the pains of producing this book, I find it fairer to reverse the traditional order of things and first thank my wife, Barbara, for the continued support, material and inspirational, without which this work would never have been completed.

I owe a great deal to Laurence Hull and Elizabeth Clontz of the Cannon Memorial Library in Concord, North Carolina for obtaining and processing the hundreds of sources so essential to the research upon which the factual material of this work depends; my obligation for their services can never be expressed in mere words. In like manner, I am indebted, as always, to Martin L. ("Marty") Wilkerson for his patience and cartographical skills in converting my words and crude drafts into the finished maps and figures that help the reader to follow the turn of events in the campaigns and battles. So also my debts extend to the professional skills, patience, and plain human understanding of my editor Daniel Eades and his colleagues Jason Azze and Scott Wich at the Greenwood Publishing Group. Another professional to whom I am indebted is my computer consultant—guru if you will—Timothy Smith, who, on less than memorable occasions, prevented me from taking an axe to my computer and its associated hardware and software, thus saving this creation for whose shortcomings and imperfections I alone remain responsible.

PART ONE

THE SANDWICHED WAR

The best way I know of persuading you of anything is not to plead with you to trust me, not to invoke authority in general, to even call upon some expert, but to show you just what it is that persuaded me.
—Dr. Philip Morrison, Massachusetts Institute of Technology

CHAPTER 1

The American Civil War in Western History

"I want Pope to be suppressed." Those six words were the essence of Robert E. Lee's orders to Stonewall Jackson, already itching to strike out on his own in independent command against a new opponent in a campaign just beginning to take shape. In this fateful summer of 1862 the month of July had seen the ending of the Seven Days Battles, in which Lee had thrown back McClellan's overcautious advance against Richmond, as well as the stalemate that followed.

Now, on 27 July as he was writing his orders to Jackson, Lee had begun to conceive the strategy he would employ to keep McClellan off balance while he and Jackson jointly took the strategic offensive against Union forces in northern Virginia. An essential element of that strategy had been Lee's doubling the strength of Jackson's corps to 24,000 while Lee continued to hold at bay McClellan's army in its bases on the Peninsula between the York and James Rivers east of Richmond (see Map 1.1). To an ordinary general, Lee's present situation would have seemed nothing less than precarious, as he faced McClellan's army of 90,000 with a Confederate army only two-thirds the strength of his enemy's. But to Robert E. Lee it presented the opportunity to strike at the newly formed Union army under General John Pope, who was already beginning to deploy it in a manner that could threaten Virginia from the north. Yet how could Lee conceive such a daring plan in his present situation?

In essence, Lee's plan, as it grew from conception to action, was to depend upon reinforcing Jackson (as he was now doing) while Lee slipped away from his confrontation with McClellan and moved the bulk of his army northward to outmaneuver Pope and destroy his newly created army before McClellan or any other major Union force could react in time to counter his strategy.

Map 1.1

Courtesy Martin L. Wilkerson.

That is why Lee's orders of 27 July to Jackson ("I want Pope to be suppressed") were followed on 7 August by Lee's additional instructions, which contained assurance of his confidence in Jackson's ability to act on his own while Lee was keeping McClellan occupied during the initial phase of his overall strategic maneuver: "Being on the spot you must determine what force to operate against. . . . I must now leave the matter to your reflection and good judgement. Make up your mind what is best to be done under all the circumstances which surround us and let me hear the result at which you arrive. I will inform you if any change takes place here [east of Richmond] that bears on the subject."

Even before he had received either of Lee's letter orders Jackson had already seized the initiative and moved his corps north to Gordonsville, the strategic point where three vital railroads converged from south, east, and north. The bold move was a symbol of Jackson's style of acting swiftly and decisively in independent command. The hawk had been loosed from the falconer's wrist and was seeking out his prey.

On 7 August, the same day that Lee was writing his latest letter order to Jackson, the latter was reviewing his latest intelligence sources—a patchwork made up mainly of spies and loyal country folk—and confirmed that his adversary, Pope, had started advancing a sizeable portion of his forces to Culpeper, about twenty-five miles to Jackson's north. The intelligence had also convinced Jackson that Pope's advance elements in and around Culpeper were presenting him with an opportunity that fitted his offensive style. By a sudden blow he could destroy Pope's advance force before Pope could concentrate his whole army.

In characteristic fashion, following his personal evaluation of the intelligence, decision followed reflection. No time was lost in framing and sending out the orders which would start the long columns of Confederate infantry uncoiling from their bivouacs to raise clouds of choking dust along the Virginia roads in the scorching heat of August.

Two days later and miles to the north a Union general was coming to terms with a decision that could bring him to a confrontation with his enemy approaching from the south. Major General Nathaniel Banks, commanding the II Corps of Pope's army, had just listened to the verbal orders from Colonel Louis Marshall, a senior aide dispatched by General Pope. Banks had listened with growing irritation, realizing that the orders were of too critical a nature to be received in such a fashion, and directed Marshall to dictate them to a staff officer who wrote them down:

General Banks to move to the front immediately, assume command of all forces in the front, deploy his skirmishers if the enemy advances, and attack him immediately as he approaches, and be reenforced from here.

Now, if the reader could be enabled to look back from his vantage point at this picture of opposing Civil War generals moving toward battle, he should be aware of the late twentieth-century "advantages" that Civil War commanders would not have had at hand—or couldn't have conceived in their fondest dreams. Just what sort of material advantages would our two commanders (and all their peers) have been lacking?

In the first place they would have no electronic technology under their command: no telephones, radios, or computers, and no airborne or ground surveillance systems to observe the movements of enemy forces. And obviously air support would be out of the question; after all, the Wright brothers wouldn't arrive at Kitty Hawk for another forty-one years. Nor would there be motor transport of any kind to move troops, and the soldiers wouldn't be able to rely on long-range artillery fires to cover them when they were committed to combat.

The inventory of missing advantages could go on and on, but there were equally serious shortfalls on the human side. No cadres had been made available—no professional officers and noncommissioned officers—at the outset of the war to provide the training, battle discipline, and backbone so essential to fielding battle-ready companies and regiments. Nor could either commander count on having a professional staff to carry out the tasks so vital to the command and control of his forces, made up of thousands of men.

Finally, there was the lack so painfully felt at higher levels of command, dating from the earliest days of the war, the heartfelt need which rides every senior commander's back like Sinbad's Old Man of the Sea. Each was keenly aware of his want of the military education and experience requisite to the command of large forces in war. So it was inevitable that the generals we have observed, like their officers and soldiers, had to learn their trade in the hard school of war. Unlike their soldiers, however, our generals had to carry that most stressful of burdens, the ultimate responsibility for mistakes, measured in the toll of dead and wounded. In view of all these shortcomings, we today feel entitled to ask what conditions prevailed to put the opposing commanders in such a fix. Indeed, what kind of a war brought about such conditions?

These questions are best addressed by taking up the latter first. Since this book is concerned with an aspect of Western history, it isn't too much to ask that the place of the American Civil War be clearly seen in that context. Unfortunately, the *real* place has been blurred by historians who continue to label the war as the "first modern war." The label has stuck, because the war, in that way of characterizing it, supposedly determined the nature of future war, especially that of the First World War. When the characterization is examined objectively, however, it is revealed as a focus on inventions which were conceived just before or during the war: rifled small arms and artillery, the machine gun, the telegraph, the armored warship, aerial observation (the balloon), and the strategic use of railroads—to name a few.

The misleading label has gained acceptance at the expense of the influence of military thought on military leaders who had to fight the war. Moreover, that acceptance has skewed our twentieth-century way of looking at the war, so that we fail to see it in a meaningful perspective: as a war sandwiched between the end of the Napoleonic Wars and the wars that Prussia fought in 1866 (the Austro–Prussian War) and 1870–1871 (the Franco–Prussian War) to make possible a united and imperial Germany. The true perspective is not a simplistic way of adhering to a chronology; instead it allows one to view realistically the rightful place of the American Civil War in Western history. Of equal importance, it serves to clear away two other misconceptions.

First, the war did not, in itself, produce the tools that shaped modern warfare. It simply provided some rudimentary forms which had to be redrawn on the tactical drawing board before they could influence the outcome of battles. The draftsmen who made the basic transformation were the reformers of the Prussian army whose efforts in the mid-nineteenth century—under the military eye of Moltke and the political backing of Bismarck—resulted in the victories over Austria and France that astounded the participants as well as the rest of Europe. In actuality, the mere invention of such weapons as breech-loading rifles and rifled cannon was no guarantee of their capability to win battles. Until they were put in the hands of soldiers trained in their efficient use, that is, in tactical units ready to employ them en masse, they could not influence the course of a war. And when progressing from the tactical to the strategic, it was only when the railroads were exploited by Moltke and the general staff for their real strategic potential that they could provide the key to the timely assembly and movement of mass-mobilized armies in the opening phases of a war.

The second misconception follows from the first: commanders on both sides in the American Civil War were practicing an art of war which had evolved from military thought based on the weapon systems of the time. Nothing could be further from the truth. The hard fact—a main concern of this book—was that the military thought which should have provided the guidance for commanders became so misdirected that the leaders on both sides in the "sandwiched war" went to war lacking a realistic fighting doctrine. To see that they needed one, and why it never materialized, is a first step toward understanding why Union and Confederate commanders fought the war the way they did—why Stonewall Jackson and Nathaniel Banks fought their upcoming battle employing an art of command that each had to fashion in his own way.

CHAPTER 2

Pre–Civil War American Military Thought

A detailed exploration of the evolution of military thought in the antebellum period could deservedly be the subject of several volumes. What follows in this chapter is a more general look at the tactical and strategic theory which supposedly provided guidance for leaders in the Civil War.

The officers of the antebellum U.S. Army who would be directly affected by military theory were West Point graduates whose thought, in widely varying degrees, was shaped by three major influences: their all-too-brief exposure to the "military art" as cadets in the classroom, their own reading on military theory, and their combat experience in the Mexican War (1846–1848).

The battles of the Mexican War had been won by American infantry, employing the smoothbore musket and bayonet, using linear tactics developed in the eighteenth century. Infantry advanced in the attack in close-ordered ranks, to exchange volleys with an enemy in similar formations. When the attacker gained fire superiority, as the Americans almost always did in Mexican War battles, he finished off the action with a bayonet assault. Soon after the war, however, proponents of a new "rifled musket" were quick to proclaim that the new weapon in the hands of *defending* infantry could slaughter an attacker who continued to use the old linear tactics, which were characterized by shoulder-to-shoulder lines advancing at the slow pace required to maintain cohesion and fire discipline.

The backers of the new weapon proved to be right. The rifled musket (or simply the rifle, as it became known) had such a vastly improved range and accuracy over the old smoothbore musket that it was inevitable that it would change forever the way that battles had been fought throughout the period of gunpowder warfare. This realization, according to the rifle backers of the time—and some modern military historians—was bound to bring on a "rifle revolution" in infantry tactics. Why the revolution never materialized is not as surprising as it is ironic from the viewpoint of today's military analyst. Unfortunately for both soldiers and theorists before and during the Civil War there were no such objective analysts available, no armchair evaluators blessed with the gift of twentieth-century hindsight. Nor were there high-level military schools, military think tanks, or government contracts for academics with a military bent.

In place of a rifle revolution a controversy grew that centered on the writers of infantry drill manuals and the authors of a few works on military theory. As it turned out, none of the drill manuals did anything to arouse in their users an awareness that they were participants in a tactical revolution. All of the manuals, published before or during the Civil War, held steadfastly to the principles of the linear system. What "revolutionary" changes they set forth were no more than increases in the rate at which attacking formations were moved at the "double-quick step" or "double-quick time," ostensibly to enable them to avoid losses to the defender's rifle fire while exposed at the most vulnerable time. There were other, similar changes which, when troops moved from theory on the drill ground to the brutal reality of the battlefield, proved to be worse than useless. As long as troop units continued to attack in linear formations they were doomed to suffer casualties at such unacceptable rates that Civil War attacks were often dashed to pieces or driven to ground.

Since the authors of the drill manuals, in the cold light of reality, had failed as revolutionaries, it would seem that other theorists would come up with solutions to the problem of the defender's firepower destroying the attacker's capability for decisive action. Undoubtedly the foremost American theorist in the antebellum period was the formidable Dennis Hart Mahan, professor of military art and science at West Point and the father of Alfred Thayer Mahan, the great-to-be authority on the influence of sea power on warfare. The elder Mahan, who taught cadets the principles of engineering and the art of war, probably exercised greater influence on military thinking through his writing than he could have in the classroom. "Probably" for three reasons: first, because that part of the West Point curriculum devoted to the art of war was actually a miniscule part of a cadet's overall military education; second, by far the greatest emphasis—in place of the art of war—in the four-year curriculum was on military engineering; third, the faculty at West Point did not have as its principal goal (in contrast to enduring popular opinion) the production of future generals, but had its hands full simply trying to turn out second lieutenants qualified to fill vacancies in the branches of the army.

The most influential of Mahan's works could discourage a modern reader by its awesome title, *An Elementary Treatise on Advanced Guard, Out-Post, and Detachment Service of Troops, and the Manner of Posting Them in the Presence of an Enemy* (1847). In spite of its title, the book actually focused on the employment of major forces in the offense, and did that so well that its concepts formed the basis of pertinent parts of the Army Regulations of 1857.

Linear Formations As the Drill Manuals Portrayed Them

The emphasis on offensive concepts, however, might seem to have been contradictory to an earlier work, *A Complete Treatise on Field Fortifications*
(1836). The two, in any case, were not inconsistent, since Mahan believed,
understandably, that both offense and defense had their place in operations.
Yet it was mainly the earlier work that was to prove Mahan's foresight sound,
especially in the later battles of the war from 1863 to 1865. Then it was to
become clear that the rifle was to force both sides into more and more digging
in, thus validating Mahan's contention that "the spade, implementing the terrain, went hand in hand with the rifle and bayonet."

There were of course other American theorists whose writings were published during the same period as Mahan's, enough to have occupied the attention of too many modern-day academics to mention, let alone explore, in
this overview of antebellum military thought. It is enough to say that all American thinking of the sort at midcentury, including Mahan's, was profoundly
influenced by the works of the Napoleonic historian and military analyst, Antoine Henri Jomini (1779–1869). His voluminous works on military history
and theory were climaxed by his *Précis de l'Art de Guerre* (Summary of the
Art of War, 1838), wherein Jomini managed to treat operations in all types of
war, with an emphasis on strategy. Although the book was a masterpiece, both
in its content and in the way that its author had summarized most of his
teaching in one work, Jomini, like some other geniuses, overlooked the fact
that his readers lacked his depth of knowledge and experience, and thus were
unable to apply his theoretical examples in a real world. This was especially
true when his American readers tried to apply his teachings in developing
their own strategies in planning operations and fighting battles in the Civil
War—*real* campaigns and battles which the master had tried to teach through
examples based entirely on abstractions that tended to institutionalize warfare.
The result of misapplying Jomini's theory has been aptly expressed in the
words of the military historian John R. Elting:

American generals of 1861, facing a military problem as vast as Napoleon's invasion of
Russia, studied Jomini in the misguided faith that they were studying Napoleon. They
marched against strategic points—Corinth, Richmond, Atlanta—content to let
Confederate armies escape to fight again, so long as they could occupy this real estate.
And so the war worried on, until other commanders emerged, possessing the true,
brutally clear Napoleonic appreciation, "There are too many good generals . . . but they
see too many things, I see only one: masses. I seek to destroy them, knowing well that
the accessories will then fall of themselves."[1]

In short, it is enough to say that the result of pre–Civil War writers' thinking—and that of their followers—was not only the failure to solve strategic
problems, but also the failure to find a realistic solution to the tactical dilemma:
how the attacker could overcome the defense's firepower without suffering
unacceptable casualties. An unfortunate result turns tragic when seen from

Linear Formations As They Actually Appeared in Battle

A Line of Skirmishers, the Precursor of a Realistic Infantry Formation our twentieth-century viewpoint, for now it is clear that only half the problem was addressed by both the drill manuals (increased rates and manner of movement) and the theorists (the continued reliance on the maneuver of thinly disguised linear, close-ordered systems). The *whole* of the problem is visible to us through hindsight, a form of insight never granted to antebellum writers and soldiers. That unseen half of the problem should have dealt with the control of tactical units *within their formations*. It was to become all too clear to attacking infantrymen on battlefields of the Civil War that dispersion—the complete breaking away from the compact, rigid ranks of linear formations into widely dispersed teams which could take advantage of terrain cover—was the answer to reducing casualties. Why weren't such measures foreseen and taken at the outset?

The reason was as old as gunpowder warfare. Junior leaders—the captains, lieutenants, and sergeants—had an inherent fear, fostered and shared by their seniors, that once their soldiers had dispersed enough to act on their own, personal control, by voice and physical presence, was irretrievably lost. The dilemma was to become increasingly felt as recruits became veterans and increased casualties became a general concern. It was then that entrenching became the rule when attacks, still in linear formations, were driven to ground by the rifle fire of the defense—proof that Mahan had been right in contending that the spade went hand in hand with the rifle and bayonet.

Even with that realization, however, the problem of the attacker was not really solved for over half a century, until the German general Oskar von Hutier developed what became known as "Hutier tactics." Based on self-sufficient infantry detachments, attacks bypassed enemy strong points to seize deep objectives, while follow-up, supporting units mopped up remaining resistance. The key to the success of Hutier tactics was not solely infiltration, important as that may have been; rather, it was the reliance upon highly trained and motivated junior leaders whose initiative and aggressiveness assured their acting on their own to accomplish their missions.

With both their tactical and strategical problems unsolved, it may be concluded that leaders on both sides went to war in 1861 without a body of realistic military doctrine to guide their thinking and their actions. The lack in the case of the generals posed perhaps the greater void, since they had not been given strategical guidance of any kind by their governments. This greater void raises the question: were there not lessons from the Napoleonic Wars that would have filled the gap and provided higher-level commanders with guidance for planning and conducting their operations—guidance which would have enabled them to plan campaigns and win battles?

CHAPTER 3

"Lessons" from Napoleonic Warfare

If suggesting that Civil War leaders might have looked back to Napoleonic warfare for enlightenment seems reaching too far back in time, our perspective is sharpened if we bear in mind that they were no more distant in time than we are today from the Second World War. It should be remembered too that American military leaders and theorists were keenly aware of the dominance of French military arms in Europe during and after the Napoleonic Wars. Our historical perspective is further aided by recalling the expanse and scope of the many wars waged by French armies in Europe.

The wars of the French Revolution and Napoleon may be seen as an almost constant state of war for the twenty-three years from 1792 to 1815, actually a state of war only briefly interrupted by treaties, shifting alliances, and periods of truce used to catch breath and reorganize. In expanse the war swept back and forth across Europe, from the coasts of France to Moscow, from the Baltic to Spain, and even across the Mediterranean. French armies fought across the borders of the major powers of Europe, employed by their commanders under all sorts of strategies and tactics, over all kinds of terrain. With such a background it is scarcely remarkable that Napoleon's *Grande Armée* at its zenith came to be regarded as the world model of a fighting machine.

With that picture in mind, it may seem odd to late twentieth-century viewers that, for all those tumultuous twenty-three years, neither Napoleon nor his administrators had taken the time to compose the collective experience of the emperor and his generals into some form of published doctrine. What they did do, in actual practice, was to adapt the tactics of the famed *Ordinance of 1791* to their own purposes in such a variety of eclectic ways that historians and theorists never caught up with the results until far later than the end of the Napoleonic era. In fact, the only historians who have given us useful insight into Napoleonic warfare—Colin and Camon in France and Becke in England—were never published until the early twentieth century, far too late for their lessons to be of value, except for interested historians in our times. And even Napoleon's Maxims (based on memoirs and correspondence) were only encapsulated principles dealing in a general way with some basic concepts. Thus the down-to-earth lessons of conducting operations and fighting battles never became available in "tactical manual" form to American Civil War commanders who could have profited from them. Still, it is of value to us when examining Civil War generalship to compare the aspects of Napoleonic warfare that may have aided those commanders in developing methods of their own. Of the several such paradigms there are at least four deserving attention.

First, his "grand tactics" provide the key to an understanding of the linkage between Napoleon's strategy and his victories on the battlefield. Simply stated, the term stood for the climaxing of his offensive strategic movements by pinning down the enemy's main body with a maneuvering force, no matter if that force was initially outnumbered, until other French corps could move to its support in time to bring on a decisive battle on Napoleon's terms. Another way of looking at grand tactics, from today's perspective, would be to think of the concept as a parallel to the art of war at the operational level as defined in U.S. Army doctrine: "The operational level is the vital link between national and theater-strategic aims and the tactical employment of forces on the battlefield;"[2] that is, it is the doctrinal link between military strategy and tactics.

Second, the basic maneuvering and fighting force, in both Napoleon's strategy and grand tactics, was the *corps d'armée*. This flexible force was in effect a miniature army, commanded nominally by a marshal who had under his command the three combat arms. The corps consisted of at least two infantry divisions (the number varying with the marshal's mission), a cavalry division or brigade, and at least one battery of corps artillery. It also had supporting services and a small corps staff. The number of infantry divisions varied with the operation plan and could be changed in accordance with changes in the strategical situation. Because the corps was a self-sufficient force it was expected to engage a major enemy force on its own for at least a day. Equally important, the corps could march independently, usually within a day's march of neighboring corps. The various corps of the *Grande Armée*, as will be seen, were then enabled to move like a vast, widely dispersed net, more swiftly and flexibly than the enemy army, until it could be concentrated against the opposing army.

Third, the advancing net was maneuvered by Napoleon's *bataillon carré* system, the crown of his grand tactics and the despair of slower-moving enemy commanders. The net of the *bataillon carré* (so called from the diamond-shaped formation which, on the map, may have roughly resembled a lower-order battalion square) enabled several corps to move in a time-and-space disposition that facilitated the army's concentration in any direction, usually allowing two or more corps to come to the support of an engaged corps and bring on the battle Napoleon was seeking (see Figure 3.1).

Fourth, the Napoleonic battle was the culmination, the payoff, of his strategy and grand tactics. In this sense the battle would be the decisive strike that would end a campaign and thus bring an end to the war. The battle, fought under the emperor's personal command, can be thought of as taking shape in three phases, or as General Camon, the French Napoleonic historian, would have it, in three acts. Act I consisted of the "Preparation for the Decisive Battle" to follow. The *masse de manoeuvre* (heretofore several of the corps making up the *bataillon carré*) would engage the enemy army all across its front in the *combat de neutralisation*, thus pinning down the enemy army and forcing its commander to commit most of his major elements. While the enemy was thus occupied, Napoleon's enveloping force, the *masse débordante*, would be moving up to attack positions on an enemy's flank, taking advantage of any cover the terrain afforded—hills, ridges, woods, and the like. On Napoleon's command (a prearranged "signal" of a volley from a battery of massed guns or an order carried by a senior aide) the *attaque débordante* would be launched by the enveloping force, which would make an inescapable threat to the enemy commander's flank and rear. Once that commander had been forced to commit his reserves, having had in effect to throw all his resources into the battle, the stage was being set for the next act.

In Act II, the "Decisive Battle," Napoleon had already formed the *masse de rupture*, his striking force, in positions from which it would be launched in the deciding attack of the battle. This was a force made up of the combined arms: fresh infantry divisions, cavalry brigades or divisions, and massed artillery batteries, to be positioned to blow holes in the enemy line, thus paving the way for the infantry and (possibly) cavalry attacks. When the striking force was ready and the weak point in the enemy line had been selected as the aiming point for its initial thrust, Napoleon took personal charge of what he liked to call *l'événement*, "the Event," so called because at this point time was all-important. After waiting, even with watch in hand, the emperor gave the order to launch the attack. What followed has been succinctly summed up by the British military historian J. F. C. Fuller:

The attack was based on the following principles: (1) While the columns advanced, the artillery compelled the enemy to remain in line—that is, in the least vulnerable formation to case and round shot fire; (2) just before they deployed, the cavalry, by threatening the enemy, compelled him to deploy from line into squares—that is, not only in the securest formation to meet cavalry, but also in a very vulnerable one to meet infantry and artillery fire; (3) next, under cover of cavalry, the columns [of infantry] deployed in order to bring to bear on the squares a heavier fire than the squares themselves could deliver, which was supplemented by fire from the regimental [artillery] guns; and (4) lastly, when the squares were thrown into confusion, the assault with the bayonet was made, and the cavalry finished off the enemy by annihilating the fugitives.[3]

Figure 3.1
The *Bataillon Carré* in Action

Courtesy Martin L. Wilkerson.

Once the decisive attack had succeeded, the cavalry, as indicated, was already opening the last act of the drama.

Act III, the "Exploitation," was the cavalry's great day in the sun. This was the dramatic, Napoleonic final touch, designed to complete the destruction of the enemy army with an all-out pursuit. This was the end that Napoleon always sought when planning his grand strategy and military strategy, even though the decisive battle, as such, could not then be discerned. Unfortunately for American commanders, this kind of exploitable and dramatic end was seldom possible and hardly ever achieved in Civil War battles, and never in those that might have been decisive in a campaign. While the above sequence and the superb handling of the combined arms cannot be taken literally as tactical models, the depiction of the Napoleonic battle does represent what French leaders were able to accomplish under ideal conditions.

The examples of Napoleonic strategy, grand tactics, and battlefield tactics represent paradigms which might have served as guidance for American commanders if they had really aspired to bring about decisive ends to their campaigns and battles. On the other hand it may be argued that American generals led forces made up of green volunteers who couldn't begin to compare with Napoleon's veterans in combat effectiveness. Given that the argument is a valid one, it remains that the above models could have served as points of departure—with the obvious modifications needed to adapt them to an American way of making war and the American terrain. Later in our exploration, when the art of command is being observed in action, certain of the four Napoleonic examples will be compared with an actual operation in such a way that one may arrive at one's own conclusions regarding the way a commander might have performed under the conditions imposed on him.

CHAPTER 4

Defining an Art of Command

The historian Sir Moses Finley has stated the problem with unargued clarity: "The historian's evidence (whether documents, literary texts or objects) propounds no questions. . . . Therefore, the historian himself must ask the right questions . . . and provide the right conceptual context."[4] Two such questions were asked in Chapter 1: What conditions prevailed at the outset of the Civil War to put opposing commanders in such a fix that they were forced to learn their trade in the brutal school of war? Indeed, what kind of a war brought about such conditions?

It is time, in this chapter, to complete the answers to the questions by looking deeper into the evidence. Such an exploration should lead to an appreciation of the challenges that Civil War warfare thrust upon untried commanders. But the explorers should never lose sight of the landscape around them—the background of the whole picture. For the first time in American history massed armies had to be formed and led into battle, armies of a size inconceivable in the past. Hundreds of thousands of civilians had to be welded into fighting forces that were expected, by both sides, to win nothing less than total victory. And where did the masses of civilians come from?

In both North and South, over half the rank and file were farmers and the next greatest mass was made up of common laborers. Lastly, there were skilled workers such as carpenters, clerks, and mechanics; and of course there were the students. Yet all—with the possible exception of recent immigrants who had seen service as conscripts in European armies—shared two common bonds: first, they were all rank amateurs when it came to soldiering in a war; second, until the draft came and the flood of recruits had dwindled to a trickle (in the South in 1862 and the North in 1863) they were all volunteers. How the hordes of volunteers were shaped into armies has been the subject of countless volumes, from diaries to histories; so it is sufficient to say here that the magnitude of the task must have seemed overwhelming to both soldiers and officers. From the viewpoint of the former it could be just plain onerous: "A Pennsylvanian [volunteer] wrote after about six months service: 'The first thing in the morning is drill, then drill, then drill again. Then drill, drill, a little more drill. Then drill, and lastly drill. Between drills, we drill and sometimes stop to eat a little and have a roll-call.' "[5] From the viewpoint of the officers—lieutenants and captains elected by the soldiers of their companies and majors and lieutenant colonels elected by the lieutenants and captains— who had to supervise the drilling, their duties had to seem never-ending.

After a day of drill, junior and senior officers alike faced nighttime sessions of study and regimental classes just to keep a step ahead of their sergeants and soldiers for the next day's training. Even Grant could recall his 1861 experience as the newly appointed colonel of the 21st Illinois Infantry Regiment: "I had never looked at a copy of tactics from my graduation [from West Point]. My standing in that branch of studies had been near the foot of the class. . . . The arms had changed since then and [other] tactics adopted. I got a copy . . . and studied one lesson, intending to confine the exercise of the first day [with his new regiment] to the commands I thus learned. By pursuing this course I thought I would soon get through the volume."[6] Needless to say, the future general didn't find his way "soon" to his goal. And unfortunately for all concerned, the grim picture of such trying times turns even darker when we moderns take note of the contents of the "tactical manual" that Grant referred to—that is to say, actually one of the drill manuals referred to in Chapter 2. Those tiresome volumes—focusing on the "school of the soldier, company, battalion, and brigade"—were hammering home the fundamentals of the linear tactics which were to lead to such bloody effects on the battlefield, appalling sights that neither leader nor led could have dreamed of in 1861. Dreams aside, the conscious thought that came increasingly to the fore in the minds of both was one that has for centuries troubled untried soldiers on the eve of battle: what will it really be like—and how will I behave?

Attempts to find and portray answers that would satisfy the public's fascination with the subject have been made for generations in every conceivable form—from the historian's traditional tools (diaries, journals, unit histories, and the like) to the novel, poetry, and now the cinema. But the more enduring form, over the passing of time, seems to have been the novel, followed by the personal narrative. The most lasting protagonists in literature (not heroes, who tend to be less real and therefore less believable) have been the likes of Tolstoi's Pierre Bezukhov at the battle of Borodino (*War and Peace*) or Stendhal's Fabrizio del Dongo at Waterloo (*The Charterhouse of Parma*). But by far the most familiar to American minds is Stephen Crane's Henry Fleming in *The Red Badge of Courage*, whose introduction to battle in the Civil War, supposedly at Chancellorsville, continues to be as stirringly vivid today as it was to nineteenth-century readers. The experience of farm boy turned soldier on that first terrifying day, alongside his equally green comrades, is shown in these excerpts from the novel:

The brigade was halted in the fringe of a grove. The men crouched among the trees and pointed their restless guns out at the fields. They tried to look beyond the smoke. Out of this haze they could see running men. Some shouted information and gestured as they hurried. The men of the new regiment watched and listened eagerly, while their tongues ran on in gossip of the battle. They mouthed rumours that had flown like birds out of the unknown. . . .

The din in front was swelled to a tremendous chorus. The youth and his fellows were frozen to silence. They could see a flag that tossed in the smoke angrily. Near it were the blurred and agitated forms of troops. There came a turbulent stream of men across the fields. A battery changing position at a frantic gallop scattered the stragglers right and left. A shell screaming like a storm banshee went over the huddled heads of the reserves. It landed in the grove, and, exploding redly, flung the brown earth. There was a little shower of pine needles. Bullets began to whistle among the branches and nip at the trees. Twigs and leaves came sailing down. It was as if a thousand axes, wee and invisible, were being wielded. Many of the men were constantly dodging and ducking their heads. . . .

Wild yells came from behind the walls of smoke. A sketch of red and grey dissolved into a moblike body of men who galloped like wild horses. The veteran regiments on the right and left of the 304th immediately began to jeer. With the passionate song of the bullets and the banshee shrieks of shells were mingled loud catcalls and bits of facetious advice concerning places of safety. . . .

Across the smoke-infested fields came a brown swarm of running men who were giving shrill yells. They came on, stooping and swinging their rifles at all angles.

A flag tilted forward, sped near the front. As he caught sight of them the youth was momentarily startled by a thought that his gun was not loaded. He stood trying to rally his faltering intellect so he might recollect the moment when he had loaded but he could not. . . .

He got one glance at the foe-swarming field in front of him, and instantly ceased to debate the question of his piece being loaded. Before he was ready to begin—before he had announced to himself that he was about to fight—he threw the obedient, well-balanced rifle into position and fired a first wild shot. Directly he was working at his weapon like an automatic affair. He suddenly lost concern for himself, and forgot to look at a menacing fate. He became not a man but a member. He felt that something of which he was a part—a regiment, an army, a cause, or a country—was in a crisis. He was welded into a common personality which was dominated by a single desire. For some moments he could not flee, no more than a little finger can commit a revolution from a hand. . . .

The men dropped here and there like bundles. The captain of the youth's company had been killed in an early part of the action. His body lay stretched out in the position of a tired man resting, but upon his face was an astonished and sorrowful look, as if he thought some friend had done him an ill turn. The babbling man was grazed by a shot that made the blood stream widely down his face. He clapped both hands to his face. "Oh!" he said, and ran. Another grunted suddenly as if he had been struck in the stomach by a club. He sat down and gazed ruefully. In his eyes was a mute, indefinite reproach. Farther up the line a man, standing behind a tree, had had his knee joint splintered by a ball. Immediately he had dropped his rifle and gripped the tree with both arms. And there he remained, clinging desperately and crying for assistance that he might withdraw his hold upon the tree.

At last an exultant yell went along the quivering line. The firing dwindled from an uproar to a last vindictive popping. As the smoke slowly eddied away, the youth saw that the charge had been repulsed. The enemy were scattered into reluctant groups. He saw a man climb to the top of the fence, straddle the rail, and fire a parting shot. The waves had receded, leaving bits of dark *debris* upon the ground.[7]

Before reflecting on the behavior of men in battle, it might be wise to look at a comparable picture from another perspective, in this case from the experience of an *actual* participant in battle. And for the purpose, what could be more appropriate than the personal experience of a military historian who, in the words of John Keegan, "bestrides the military historian's landscape"— "the great nineteenth-century Prussian, Hans Delbrück, a pupil of pupils of Ranke, the first Rankeian to concern himself with military history and therefore the pioneer of the modern 'scientific' and 'universal' approach to the subject."[8] Delbrück is perhaps better known in America for his masterwork (translated by Colonel Walter J. Renfroe, Jr.) *History of the Art of War— Within the Framework of Political History*. Delbrück will be represented in this case by an excerpt from a letter written by the future historian when, as a reserve sub-lieutenant in the 29th Rhenish Infantry Regiment, he saw combat firsthand in the Franco–Prussian War in the battle of Gravelotte–St. Privat:

We [Delbrück and two of his German comrades who had been on a reconnaissance mission] hurried back to our regiment, and soon the main battle began. The shells began to scream, without striking the ground, the cannons became ever more intense. Quickly we passed through a village and were out into the open fields. Here we had to expose ourselves to the most terrible shells, *mitrailleuse* and chassepot fire, running as long as we could, then resting. During the open field run our regiment became scattered and lost all order. In a gulley in the middle of the field many tried remaining lying down, as it was pretty safe. They could scarcely be moved to go forward. In the confusion two or three hundred men from different units became mixed together. Leadership did not exist or it was poor and the soldiers showed no courage: it was a pitiful sight. Finally we came to the outskirts of a woods, filled with nearly impassable underbrush. Scarcely had we begun to advance forward into it than a murderous fire began against us and we had to retreat. The French stood a few hundred feet before us in a prepared and protected position and fired, without our being able to see them. Fortunately about thirty yards from the edge of the woods, there was a deep gorge, which was absolutely safe, but the bullets went showering overhead. With our small numbers an attack was unthinkable. A reserve lieutenant commanded and sent me back three times to bring more men. I had to bring them forward with sword in hand and with threats to use it.[9]

A Civil War Hasty Entrenchment under Enemy Fire

Aside from the all-embracing fear that runs through all ranks, there emerges a condition common to all battle experiences, the confusion that reigns once the fighting has begun. Veterans of all wars in all times continue to remark upon the condition. From the histories of Polybius to interviews with Vietnam veterans, soldiers never cease to remark on the cacophony that seems to assail the senses at the same time. All the mingling sights, sounds, and general uproar combine to create an overall sense of chaos that prevails when men are locked in combat.

In the two examples (after taking note of the contrast between Crane's "youth" in his first battle and the young Delbrück, the Prussian officer from the finest war machine in Europe), one cannot escape their common reaction, the awareness of confusion and an overall sense of a lack of control, like an unsounded cry for help—for someone or something to restore a sense of order. Yet, as an experienced observer is well aware, all the months of training to instill discipline and all the efforts of junior leaders on the spot will never suffice to remove the chaos that is at the heart of battle. Consequently, all that the committed officer and soldier can do is what he was trained—and ordered—to do. Yet, as we are equally aware, it would make no sense at all to commit men to battle unless there was a reasonable chance of winning it. And with that perception in mind, one enters the province of higher command, literally onto a higher plateau of command that is, of necessity, removed from the chaos of battle. It is the exploration of that province of command that is the ultimate aim of this work. And since an exploration must have a starting point, research has revealed a contemporary source which combines an insight in depth into the minds of higher-level commanders—at army, corps, and division levels—with a broad range of combat command experience derived from interviews and surveys with over eighty U.S. Army commanders who had held command in the Second World War at the above levels.

The source was the *ARC Study: Art and Requirements of Command*,[10] which represented not only a timely approach—for the first time in American military history taking advantage of senior commanders' collective memories and personal sources while they were still fresh in mind—but also an unequaled opportunity to exploit a mine of a richness that historians dream of but rarely discover. There are, however, two points that demand caution. In the first place, the study represents only one point of departure for this book's appraisal of Civil War generalship. Secondly, the so-called principles of command established by the study should be regarded as conceptual in nature; however, they can provide us with insights into critical areas that relate to observing Civil War commanders in action, especially into how they developed their own methods of command. The critical areas will become evident as one observes the actions of selected commanders in the campaigns and battles that will be observed.

The areas of interest include (but are not limited to) a commander evaluating his mission and available intelligence, making decisions and formulating orders, supervising combat and logistical operations to assure that orders are being carried out, and handling command relationships with subordinate commanders. Of equal if not greater importance is the fact that our areas of interest make up essential elements of what has become known as the art of command. It is important to note that the *ARC Study* was undertaken "on the premise that high-level tactical command . . . *is a highly personalized art* [italics added] as well as a clearly defined professional discipline." Since such an art has been recognized and accepted in countless cases by both military professionals and historians, it deserves further definition if it is to be of use in this work. Unfortunately, and in spite of the many works devoted to the subject, the art of command apparently continues to demand a concise definition.

Not surprisingly the search for a useable definition uncovers a broad spectrum, stretching from a denial on one extreme to a master warrior's point of view on the other.

The first is an opinion expressed in a work on tactical genius: "Although battle is a confrontation of technologies, the skill of the general is not a science and certainly not an art."[11] At the other extreme one finds Napoleon's Maxim LXVI: "In war the general alone can judge of certain arrangements. It depends on him alone to conquer difficulties by his own superior talents and resolution."[12]

Lest my search for a useable definition get us entangled in a briar patch of abstractions and hypotheses, it would be useful to consult scholars who have examined both the theoretical and the practical. A model would be Clausewitz, who, if anyone, looked deeply into the ways that a commander could turn theory into practice: "The closer it [theory] comes to that goal [of putting theory to practical use], the more it proceeds from the objective form of a science to the objective form of a skill, the more effective it will prove in areas where the nature of the case admits no arbiter but talent. It will, in fact, become an active ingredient of talent."[13] Clausewitz' argument has been couched in simpler terms by Roger Beaumont in conclusions from his insightful study on command method: "In analyzing the practice of command as an 'art,' dangers of abstraction and reduction quickly emerge, the very bane of military history and analysis along with hindsight. . . . For some time to come one may expect, as with quarterbacks, that military leaders will learn as the game is played."[14] In acknowledging conclusions like the above, I would submit the following as a useful definition for the art of command: *the skill, in warfare, in employing the methods whereby military forces are controlled by a commander to accomplish his mission.* Equipped with this definition, one may proceed from abstractions to realities, from the realm of theory to the application of an art in practice.

PART TWO

CEDAR MOUNTAIN: MEETING ENGAGEMENT

The accidental meeting of two armies on the march gives rise to one of the most imposing scenes in war. . . . A great occasion of this kind calls into play all the genius of a skillful general and of the warrior able to control events.

—Jomini, *Summary of the Art of War* (1838)

Meeting Engagement—a combat action that occurs when a moving force, incompletely deployed for battle, engages an enemy at an unexpected time and place.

—Department of Defense, *Dictionary of Military Terms* (1988)

CHAPTER 5

Stonewall Jackson Plans and Conducts His Campaign

Our world of today, composed of readers and historians alike, has always known him as Stonewall Jackson. By the late summer of 1862, the dust-covered men in the marching columns of Confederate infantry had come to know him as "Old Jack," the nickname used as much in awe as affection. The awe had come to them the hard way, born of aching joints and sore feet, the common denominator of Jackson's "foot cavalry" in the Valley Campaign, where they and their leader had become the darlings of the South only two short months ago. Those action-filled months of May and June in the Shenandoah had seen defeats forgotten and victories magnified by a Southern press that had heralded their leader as the strategist who had saved Richmond by thrashing a combination of Northern armies outnumbering his little army three to one. That the overall strategy came from the concepts of Johnston and Lee never mattered to the press and thus never occurred to Jackson's adoring public. Indeed, Jackson's rise to fame, from the *Richmond Dispatch*'s glowing story of "Stonewall" at Bull Run to the latest accounts of the Valley Campaign, was almost entirely due to Southern newspapers. And in August 1862, Jackson's reputation exceeded even that of Lee, who, if known to the public at all, had been regarded (prior to the Seven Days Battles) as the theorist who had advised President Davis to fortify the approaches to Richmond. Jackson's renown was to become so fixed in Southern minds that such praise as that voiced in the *Southern Literary Messenger* was not at all uncommon: "He is the idol of the people, and is the object of greater enthusiasm than any other military chieftain of our day."[15] That kind of adulation prompts a question when one observes what happened before and during the meeting engagement that came to be known as the battle of Cedar Mountain: what

Stonewall Jackson

kind of general—what kind of man—really existed behind the newspaper accounts and public image of Stonewall Jackson?

Every commander's plans and subsequent actions begins with his *mission*, usually coming from higher authority, military or political. In Jackson's case, as we have seen, his mission came directly from Lee in the form of a series of letters or letter orders. There was something highly significant about those orders—both in how the writer conveyed his strategical concepts and how the recipient proceeded to translate those concepts into action. In today's military language, Lee's letter orders to Jackson would be called "mission type orders," meaning that the receiving commander is told *what* to do, but not *how* to do it. Lee had made that quite clear by inserting "I now must leave the matter to your reflection and good judgment," a statement typifying the command relationship that history has recognized so well. As for Jackson's "reflection" on his mission, we have already seen how he had begun to interpret it by putting his whole force on the march with the full intent to spring on—and destroy—Pope's advance elements at Culpeper.

Long before Jackson had put his corps on the march it is evident that his interpretation of his mission had, as always, been guided by his strategical insight, the quality which Lee had come to trust so much in this general. It was Jackson's perception of the overall strategic picture—not only the military but the political factors behind a strategy—that enabled him to see the whole while perceiving what part his mission played in it. It was largely this quality that had allowed him to see how the effects of his own strategy in the Valley Campaign could upset Lincoln's grand plan to direct his armies in a converging offensive to capture Richmond. Yet it was not this prescience alone that had gained Lee's respect; it was Jackson's relentless drive to maintain the offensive and strike his opponents that had earned the respect of his enemies as well. Underlying those qualities was another which history seems to have reserved for her greatest generals, the exploitation of surprise, the ability to strike the enemy at an unexpected time and place. The essential accessory of surprise is secrecy, and it was Jackson's obsession with the latter that became both a source of strength and of weakness in the planning and execution of his troop movement orders. His obsession with keeping his plans solely to himself—for over a century the target and despair of historians' research— had become a continuing cause of frustration to his subordinate commanders. Even one of Jackson's staff, on observing the divisions of the corps on an earlier march, was heard to comment, "It seems strange to see a large body of men moving in one direction and only one man in all the thousands knowing where they are going." On another occasion, Major General A. P. Hill, commander of Jackson's largest and newest-joined division, when asked where a marching column was headed, "replied that he supposed that we would go to the top of the hill in front of us, but that was all he knew."

Secrecy aside, Jackson's orders for the march of his corps toward Culpeper, issued on the night of 7–8 August, were clear enough about the order of

Map 5.1

Courtesy Martin L. Wilkerson.

march. The three infantry divisions of the corps were to move in the following
order: Ewell's division leading, followed by Hill's, with Winder's in the rear.
The march was to start at "early dawn," about a half hour before sunrise, that
is, about 4:15 A.M. Its main direction of advance, as conceived by Jackson, led
from Orange Court House northward toward Culpeper (see Map 5.1). Thus,
the axis of advance on the map would have been the road that ran parallel to
the Orange and Alexandria Railroad to Culpeper, twenty miles to the north.
It would have been a feasible day's march for Jackson's "foot cavalry" of the
Valley Campaign, but three obstacles intervened to cut short the march: two
could have been foreseen; a third, as it happened, was not. The foreseeable,
the weather and the enemy, have always been uppermost in the mind of any
commander launching an operation. In this case, the heat of a Virginia August
and the dust clouds rising from dry roads were bound to slow down any
infantry, while an active Union cavalry screen had for days advertised its
whereabouts to Jackson. It was the unforeseeable third factor—at least in part
due to Jackson's mishandling of his own logistics—that was to upset the orderly advance of his whole corps.

Sometime during the same night that Jackson had sent his march orders to his division commanders, he changed his mind about Ewell's routing and redirected him to march his division (leading the corps advance) on roads more to the left (westward) of the original route. This meant that Ewell was now to move through Liberty Mills on the Rapidan River, thence up roads on both sides of the Rapidan to the Orange Court House–Culpeper highway. There were no doubt good reasons for the change, but it was the transmission of the new order that may have caused the confusion that ensued. Ewell and Winder received the change in march orders, but evidently Hill, who was literally in the middle (his division being the center in the order of march), did not. The result was the kind of logistical nightmare that could threaten the plans of any major force commander, the confusion caused by one of his large units crossing the march route of another.

When Jackson rode out at an early morning hour of 8 August to check—as would any good commander—on his corps' march, he came across A. P. Hill at the head of his motionless division column, near the road junction at Orange Court House. When Jackson asked why Hill's column was halted, Hill replied, sensibly enough, that he was waiting for Ewell's division to pass. At the time, so it would appear from the record, the column then marching past Hill's halted units was taken by Hill to be one of Ewell's brigades, and so, naturally enough, Hill was waiting for it to pass so that his division could follow in its appointed place. Apparently, neither Hill nor Jackson realized at the time that the passing column actually belonged to Winder's division. Jackson ended the brief encounter without another word to Hill and curtly ordered an aide to hurry along the next column down the road. What is even odder about this chance meeting of the two commanders was that neither, at least as far as any record shows, made any attempt to ascertain to what command the passing units belonged—*at that time*. Since there are all sorts of ramifications in historians' speculations about what had happened and why, there is good reason to avoid the mess and stick to the outcome.

The red-haired Ambrose Powell Hill was known for having a temper to match, so it is evident that having waited for the other troops to pass, followed by a division wagon train, Hill was in no happy humor after two hours of killing time around Orange Court House. So a fuming Hill rode forward, past a halted column, to Barnett's Ford to find out the reason for the delay. There he found units of Winder's division waiting on a part of Ewell's troops to pass because two roads joined at the ford. Hill sent an aide galloping to Jackson with the news and, because he was already confused about wagon trains being interspersed in infantry columns, asking where Jackson wanted the trains to march. He got no reply until late in the day, when Jackson sent only a verbal order for him to bivouac his division around Orange Court House. And so, as the sun set on that unhappy day, the corps' operations came to a dismal end. Ewell's division, famed for its hard-marching qualities, had covered only a miserable eight miles. Hill's division, which might as well have stayed in camp, had made it to a point just a mile north of Orange Court House! What were the causes of the whole fiasco?

Given that 8 August was an unusually hot day, that Hill and his troops were new to Jackson's command, and that Hill's division was larger than the others and would need more road space, there are still not enough "givens" to account for the root causes. Though Jackson's staff had not served him superbly, it is in the end the commander who remains responsible for all that his command does or fails to do. Jackson had not only failed to ascertain that Hill had received the change in march orders, he had not even informed that division commander of his overall plan. Though most historians tend to dismiss the failure as a part of Jackson's famous reticence, the fact remains that a commander who keeps his plans solely to himself can hardly expect his subordinates to exercise initiative when they don't know what is expected of them during an operation. What kind of general, what kind of man, would feel himself so far above the ordinary that he felt no need to confide his concepts— even his plans—to his commanders?

An answer can't be limited to observations on generalship; there is far too much of the man within the general to look at them separately. Another factor intrudes when one considers that separation, the *myth* of Stonewall Jackson that overlays all attempts to view the man as he really was. There is so much *image* in the myth that one finds it difficult to try to look behind it. Stephen Vincent Benét in his epic poem, *John Brown's Body*, shows us a glimpse of the image:

> Hard on his followers, harder on his foes,
> An iron sabre vowed to an iron Lord[16]

Above all, he remains a bundle of contradictions wrapped in eccentricities; indeed, more than one of his general officers was not above declaring him crazy. He was deeply religious, a hard-as-nails Presbyterian who had an unswerving belief that God had destined him to destroy his enemies in battle. Yet he was the same deacon who delighted in the conversation of old ladies and ministers of the church, and who loved to play with children, who were drawn to him by his gentle manner. He would take time out from a military operation to attend church whenever the opportunity was presented, but he lived up to a reputation for sleeping through an entire service.

He lived a Spartan existence, spending hours in the saddle and sleeping on the ground whenever conditions demanded. Yet even at age thirty-eight, in 1862, though he remained as physically strong as he had been throughout his life, he continued to be overly conscious of supposed afflictions. Believing that one arm was heavier than the other, he would hold the heavier arm overhead in order to even the flow of blood. He claimed to be subject to dyspepsia pains, and restricted his diet to the simplest of foods such as corn bread, butter, and milk. His rigid regimen extended to abstaining from whiskey and tobacco. When he sat on a chair his back was ramrod straight (so that the blood would flow properly), with his heels together and the toes of his boots pointed straight ahead.

While he was curt to an extreme in the field, seldom even raising his eyes to acknowledge a message or report, his manner could be as gentle as his deep blue eyes—except when they flashed in anger at some violation of orders. Even his appearance could seem contradictory. His soft brown beard and curly auburn hair bespoke the gentleman, but this was belied by his insistence on wearing the same weather-beaten forage cap and old uniform coat that might be as dusty as his military boots. He could have been seen as a handsome six-footer, but his long-legged stride was awkward, as was his seat in the saddle. He was a good horseman, but even that was disputed by those who, while they thought his seat secure, never considered it to be graceful like Lee's or Jeb Stuart's.

The inner man, as we have seen, is another matter; one that General Daniel Harvey Hill, Jackson's brother-in-law, tried to fathom when he said, "The biographer of Stonewall Jackson is a poor philosopher who does not point out the connection between the severe struggles of the *man* with himself & the giant wrestling of the *General* with his enemies."[17] The "enemies" no doubt included the forces of evil, over which Jackson's stern Christian faith continued to triumph. There can be little doubt also that two of the strongest forces that shaped Jackson's rise to fame were ambition and his unshakable conviction that he had been chosen by the Almighty to lead the South's soldiers to ultimate victory. It was this coupling of faith and ambition that stood firmly behind his strict enforcement of discipline among his soldiers and the highest standards of performance for their officers. He didn't hesitate to order deserters shot in front of their regiments, to place a brigade commander under arrest for command failure in battle, or to prefer charges against a Virginia officer who encouraged his soldiers to use the fence rails from his own land for their winter campfires. To him, a sign of weakness was the mark of failure, a lack of patriotism, and that was the end of it. In the long run it was the consistent display of Cromwellian discipline and unrelenting high standards that made him admired, not only by Southerners but Northerners, military and civilian alike. Stonewall Jackson was probably the only Confederate general who was ever cheered by Union prisoners when they caught sight of him in the field. But above all, one attribute stands out, one that would make men follow him anywhere, one that never failed to make him the hero of the South—he won battles.

Thus it becomes evident that Jackson's stern faith formed the bedrock that supported both his ambition and his self-confidence in his military genius. As one mainstay of that genius, we have already taken note of Jackson's strategic insight. It was that quality that made him take pause at the end of 8 August and take another look at the strategic picture that was taking shape. It was an unfinished picture—as intelligence pictures usually are—showing the Con-

federate commander more blank patches than those filled in. Jackson knew
that Lee continued to confront McClellan's main body east of Richmond and
that the Union general Burnside with a force of unknown strength was assembled near Fredericksburg. Jackson's own command was confronted by a heavy
enemy cavalry screen. That cavalry was apparently supported by a strong
infantry force of Pope's around and south of Culpeper. With characteristic
frankness and less than usual optimism, Jackson summed up his situation and
decisions in a dispatch to Lee, dashed off before he took to the saddle in the
early morning of 9 August:

General: I am not making much progress. The enemy's cavalry yesterday and last night
also threatened my train. . . . Hill (A.P.), though at Orange Court House yesterday
morning, having encamped in a mile of the town on the other side, reported last night
that he was not more than a mile on this side, thus making only 2 miles yesterday.
Ewell's division, which is near this point (12 miles from Culpeper Court House) and
in front, marched about 8 miles. Yesterday was oppressively hot [96 degrees F.]; several
men had sunstrokes. . . . I fear that the expedition will, in consequence of my tardy
movements, be productive of but little good. My plan was to have been at Culpeper
Court-House this forenoon. Should I learn that Burnside has gone in the direction of
Richmond I will try to cut him off. . . . The enemy's infantry, from reports brought in
last night, is about 5 miles in front; his cavalry near ours.[18]

    The order of march of Jackson's corps, as it renewed its northward advance,
was now as follows (see Figure 5.1): Ewell's division in advance, followed by
Winder, with Hill's division bringing up the rear. The corps cavalry covered
the advance, four regiments and two detachments under Brigadier General
Beverly H. Robertson. Unfortunately for Robertson—and the corps as a
whole—Jackson had taken a personal dislike to Robertson, perhaps brought
on by the latter's haphazard performance as the commander of the corps'
major reconnaissance element. Earlier in August Robertson had ridden up to
Jackson, who, in one of his few light moments, had been joshing his medical
officer about eating a raw onion to allay his thirst. When he recognized Robertson, Jackson at once dropped the levity, and wheeled on him with the
question always uppermost in his mind in regard to his cavalry, "Where is
the enemy?" An apparently unembarrassed Robertson replied, "I really do not
know." Though he might have gotten an A for honesty, Robertson's answer
left much to be desired from a force commander's viewpoint. Jackson's reaction spoke his disgust; he turned his back on the cavalryman without another
word. The disgust may have still rankled Jackson, for from early morning
onward he was persistent in pushing Robertson for information about the
enemy, and getting back only the word that his men were straggling, news
that was sure to turn Stonewall's dyspeptic stomach even more sour.
    Meanwhile the infantry, blessedly unaware of the cavalry's sloppy perfor-
mance, had stepped out smartly, in spite of the rising heat of the day. Ewell's

Figure 5.1
Jackson's Corps Organization

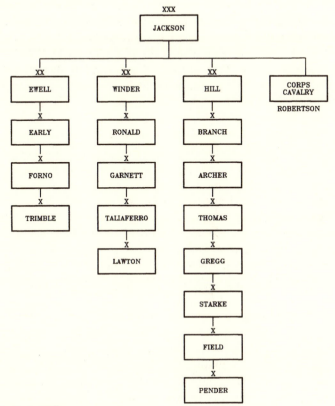

Courtesy Martin L. Wilkerson.

division was preceded by one of his brigades made up of five Louisiana regiments and the 12th Georgia, and commanded by Jubal A. Early, "Old Jube" to his troops. Early had dropped off security pickets on both sides of the road as he advanced, following the instructions of Ewell, who shared Jackson's concern about the threat of Union cavalry.

Early's leading regiment came to a halt about midmorning, when its commander found units of Robertson's cavalry in the process of scouting out Union cavalry to their front, some of which could be seen crossing a ridge about 800 yards to the right front. Soon Early was on the scene, joined shortly by Ewell. While the two were meeting, a battery of Old Jube's artillery had unlimbered and was firing ranging rounds at the enemy cavalry. When the Union cavalry disappeared behind the ridge, something happened that was to halt the forward march of Jackson's lead elements. The fire of Early's artillery was suddenly returned by that of Union guns. So, if enemy artillery was already there in firing position, there must be enemy infantry somewhere out there too! And waiting for a fight? Ewell wasted no time in ordering Early to reconnoiter to the front.

While Early and Ewell were meeting, Jackson, following his custom, had already ridden forward to see things for himself. He had left his forward headquarters to establish a command post at the house of the widow Petty while he and his command group rode on to a hilltop where he got his first glimpse of enemy cavalry. They seemed to be scouting off to his right front, to the east of the main Orange–Culpeper highway, near the so-called Critten-den Lane, a farm road leading from the highway to the Crittenden house.

Jackson then rode on to catch up with Ewell, who, while waiting for Jackson, had dismounted and was playing with the children on the porch of a farmhouse. When Jackson came up to the porch and an aide had handed him his map, the two generals spread it out before them and began a map study of the terrain. The chief feature of the terrain, one that would largely influence any battle plan, was the Orange–Culpeper highway, which had formed the axis of advance of Jackson's corps. A close inspection of that road shows (see Map 5.2) that its southern extreme is marked by the Crooked Run Church. From that point the main direction of the road runs generally north-northeast until it reaches the Gate (so labeled on the map) to the lane leading to the Crittenden house. Then, from the Gate, the highway runs northeast for a mile and a half before it finally turns straight northward. Other significant features include the Y in the highway where a leg splits off to run to Madison Court House. There were some open farm fields enclosed in large part by woods (all to figure later in the battle), a couple of small streams (no military obsta-cles), and the dominant topographical feature, Cedar Mountain, also known at the time as Slaughter's Mountain, named after the original owner of the land.

It was Cedar Mountain that caught Jackson's eye as the critical military feature of the area, the one on which he had begun to form a plan of action. The other factor influencing his upcoming decisions was his assumption that the main enemy force—if there really were one—was waiting *east* of the Orange–Culpeper highway. From that assumption and his terrain study, Jack-son conceived his plan. He decided to deploy whatever part of his corps would be required as follows: first, he would sweep aside any small Union force that might be impeding his corps' advance; second, if a larger enemy force were to be uncovered, he would maneuver his divisions in a double envelopment to destroy it. It is important to note that Jackson, in keeping with his as-sumption about the location of the enemy main force, did not order a recon-naissance by any commander to cover his corps' left flank.

Accordingly, the main effort would be made initially by Ewell, who would employ two brigades to sweep past the west slope of Cedar Mountain, thus ensuring its retention by following elements, and continue his maneuver to turn the enemy's left flank. Early, with Ewell's remaining brigade, was to continue to move forward, using the main highway as his axis of advance.

Map 5.2
Jackson's Plan of Maneuver

JACKSON'S PLAN OF MANEUVER
(Not To Scale)

Courtesy Martin L. Wilkerson.

Winder's division was to follow Early, supporting him. At the same time Winder would extend elements of his division westward in order to turn the enemy's right flank. Hill's division was to serve initially as the corps reserve, until the employment of its elements could be determined. A final essential factor in the plan—certainly stemming from Jackson's eye for terrain and from the

mind of Jackson the artillerist—would be flanking fire from Confederate batteries that would enfilade the enemy from Winder's left flank and from Ewell's
guns on the commanding slopes of Cedar Mountain on the corps' right.

The orders given, both Jackson and Ewell took a break in the shade of the
farmhouse porch. That Jackson could calmly snatch brief rest periods, even
in the course of an action, is well known. What remains unknown is what
might have gone through his mind as he stretched out to relax. It is tempting
to wonder if he reflected on an earlier moment of that morning when Hunter
McGuire, his staff medical officer, had asked him if he expected to fight a
battle before the day was over. Jackson had smiled and replied, "Banks is in
our front and he is generally willing to fight, and he generally gets whipped."

CHAPTER 6

Nathaniel Banks and the Advance to Cedar Mountain

Indeed it was Banks in front of Jackson—Nathaniel Prentiss Banks, Major General, U.S. Volunteers, commanding II Corps, Army of Virginia. It was the same Banks who was still smarting from the outmaneuvering and defeats suffered at Jackson's hands in the Shenandoah Valley less than three months before this coming confrontation. How Banks arrived at Cedar Mountain shapes the story of what follows.

Back on 26 June, the same day that Lee moved to attack McClellan in the Seven Days Battles, Lincoln signed the executive order that created the Army of Virginia and appointed Major General John Pope as its commander. The order, in effect, consolidated widely spread forces in the Shenandoah and south of Washington into one army made up of three army corps: I Corps under General Sigel, II Corps under General Banks, and III Corps under General McDowell. The new army's mission—curiously misinterpreted in some histories—was spelled out clearly enough in Lincoln's order:

The Army of Virginia . . . while protecting Western Virginia and the national capital from danger or insult, it shall in the speediest manner attack and overcome the rebel forces under Jackson and Ewell, threaten the enemy in the direction of Charlottesville, and render the most effective aid to relieve General McClellan and capture Richmond.[19]

The order also implied that the army's operations, while they were shielding Washington from the threat of enemy forces, should draw away a part of Lee's forces, thus aiding McClellan in any renewed offensive against the Confederacy's capital, an implication not lost on Pope. While all this seems clear enough in retrospect, the tasks confronting Pope were not so simple. He was

Nathaniel Banks

Map 6.1

Courtesy Martin L. Wilkerson.

taking command of forces that, in late June, were scattered from the Shenandoah Valley to Manassas and thence to the upper Rappahannock River (see Map 6.1). While his first concern was to concentrate the corps of his new army east of the Blue Ridge Mountains, he had to bear in mind the requirement to coordinate his upcoming operations with McClellan, who characteristically regarded any other force's operations on the North American continent to be automatically satellited upon his intentions and plans. John Pope characteristically saw *his* role as an army commander placing him on an equal footing with McClellan, who had already demanded of Lincoln a reinforcement of 35,000 troops in order to contend with Lee's imagined army of

200,000 standing between him and Richmond. So, when Pope made a tele-graphic overture to McClellan suggesting that the two armies coordinate their upcoming operations, the "Little Napoleon"—who, during his botched oper-ations in the Seven Days Battles, had managed to antagonize everyone of importance in Lincoln's war administration—replied only with the comment that Pope should concentrate his forces while, at some time in the future, he (McClellan) *might* move against Richmond in the event that Lee should move his main force against Pope.

The rebuffed Pope, while still in Washington, began to formulate his own strategy. Following meetings with Lincoln and Halleck, the president's com-mander of the armies, Pope telegraphed his initial orders to his field com-manders that would start the concentration of the major forces of his Army of Virginia: Sigel's I Corps was directed toward Sperryville; Banks' II Corps was to move to the vicinity of Little Washington, northeast of Sperryville; and McDowell's III Corps' two divisions were positioned initially with Rickett's division near Waterloo while King's division remained around Fredericksburg.

Another part of Pope's aggressive strategy was a directive to Banks to push forward with the cavalry of his II Corps toward Gordonsville, to seize that town and destroy the railroad east of it in order to disrupt Confederate com-munications. Although Banks did order Brigadier General Hatch, his cavalry commander, to carry out that mission, Hatch managed to bungle things right from the start. Instead of moving out with a mobile, purely cavalry force, he moved with a command that included both artillery and supply trains, thus making such slow progress that, as we saw earlier, Stonewall Jackson's offen-sive strategy had already enabled his forward elements to occupy Gordonsville in mid-July.

When Pope was informed of the aborted effort, he was determined to offer Banks a chance to show renewed aggressiveness by instructing him to send Hatch out again, this time to destroy the railroads west of Gordonsville in the direction of Charlottesville. Again Banks dispatched Hatch on the mission, and again Hatch—for reasons that are not clear—made such a feeble effort that he had to be recalled. Pope wasted no time relieving Hatch and replaced him with Brigadier General John Buford as Banks' new chief of cavalry. Fi-nally, Pope was ready to leave Washington and take command in the field. By 29 July he had joined Banks at the latter's command post southeast of Little Washington for a final look at the situation before issuing his latest orders to his three corps commanders. What opinion Pope might have formed of Banks' competence as a commander at this point is unknown, but aside from that particular viewpoint there is enough background information to pro-vide us with a picture of Banks, the man and the general, in 1862.

To his soldiers, as he rode past their regimental ranks, he was (with def-erence to Gilbert and Sullivan) "the very model of a modern Major-General," in immaculately tailored uniform gleaming with rows of brass buttons and the twin stars of his rank, yellow dress gloves that contrasted smartly with the dark blue of his uniform coat, and his saber at his side. Moreover, he had the comportment to match his martial appearance. Seeming taller than his five feet, eight inches, he had an erect, graceful carriage, an earnest look about him, and a melodious but powerful speaking voice. He rode his horse well, having taught himself to keep an erect posture on horseback, and to maintain a set jaw and stern demeanor befitting the soldiers' image of their general. His neatly brushed dark hair, heavy brows, and military moustache served to complete the picture.

Behind the image, however, there remained the hard fact that he had no military experience at all prior to his appointment by Lincoln, who had no other recourse at the time than to appoint political backers to high military rank—after having exhausted his meager supply of regular army possibles. In Banks' case, Lincoln's political debt was a huge one—to a nationally recognized antislavery Republican leader who had served in ten sessions of Congress and had risen to Speaker of the House of Representatives, a position only matched by his subsequent election as governor of Massachusetts, an office which he held from 1858 to January 1861. After the fall of Fort Sumter he had been quick to tender his services to the president, who commissioned him a major general of volunteers in May 1861.

Banks' rise to high political office was as traditionally American as Fourth of July speeches and bunting-decked speakers' platforms. Born one of seven children to hardworking, lower-middle-class parents in Waltham, Massachusetts, he was fortunate to have gotten even the barest of common-school educations before he had to go to work in the cotton mill where his father served as a foreman. Earning two dollars a week as a bobbin boy, he not only had begun to find his start in life but was able to cash in, later in his mature years, on the political nickname "the Bobbin Boy of Massachusetts." Pushed by insatiable ambition, he pursued two interests that were to take him out of the mill and form the bases which would lead to a real future. First, he took part in local debates and even began lecturing against intemperance. Second, he undertook studies on his own that would eventually enable him at age twenty-three to win admittance to the bar, and though he never practiced law in the courts he had opened a door to a career in politics.

The door, at first, didn't open easily. During those formative years—aside from a brief fling at studying acting which may have contributed to his public speaking abilities—he was a six-time, unsuccessful candidate for the lower house of the Massachusetts legislature. His seventh try in 1848, however, landed him a seat in that legislative body, and he was on his way—on his way to the only profession which (outside of his Civil War military service) would provide him with an income for life.

After four years this self-made man, at age thirty-seven, was ready to try for bigger things. In 1853 he was elected to the U.S. House of Representatives, where he made such a name for himself that, in only three years, he was proposed for the leadership role of Speaker of the House. His assumption of that role was not any easier than had been his seven attempts as a candidate for his first election; it took no less than 133 ballots—something of a record in itself—before he was confirmed as the Speaker. In spite of what must have been a stormy in-house battle, Banks soon proved himself to be a political leader to be reckoned with on any ground. He soon gained recognition for outstanding qualities that were to serve him well throughout a lifetime in politics. Not only rated as a brilliantly effective public speaker, he became widely known as a skillful negotiator, a tactful administrator, and a pragmatic party leader who, in his role as Speaker of the House, never had a decision overruled—and that in a period of tempestuous partisanship.

In fact, Banks' reputation as a political leader had by now become so firmly established that he was offered his party's nomination for the presidency in the campaign of 1856. Banks, however, declined the nomination, and in the following year looked homeward to another nomination—for the governorship of Massachusetts. He accepted the challenge and, against a firmly entrenched, three-time incumbent, took the innovative step of taking to the hustings in person, a move considered overly risky by politicians of the day. Banks, however, won by a large majority, and took office in 1858. Although his term in the governorship proved him to be a capable and effective executive, when Banks finished his term he offered his services in a military capacity to President Lincoln, following the fall of Fort Sumter. When one considers Lincoln's overnight appointment of a prominent political figure with no military experience to high military rank, the inevitable questions come to mind: How did he manage the adjustment? How well would he function in high command?

It may not be surprising to find that Banks started his military career by gaining an immediate popularity with his raw amateur soldiers of 1861. The personal appearance of such a smartly turned-out general was bound to impress the green farm boys and working-class volunteers who made up the ranks of the regiments on parade. And the personal picture was rounded by the background of a splendidly mounted staff and the general's bodyguard of red-fezzed Zouaves decked out in scarlet trousers and white leggings. Such a martial show was not an uncommon practice among amateur generals of the time, who thought they had to substitute image for lack of professional know-how.

In spite of the martial show and image creation, it would only be fair to point out that Banks showed a number of redeeming qualities that became evident soon after he took command. He showed a real and persistent interest in looking out for his men by seeing that they had such basics as rations and clothing. Also, he set a personal example of temperance, and put down rampant drunkenness by throwing out the whiskey and its suppliers. He stamped out prostitution rings in his camps by having the women rounded up and shipped back by the wagon load to Washington—where they no doubt found gainful employment.

He was not as effective overall in dealing with discipline, due to a tendency toward indecisiveness—even reversing decisions on occasion—in dealing with serious problems like desertion and looting. In one case, that of an offender in the 2nd Massachusetts who was ordered strung up by the thumbs as an example to the regiment, Banks approved the sentence, and ordered cavalry and artillery units to back up the execution of the sentence. However, when an outcry of objections came from a neighboring regiment, Banks called off the outside units, changed the location of the demonstration to a secluded area, and then failed to witness it in person. The colonel of the 2nd didn't hide his disgust, and another officer sounded off publicly, with words to the effect that their general lacked the military backbone to carry out his own orders. Later on, in the Shenandoah campaign, Banks issued strict orders against the looting of Valley farmsteads, but the orders were never effectively enforced, leading campfire wags to observe that "officers shut their eyes whenever a rooster crowed."

In other matters relating to command, Banks was either plain unlucky or a victim of his lack of military acumen. When it came to selecting and organizing a staff—a matter whose importance to a commander could hardly be overemphasized—he was faced with a problem shared by all Civil War commanders: trained, professional staff officers simply did not exist; thus, every commander was thrown back on his own resources. Banks tried to make do with what he considered the best available, but it seems that his basic criteria for selection of staff officers were based on outward qualities such as obvious intelligence, evidence of an educated background, and a confident bearing to match. What was lacking was professional training and experience, but equally damaging to Banks' command structure was the fact that too much self-assurance in a staff officer's bearing—when viewed from "below," from the viewpoint of subordinate commanders, their staffs, and the troops—was taken as arrogance, and thus reflected badly on the commander and his command relationships.

In another command aspect, Banks has been compared with Stonewall Jackson in his manner of concealing his operational plans from his subordinate commanders.[20] While it is probably true that Banks may, on occasion, have confused his subordinates with incomplete or faulty orders or failed to confide in them in clearing up matters, the comparison with Jackson's modus operandi does not stand up in the light of historical evidence. Jackson, while keeping future operations to himself, undoubtedly had a complete concept of operation in mind, thus knowing exactly what he wanted accomplished—when, where, and by whom. Banks, on the other hand, must have appeared secretive, when in all probability he was hiding the fact that he hadn't formulated a coherent plan or that he was unsure of the orders he should issue to execute a plan. In either case—or in a combination of the two—he must have kept his thoughts to himself until the situation forced him to act.

In assessing a tactical situation, Banks showed other shortcomings in fields that are essential parts of a combat commander's capabilities: he was not good at reading maps nor at the conjoint skill of terrain and combat reconnaissance, that is, the ability to assess the significance of terrain features in relation to the movement of troops on the ground. And although those capabilities might have been acquired—even the hard way through trial and error in active campaigning—it seems that Banks never did master those skills, at least to the degree of being confident of his ability to outmaneuver an opponent before or during an engagement.

All things considered, Major General Banks, the politician-cum-soldier, had to struggle with so many obstacles in making the transition from a skilled political leader to a high-level military commander that one wonders that he was able to manage at all. But manage he did, and therein lies the key to understanding his ability to function in the job: he was essentially a *manager* and not a *leader* of soldiers whose fate in war was his responsibility. If that seems to be a singular way of looking at Banks' attempt at making the transition, one should be aware that today's U.S. Army still has to cope with the problem—even though restricted nowadays to professional soldiers—of sorting out the differences between management and leadership.

In looking at Banks' problems from any angle, it becomes evident that—in spite of his undoubted personal courage, the fact that he was able to inspire men through his oratory, and his ability to oversee their well-being—his generalship was about to be tested in the crucible of battle in ways that he had never faced before and would never again face in the same way.

Turning again to Pope's Army of Virginia operations, by the end of July Pope had determined to begin concentrating his forces in the Culpeper Court House area. He had earlier disposed his cavalry to cover his army's front, all the way from the Blue Ridge Mountains in the west to the juncture of the Rappahannock and Rapidan Rivers in the east. Specifically, Buford's cavalry covered the western portion of the army front from Madison Court House to Barnett's Ford; while Bayard's cavalry covered the eastern front along the Rapidan River from Barnett's Ford (where he had linked up with Buford's cavalry pickets) to Rapidan Station.

At this point it is important to note that, while the Army of Virginia's official strength returns showed an overall total of 72,000 troops, the troop strength in the area of operations (i.e., where Pope was now concentrating his three corps) was actually slightly less than 44,000. Even more important, Banks had, on 31 July, reported II Corps total strength at some 15,000 troops, but his actual strength on the ground was actually only 8,800 men.[21] Such a discrepancy would, when viewed from a twentieth-century military viewpoint, be nothing less than incredible. In Banks' case, the difference has never been fully explained, but the shock is lessened when one takes into account the number of detachments Banks would have made to guard his logistical rear (a worrisome burden that seemed always uppermost in his mind), involving sizeable combat units detached to safeguard his communications.

On 6 August two of Pope's three corps had begun their march toward Culpeper Court House. McDowell was directed to move Rickett's division of his III Corps from Waterloo to Culpeper; Banks to move his II Corps from Little Washington to the point where the Sperryville–Culpeper Turnpike crossed the Hazel River. Initially, Sigel was directed to remain at Sperryville until ordered to move forward. As a result of Pope's march orders, by 7 August all of his infantry and artillery (with the exception of King's division of Mc-Dowell's III Corps at Fredericksburg) was strung out along the axis of the turnpike from Sperryville toward Culpeper.

On that same day, 7 August, Pope had arrived at Sperryville, where he had gone to check on Sigel's I Corps. While there he received cavalry reports that enemy infantry had begun to cross the Rapidan River between Liberty Mills and Barnett's Ford. Bayard also reported that he was pulling back his cavalry screen in the direction of Culpeper. So, by now there was little doubt that the enemy was moving in force toward Culpeper, and Pope rode forward himself to make his own estimate of the situation. By the morning of 8 August he was at Culpeper, where he decided on his next moves. Banks was ordered to accelerate his march to Culpeper and Sigel was directed to follow Banks and join the concentration of the army's forces in the Culpeper area. More-over, Banks was further directed to send forward Crawford's brigade in the direction of Cedar Mountain with orders to support Bayard's cavalry elements as they withdrew.

Although Banks was prompt in getting his corps on the road, the marches of 7 and 8 August went forward under rough conditions due to the extreme August heat. George H. Gordon, one of Banks' best brigade commanders, recalled that "clouds of dust hung over us, there was not a breath of air, and the road was like a furnace. . . . many of our men fell out from weakness."[22] The experience of Gordon's brigade was typical, but in spite of the adverse conditions Banks had pushed forward resolutely and closed his march at Cul-peper on 8 August. In contrast, Sigel was so slow in getting his I Corps on the road (if one can imagine a corps commander querying the army staff on which road to take when there was only one, the turnpike from Sperryville to Culpeper!) that he was a day later than Banks to reach the Culpeper area—a vital factor in any pending engagement, since Pope must have been relying on Sigel's corps as his chief means of reinforcing Banks if the need arose.

As Banks oversaw the forward movement of the two divisions of his corps (see Figure 6.1), he must have had at least two pressing bits of counsel from Pope in the back of his mind. The first had been that part of Pope's now infamous bulletin addressed to the officers and soldiers of the Army of Virginia shortly after he had assumed command: "Let us disregard such ideas [of taking strong positions and holding them . . . of lines of retreat]. The strongest posi-tion a soldier should desire to occupy is one from which he can most easily advance against the enemy."[23] The other, in a letter from Pope to Banks, admonished him that "retreat is over. I shall not in any case act on the de-

Figure 6.1
Banks' II Corps Organization

Courtesy Martin L. Wilkerson.

fensive, but should the enemy advance against us, I shall . . . do the attacking myself. . . . Impress upon your troops the certainty that the attack will hereafter always be made by us, teach them to look forward and not backward."[24] How much those admonitions occupied Banks' thoughts during 8 and 9 August is, of course, unknown, but the course of events has shown that he had taken the warning to heart. That he did so with confidence in his ability to follow them is evident in the letter that Banks wrote to his wife in the evening of 8 August: "The day we have waited for so long has at last come. I am glad."[25]

By the early morning of 9 August the last elements of Banks' corps had reached their assembly areas near Culpeper, and by that time Pope had made up his mind to direct Banks forward to block the advancing Confederates until he could complete the concentration of his army around Culpeper and, presumably in keeping with his spirit of the offensive, move against his opponent. Accordingly, he sent a senior aide, Colonel Louis H. Marshall, over to Banks to deliver verbal orders to that effect. Banks, however, was careful to see that the orders were transmitted in writing and had an adjutant take them down at Marshall's dictation:

Culpeper / 9:45 A.M., Aug 9"62 / from Col Lewis [*sic*] Marshall—Genl Banks to move to the front immediately, assume command of all forces in the front—deploy his skirmishers if the enemy approaches and attack him immediately as soon as he approaches—and be reinforced from here.[26]

Banks then issued his march orders to start II Corps forward toward the Cedar Mountain area, where Crawford's brigade was already taking up positions to support Bayard's cavalry. Once his corps had been set in motion, Banks rode over to the army command post for a final check with Pope on the situation. Upon his arrival Pope informed him that he had already sent forward Brigadier General Benjamin S. Roberts, Pope's chief of staff, who knew the Cedar Mountain terrain and who would "designate the ground you are to hold." If, at this time, Banks questioned the term "to hold"—in the light of Pope's just-issued order and his repeated admonitions about staying on the offense—it appears that he kept any misgivings to himself. In any case, he rode on toward Cedar Mountain, prepared to deploy the two divisions of his corps with the help of General Roberts.

It was shortly after noon when Banks met up with Roberts, and the two began to look over the ground on which Banks would deploy his divisions. Because Roberts was familiar with the area and because Crawford had already drawn up his brigade in line of battle, Roberts pointed out Cedar Run (actually the north fork of Cedar Run) as a terrain feature which Banks could use initially as a guide for starting his deployment. Gordon's account of the meeting includes the following exchange: "When Banks came up, he said to Roberts, 'General Pope said you would indicate the line I am to occupy'—'I have been over this ground thoroughly,' replied Roberts, 'and I believe this line,' meaning the one which Crawford's brigade then held, 'is the best that can be taken'—'In this opinion I concurred with him,' says Banks, 'and placed my command there.' "[27]

During Banks' terrain ride with Roberts the latter apparently dropped a comment that seems not only uncalled for but one that rankled Banks to the extent that he remembered it in correspondence and testimony some twenty years later. Roberts, a West Pointer who was known to dislike political generals, reportedly remarked to Banks that "there must be no backing out this day." The remark stuck in Banks' memory because, he later wrote, "I hear the sound of his voice. It referred to our retreat from Strasburg [following defeats by Jackson in the Valley Campaign some two months earlier] before the same Stonewall Jackson."[28]

Small wonder then that the two commanders who were about to confront each other again in battle would recall the other with such contrasting feelings: Jackson with professional scorn for an old adversary; Banks still smarting from a well-recalled drubbing, and burning to reverse the score.

CHAPTER 7

The Battle of Cedar Mountain

When Jackson and Banks first became aware that each was confronted by a sizeable enemy force, their overriding and common concerns were the deployment of their troops and the terrain over which they were to move. In Jackson's case we have had a cursory look at the terrain on which he had begun to plan the maneuver of his corps' leading elements. It would be helpful now if we could take a closer look at the ground (see Map 7.1), first as Jackson would have seen it.

THE TERRAIN

The Orange–Culpeper highway, on which the advance of his whole corps now depended, extended from the Y (marked by Major's School House) to the northeast. As Jackson looked up the road toward Culpeper, off to his right at a distance of about a mile and a half was Cedar Mountain, which was already being secured by Ewell's division on the right flank of Jackson's corps. To Jackson's left, on the north side of the highway, were farm fields in the shape of an inverted L; these fields were surrounded on three sides by dense woods, with the open side of the fields adjoining the highway. Farther up the road, on its right side, were cornfields whose tall-standing corn could provide concealment for troops inside them. In general terms, the terrain (with the exception of the woods) was open enough for maneuver and to provide fields of fire. That is not to say, however, that the ground was an ideal battlefield. Though its nature was gently rolling, it was made up of many low ridges or folds which could provide troop cover, and the woods not only were thick with trees but also contained dense underbrush, features which were tactically

Map 7.1

Courtesy Martin L. Wilkerson.

significant because they could conceal troop movements and at the same time could slow down those movements, while obscuring fields of fire.

Turning to Banks' viewpoint, when he was reconnoitering the ground in the company of General Roberts he had observed that Crawford's brigade had deployed with its line roughly parallel to the north fork of Cedar Run and north of the highway. Looking to his front he could see the near edge of the woods described above; he could also see that the same woods extended far enough to his right to conceal either the advance of his troops or that of approaching enemy troops. Also, when he looked forward from Crawford's line he would note that the ground sloped gently down to the north fork of Cedar Run and from thence rose gently up to that woods to his front. To his left lay the highway and beyond it the cornfields. From his location at Crawford's line neither Banks nor his troops could see the cleared fields north of the highway because they were obscured by the woods to their front. By the same token, Confederate troops on the far side of the cleared fields were prevented from observing any advancing Union troops because the latter would be hidden by the same woods.

ADVANCE GUARD ACTIONS AND REACTIONS

Jackson's plan of maneuver was to develop the situation with the lead elements of Ewell's and Winder's divisions in a manner designed to (1) overrun
any small enemy force in their front and (2) if a major enemy force were
encountered, to destroy it by a double envelopment. After he had this plan
firmly in mind, he began to oversee the operations to his front. The first
development to demand his attention was the action taken by Early's brigade
of Ewell's division. It will be recalled (near the end of Chapter 5) that it was
Early's brigade whose advance guard had first encountered enemy cavalry to
its front, and it was Early who had deployed his leading regiments to advance
and drive off the pesky cavalry screen. It was then that Early's infantry was
first taken under fire by Union artillery, and thus Early and Ewell were alerted
to the fact that there had to be more than just cavalry opposing them. After
Ewell had conferred with Jackson (end of Chapter 5) he had given his orders
to Early, who proceeded to carry out his part of the mission. In doing so he
made a quick reconnaissance to his front and decided that he could deploy
his leading regiments on the open ground south of the Culpeper–Orange highway, that is, in a line perpendicular to the highway. Once he had deployed
he advanced his line to drive the enemy cavalry off the low ridge to his front.
When his leading troops crossed the crest of the ridge they were immediately
taken under fire by batteries of Union artillery. The batteries had ranged in
so quickly and accurately that Early's lead regiments began to suffer gaping
holes in their ranks, and Early halted the advance. He pulled his line back
under cover of the ridge and sent back for reinforcements to come up on his
left. The suspended advance was not due to hesitancy on Early's part—his
character and reputation indicate quite the opposite—rather it was the necessity to wait for units of Winder's division to cover his left flank and advance
in line with him. As far as Jackson's scheme of maneuver was concerned, it
appears that he had, in keeping with his secretive nature, communicated his
plan of battle only to Ewell and Winder and no one else in the chain of
command. Notably unnotified was A. P. Hill, whose after-action report reveals
that, at the time, he knew only that he was to send a brigade forward to
reinforce a part of Ewell's division.

As Jackson's advance guard units were becoming engaged and reinforcing
units began to deploy to Early's left, Jackson was surely aware that his entire
force of over 20,000 men had to advance and deploy from one single road,
the Culpeper–Orange highway. If there was ever a need for a Napoleonic type
of advance to contact over a wide road network, this was it. Jackson, however,
had to deal with a score of limitations that even a Napoleon could not have
conceived; that aspect will be considered in due time. For now, it is important
to observe that the three brigades of Winder's division were moving up into
battle positions between 3:00 P.M. (the approximate time that Early had made
his forced halt) and 4:00 P.M. Winder's lead brigade, commanded by Colonel

T. S. Garnett, moved forward and was followed by William B. Taliaferro's brigade, and the two deployed initially on the left side of the highway, facing south at right angles to Early's front. This odd deployment was supposedly part of a maneuver intended to strike the enemy batteries in flank and clear the way for Early to advance. Garnett soon saw the impracticability of attacking across Early's front, and called off the maneuver. In the meantime, as Garnett and Taliaferro changed front to face toward the enemy, General Winder saw fit to turn his personal attention to getting supporting artillery into firing positions, rather than hurrying his third brigade into a position on his left flank—a key position, since that brigade would not only anchor Winder's division's left flank, but that of Jackson's whole force as well.

Winder's concern with supporting artillery was justified. He had observed enemy batteries moving to position from which they could pose a real threat to his deploying brigades. Brigadier General Charles S. Winder was not only a skilled tactician but also one of Jackson's most trusted commanders. He had lived up to Jackson's expectations as commander of the famed Stonewall Brigade during the Valley Campaign, and was the logical successor to command Jackson's division upon Stonewall's promotion to corps commander. He had gotten out of a sickbed—with Jackson's reluctant permission—to resume command of his division as it took up its march on this same day. In fact, Winder had ridden forward as far as possible in an ambulance until he could mount his horse and take command in the front. Another part of his immediate concern was the all too evident fact that an intense artillery "duel" was in progress, and incoming enemy rounds were already beginning to fall uncomfortably close to Poague's battery, which Winder was overseeing at the time. Wanting to observe the enemy while directing the fire of a section of the battery, Winder had dismounted and, with his field glasses to his eyes, had started to call out a command when he was horribly wounded by an incoming shell. There was no doubt that the wounds were mortal; his left arm and side were torn to shreds, and after being carried to the rear he later died. That Winder's mortal wounding would impact seriously on the course of events was soon to become obvious. His designated successor in command was Brigadier General William B. Taliaferro, whose brigade we have already seen going into action alongside that of Garnett.

Though Taliaferro was quickly informed of his succession to division command, he knew nothing at all of Jackson's battle plan, since it appears that Winder had had neither the time nor the opportunity to pass on what little he knew. In any case, Taliaferro at once took matters into his own hands, and took stock of the situation as he could personally assess it. During the shifting of brigade positions following the aborted attack across Early's front, Taliaferro had redeployed his brigade to the left of Early's, which meant that Taliaferro's brigade was then on line between Early and the highway. At about the same time Garnett had begun to deploy his brigade to the left of the highway and facing the cleared fields to his front, which would place his brigade left flank somewhere in the woods surrounding the cleared fields. That "somewhere" now became Taliaferro's immediate concern as the new division commander, and he wasted no time in riding toward the left to contact Garnett and find out things for himself. He failed to find Garnett but did meet up with Garnett's leftmost unit, the 1st Virginia Battalion, an Irish–American unit which had gone into line in the woods and had not yet made contact with the regiment to its right. Taliaferro continued his reconnaissance to his right front and came out on the highway, where he could see more clearly and direct his operations. While Taliaferro was making his way through the woods, Jackson had been informed of Winder's wounding, and had ridden forward to check on matters personally. Though he didn't find Taliaferro he did come across Garnett, whom he warned to pay careful attention to his left flank and to request reinforcements from his new division commander. Garnett at once sent a couple of aides to find Taliaferro, and one eventually found him at the front near the highway.

Jackson was equally concerned with getting up Hill's division, which not only constituted his force's reserve, but also comprised half the strength of his corps. He had already had Hill dispatch one brigade, Thomas', to reinforce Early. Thomas had gone into position on Early's right and was thus committed into action. Consequently Jackson then wished to turn his attention to the readying of Hill's other brigades for commitment in the corps center or on its left. Unfortunately for Jackson's plans, the situation on his left was soon to change so rapidly and violently that it would require all of his personal powers to restore the situation.

While Jackson's lead units were making their deployments, Banks had already arrived in the area with Augur's division and directed it to deploy to the left of Crawford's brigade (see Map 7.2). Augur's initial deployment placed his division in a line behind the cornfields, so that it was left of and perpendicular to the Orange–Culpeper highway and facing the enemy. Augur was putting his troops in position starting around 2:00 P.M., about an hour before Early had made his first advance. When Augur's three brigades came on line they were in order from right to left: Geary on the right with his right flank near the highway; Prince's brigade to Geary's left; Greene's brigade on the extreme left and somewhat farther rearward. The first two brigades were relatively strong units, while Greene's was a small unit with only two weak regiments.

These troop movements were made under Banks' watchful eye, for he had taken a forward post just across (north of) the highway opposite the right flank of Augur's division. He was there during the first phase of the artillery duel, when he got an opportunity to show his physical courage. He was leaning against a tree when an artillery solid shot struck it about a foot and a half above his head. He was uninjured but also unshaken, even when it was revealed that the round had left a gaping hole in the tree. Soon he was able to

Map 7.2

BANKS' INITIAL DEPLOYMENT
(Not To Scale)

Courtesy Martin L. Wilkerson.

make a dashing ride along his front lines, to show his presence while checking on his troop dispositions.

An important part of Augur's deployment was the ordering out (from Prince's brigade) of the 8th and 12th U.S. Infantry Battalions to act as skirmishers. These regular army units covered the entire front of Augur's division, fanning out into and under cover of the cornfields, from which they did a superb job of skirmishing, as their enemy was soon to realize. Taking full advantage of the tall corn, they kept Early's and other Confederate troops under constant sniping fire. They were even able to scare the drawers off of the cannoneers of Pegram's and Hardy's batteries (in firing positions and firing toward the cornfields), to the extent of the latter having to be saved by Early himself ordering an infantry regiment to their rescue.

Banks' II Corps' total fighting strength consisted of his two divisions: Augur's, whose deployment we have just observed, and Williams' division of two brigades. Crawford's brigade, as already related (Chapter 6), was on the field initially to back up Bayard's cavalry screen, and we have also noted the battle position that it now occupied. The two divisions were roughly equal in their fighting strengths: Augur's rounding off at 3,200, Williams' at about 3,500,[29] thus bringing Banks' II Corps total to some 6,700. When one compares that total to Jackson's available strength of some 20,000 (Jackson's corps actually numbered about 24,000, but two brigades of Hill's division had been detached to guard the corps' supply trains), one can see that the disparity on the field could have risen to as much as three to one in Jackson's favor. Be that as it may, military historians and analysts are quick to point out that numbers alone do not determine the outcome of battles: there are a host of other factors influencing an outcome, not the least of which are the massing of force at a critical point, quality of leadership, morale on both sides, and so on. Moreover, one can be certain that neither Banks nor Jackson would have had anywhere near an accurate accounting of his opponent's actual strength. In fact, it may be recalled, Banks didn't have even an accurate accounting of his own corps strength during his strategic moves before his corps moved toward Cedar Mountain.

Strength in numbers aside, Banks' obvious concern after Augur's division's deployment was the positioning of the two brigades of Williams' division. Crawford's brigade was moved forward about 400 yards, across the north fork of Cedar Run and into the strip of woods in its front. In that part of the woods the brigade could face an oncoming enemy across the cleared fields (in this case a wheat field) while remaining concealed in the west edge of the strip of woods. Gordon's brigade was deployed to the right of Crawford's, and about a half mile to its rear. These movements were completed between 3:00 and 4:00 P.M. At about the same time all of Banks' supporting artillery, forty-two guns in all, had occupied firing positions across the front: three batteries on the left of the highway, four on the right. All of the batteries were actively engaged from 3:00 P.M. to 5:00 P.M., though, with the exception of the Union skirmishers' firing, there were no major infantry units engaged during the same period.

By this time, though Banks' disposition of his force may have appeared to have assumed a defensive posture, his concept of his role in the coming engagement was to prove anything but passively defensive. As events were soon to show, he did not intend to sit tight in his present positions and wait for his enemy to attack him. Whatever his ultimate intentions might have been, at 2:25 P.M. he sent a message to Pope informing him of II Corps' situation and dispositions; the general tenor of the report indicated that, though the enemy seemed to be "taking positions," he did not appear to "intend immediate attack." However, the next message Banks sent to Pope, at 4:50 P.M., did reveal the II Corps commander's offensive spirit—that same spirit so frequently conveyed by Pope to his commanders and troops:

About 4 o'clock shots were exchanged by the skirmishers. Artillery opened fire on both sides in a few minutes. One regiment of rebel infantry advancing now deployed in front as skirmishers. I have ordered a regiment on the right, Williams' Division, to meet them, and one from the left, Augur's, to advance on the left and in front.

5 P.M.—They are now approaching each other.[30]

Whether Banks' message was intended to create a sense of suspense in his army commander's mind is, of course, indeterminate, but Pope's reaction—after listening to the sounds of cannonade that reached him at Culpeper, and taking heed of the ominous note of impending action in Banks' report—was both prudent and prompt. He immediately ordered Ricketts' division of McDowell's corps to move forward to Banks' support. Though the order was received in timely fashion, Ricketts' reaction was not so timely. Despite the fact that his command was only a few miles from Cedar Mountain, his division's lead elements didn't arrive on the field until 7:00 P.M., far too late to influence the action.

In the meantime, while Banks was about to issue his next orders to his division commanders, Jackson was fully occupied with overseeing the execution of his battle plan. As he saw the situation following Taliaferro's assuming command of Winder's division, it was imperative not only that the division secure its left flank—and that of the corps—but also that it get its leftmost units sorted out in order that the corps could advance as a cohesive force. So, just what was going on in that woods on the corps left—and what of the enemy beyond the woods?

THE FORCES ENGAGE AND THE BATTLE TAKES A CRITICAL TURN

As we have seen, Jackson's closest enemy was not beyond the woods but already in them in the form of Crawford's brigade, fully prepared to advance to the attack should the order be given. And Banks had been preparing himself to give that order. Either before or immediately after getting off his 4:50 P.M. message to Pope, he had been facing the weightiest decision of his command career. His decision depended upon his answers to two all-important questions. First, was the enemy force confronting him too weak—as it now seemed—to take the initiative and attack him? Second, were those orders from Pope that he had made Colonel Marshall convert to writing ("deploy his [Banks'] skirmishers if the enemy approaches, and attack him immediately as soon as he approaches") really broad enough to permit him to attack Jackson at this critical time?

Banks' answer to the first question depended upon his perception of what he had so far observed of the enemy's actions in front of his deployed brigades. His answer, from all indications, was in the affirmative: yes, because there were still no signs that a major enemy attack was massing, nor had the enemy shown any signs of activity other than light skirmishing and artillery firing. Banks' answer to the second question was also in the affirmative, as clearly

Map 7.3

Courtesy Martin L. Wilkerson.

shown in his command decision. There may have been a third question regarding the availability of sufficient reserves to support a II Corps attack: there was none, since, as it happened, both Augur's and Williams' divisions were fully committed to action. Moreover, Pope's assurance in his orders to Banks that you will "be reinforced from here" would depend on the army commander's capability of getting major elements of the corps to Banks' aid in a timely manner—a capability he did not possess, as demonstrated by the failure of Ricketts' division to arrive in time to support Banks' actions. As a result, Banks apparently downplayed or disregarded the need for a corps reserve to back up an attack by his whole force.

Banks did arrive at a clear-cut decision, for his next action was to order an attack by both Augur's and Williams' divisions (see Map 7.3). Augur's division (less Greene's brigade, which was left behind to secure the corps' left flank) launched Geary's brigade and Prince's brigade abreast. The attack of Williams' division was led by Crawford's brigade, which attacked across the open wheat field and into the woods beyond it; Crawford was to be supported by Gordon's brigade. The advance of the two divisions was clearly divided by the highway: Augur's to the left of the road, Williams' to the right of the road.

Both attacks were launched between 5:00 and 5:30 P.M., and fell upon Jackson's forward elements. To the south of the highway, Augur's brigades struck the Confederate brigades of Early and Taliaferro, the latter now commanded by another Taliaferro, Colonel A. G. Taliaferro, the uncle of William B. Taliaferro, who had succeeded Winder in command of the division. To the north of the highway and in the woods east of the wheat field, Crawford's brigade smashed into Garnett's brigade and (subsequently, as will be seen) into Ronald's brigade, which had been located to the left rear of Garnett.

When one looks at the whole picture *after* the opposing forces had become fully engaged, it might appear that Crawford's brigade was making the main attack of Banks' corps and Augur's division was making a secondary or supporting attack. Such was not the case for two reasons: one, Banks probably could neither have planned nor executed such a coordinated attack; two, the initial success of Crawford's attack was fortuitous from Banks' viewpoint because, in both senses of the word, it was accidental and fortunate.

What happened on the Confederate side was this. When Taliaferro had to assume command of Winder's division, there was unavoidable confusion, not only because Taliaferro was ignorant of Winder's mission (as received from Jackson; see Chapter 5), but also because he had to ride through a dense woods trying to locate other leaders and sort things out on his own. At about the same time Jackson, having been informed of Winder's fall, had gone forward to find the new division commander. After failing to find Taliaferro—small wonder, considering that all concerned were hindered by the woods and the unfolding situation—Jackson did find Garnett and, it will be recalled, after warning him to watch out for his left flank, rode back to his forward command post. Shortly after Jackson had left, Garnett had looked to his front, and there coming across the fields was the long blue line of Union infantry advancing to the attack. He sent an aide galloping to the division commander with an urgent warning.

The long blue line was the leftmost line of the three regiments of Crawford's brigade. On the brigade commander's order bayonets were fixed, and the line emerged from the woods, the men hopping over a fence at their edge of the woods and continuing their advance across the open fields. At the same time, the right flank regiments in the blue line were passing rapidly through the woods to their front, so that their line overlapped the Confederate left and took it in flank. The fired-up Union attack had struck the unprepared Confederate units of Garnett's brigade with such force that disorder reigned throughout, compounded by the change of division command at just the wrong time, with both commanders and regiments out of contact in the deep woods.

As soon as Taliaferro, as the new division commander, had received Garnett's word of the oncoming Union attack—indeed, he now saw it himself from his forward post—he sent a courier galloping to order Ronald to bring up his brigade on Garnett's left flank. It was too late. The leftmost regiments of Garnett's brigade had broken, and their dissolved remnants were streaming to the rear. Then as Ronald's brigade, the famed Stonewall Brigade, tried to make its way forward to link up with Garnett's brigade, it was met in the woods by Crawford's hard-charging line, which paused only long enough to send a volley crashing into the faces of Ronald's dumbfounded men. The Stonewall Brigade fell back in confusion that was soon turned into panic by the 1st Virginia Battalion and the 42nd Virginia, whose men broke ranks and fled rearward. The contagion of panic spread as the Union volleys could be heard crashing through the woods. Colonel Andrews, commanding the 2nd Massachusetts of Gordon's brigade, recalled that "suddenly, at about forty minutes after five o'clock, there burst forth from the direction of the wheatfield [the field and the woods being over 1,000 yards from Andrews' position] the heaviest and most continuous sound of musketry I have ever heard. It was not preceded by scattering shots, but at once became a steady roar."[31]

Crawford's attack, however, did not confine its success to breaking up the Confederate left in the woods. Indeed, the attack gathered momentum as its spearheaded units swept out of the woods, and wheeling south crashed into the left flank of A. G. Taliaferro's brigade, which was fully engaged in trying to fight off the attack of Geary's brigade of Augur's division in its front. This latest coup of Crawford's attack enabled his men, exuberant with their continued successes, to pour their fire into Taliaferro's and Early's regiments, already with their hands full in delivering defensive fire against Geary's and Prince's advancing brigades. The combined fire of Union volleys from front and flank was more than Taliaferro's and Early's troops could stand. One historian noted that "both the Forty-seventh and Forty-eighth Alabama, from opposite ends of the brigade [A. G. Taliaferro's], collapsed and fell back 'in utter rout.'"[32] A similar fate befell the regiments of Early's brigade on its left, whose ranks fragmented and broke away to the rear.

At this critical point in the battle, one may well ask: Was not Banks' decision to attack confirmed beyond his greatest hopes? Was Jackson confronted with a looming disaster, one that was inconceivable to a commander of his stature?

BANKS' ATTACK AT CLIMAX—JACKSON'S RALLY AND RECOVERY

When Jackson's combat intelligence and inherent battle sense combined to alert him to impending disaster, his reaction was characteristic—immediate but with no sign of alarm. He rode rearward and found A. P. Hill. The tenseness of the situation, now keenly realized by both men, was ripe for an instant renewal of their famous feuding. "Within a few moments Jackson found Hill and went after him. 'Jackson sharply told him he was behind time,' an eyewitness reported, 'and ordered him to deploy his regiments.' A. P. Hill had in fact been doing just that as rapidly as his men arrived and already had reason to believe that Jackson dealt unjustly."[33] Hill, however, accepted the unneeded urging and went on with his duties. Jackson wheeled his horse around and hastened back toward the scene of action.

On his way to the front he came across Brigadier General L. O. Branch, a Southern political general, who was in the middle of practicing his oratorical skills on the men of his brigade. Jackson interrupted him only long enough to order him to "push forward, General, push forward!" Jackson didn't wait to oversee Branch's compliance, but galloped on to come up to the Gate, where Crittenden Lane joined the highway, the critical point of the action as Jackson now saw it. What met his eyes didn't surprise him, men jamming the road in panicked flight, but it did arouse him to enact one of the most re-nowned scenes in his personal history.

With his inherent instinct for being at the right place, at the right time, he made use of a dramatic flair that was as effective as it seemed foreign to his nature. Pushing his horse into the midst of the milling crowd on the highway, he meant to draw his sword in a gesture intended not only to rally his men but, if necessary, to use the flat of it on the backs of the fugitives. At this point, however, the gesture switched from the dramatic to comic opera: the sword had rusted in the scabbard from nonuse, and he couldn't withdraw it. In another time and place the heroics-gone-awry would have seemed right out of Gilbert and Sullivan, but in this case Jackson was undeterred by any such mishap. "So he deliberately unsnapped it from his belt holdings and used it scabbard and all on the heads of the fleeing panic stricken troops."[34] The scabbard wielding, however, was not the end of Stonewall's rallying efforts. He grabbed a Confederate battle flag and, waving it overhead, cried out in a shout that could be heard up and down the highway, "Rally, brave men, and press forward! Your general will lead you. Jackson will lead you. Follow me!"[35] Incredible as it may seem to today's more worldly reader, the effect on the troops "was electric." Many of the men, ever sensitive to the Jackson charisma, halted and turned back to find their regiments.

While the effect of Jackson's rallying was spreading, another development— as beyond Jackson's control as it was inevitable—was the slowing down of Crawford's attack from a torrent to a trickle. At the same time that Crawford's men were running out of steam after their amazing feats, their ammunition was also running out. Moreover, Banks had no reserves, at either division or corps level, to feed in or pass through Crawford's brigade to exploit the suc-cess of the attack. Unsurprisingly, then, the momentum of Crawford's attack ground to a halt, and as a result, so did that of Geary's and Prince's brigades. Consequently, the whole of Banks' corps was becoming increasingly vulner-able to a Confederate counterattack (see Map 7.4).

These developments had become all too evident to Jackson immediately after his personal involvement in the efforts to rally the broken units of his corps left and center. By 6:30 P.M., not over half an hour after Crawford's

Map 7.4

Courtesy Martin L. Wilkerson.

attack had reached its zenith, Jackson's rallying was beginning to pay off as he began to recover control of the Confederate situation. On Jackson's left, Branch had taken his corps commander's words to heart and was indeed "pushing forward" with his brigade in perfect order as it launched into its part of a counterattack. As Branch's North Carolina regiments advanced toward the Union right flank they were met by the fugitives from the broken units of Ronald's Stonewall Brigade, mostly from the 27th Virginia. The Tar Heels kept their ranks intact, only opening them enough to let the fleeing Virginians through, no doubt with some unkind remarks to the effect that it was a shame that the latter should be running in the wrong direction over the sacred soil of their native state.

On Jackson's right, where A. G. Taliaferro's and Early's brigades had taken blows from their front, left flank, and rear, regimental officers were regaining control of their companies and beginning to reform their battle lines. In fact, on Early's right, Thomas' brigade (having gone into a reinforcing position on Early's right flank) and Early's 12th Georgia had held steadfastly and had never fallen back a single pace.

Back in the Confederate center and on the left, A. P. Hill was living up to his reputation as a fighting general. He had stripped off his uniform jacket to reveal his famous red battle shirt, and had gone to work to get his available brigades into action. It will be recalled that Thomas' brigade was engaged on Early's right and Branch was already advancing to attack the Union right. Now Hill was making sure that two more of his brigades, Archer's and Pender's, were being deployed and advancing into action. Archer led off, followed by Pender, and the two were launched against the Union right (in the meantime, Branch had inclined his brigade's advance to the right in order to take any pressure off of reorganizing units in the center and to lead the counterattack in that area). Hill was coming into his own as the salvager of the situation. In the words of one historian, he had already "forged a powerful shining weapon in the form of the Light Division, which even now was on its scrappy way to becoming the best in the entire Confederate service."[36] The Light Division, totaling half the corps strength, had now become the ideal weapon to turn the battle around, perhaps even turning defeat into victory.

On the Union side, as related, the momentum of Crawford's attack had come to a halt—and with fearful losses. Not only had Crawford lost his regimental commanders and most of his field officers; his brigade losses in killed, wounded, and captured came to a staggering 53 percent. The enormity of such a loss may be appreciated when viewed in the light of today's professional war-gaming calculations, when a unit sustaining more than 30 percent casualties is considered no longer effective in combat and is counted out of action. Banks' losses did not end with the effects on Crawford's brigade. Augur and Geary were both badly wounded and out of action, and Prince was taken prisoner even before becoming aware that the division command had fallen on him—a revealing picture of how Civil War higher commanders got personally involved in leading their troops from the front, along with what has already been seen of Jackson's rallying efforts on the Confederate side.

Looking now from Banks' overall command viewpoint, Geary's brigade had taken 40 percent casualties, while Prince's had sustained losses of some 30 percent as their attack actions came to a halt. Banks, of course, had no way of calculating percentages of losses at the time, but he was certain to have realized that the offensive capability of II Corps was shot, and the point was being driven home by the further realization that Jackson's counterattacking forces were threatening him from both flanks and even against his center. The threat, in fact, was becoming so evident that Banks had to displace his artillery batteries rearward and to look to Gordon's brigade, on the right, to save that flank from being overrun by Hill's three brigades that Jackson was throwing against it. Another sign of the mounting threat to Banks' whole force was his ordering—at the urging of Colonel Clark of the corps staff—the desperate charge of the 1st Pennsylvania Cavalry, launched head-on against Branch's advancing brigade. The gallant charge, full tilt in a column of fours down the highway, was at once taken under fire by Branch's men from the front and by three other Confederate regiments from the flank. This miniature Balaclava ended as quickly as it had been begun, with men and horses falling right and left, and the remnants (71 cavalrymen out of the original 164) falling back behind the 10th Maine Infantry, which had made a stand near the highway.

At about the same time that the cavalry was making its charge, Gordon's brigade was moving up to positions along the east edge of the woods overlooking the wheat field. From there his three regiments would attempt to cover the withdrawal of Crawford's survivors, who were retracing the same path they had taken in their attack. At the same time Gordon was expected to act as a bulwark against the ever increasing threat of Hill's three brigades against Banks' right flank and center. And to the left of that center, the brigades of Geary and Prince were making a creditably orderly withdrawal, also retracing the same ground over which they had attacked.

In summing up the result of the actions taken by both sides during this critical period (i.e., from about 6:30 to 7:00 P.M.), Banks' all-out attack had—after stunning and unexpected successes—lost its momentum due to the exhaustion of the troops and their heavy casualties. Banks' corps was making a steady withdrawal so far, after his having pulled back his artillery, and covering his right flank with Gordon's brigade, which, it was hoped, would hold off the looming threat from that direction. Also, in Augur's division the brigades of Geary and Prince were making an orderly withdrawal—orderly considering their casualties and the loss of some unit integrity that inevitably occurs during retrograde actions of the kind.

As for Jackson, he had literally snatched recovery from near disaster, and was making his command presence felt all across the field as he urged forward his corps reserves, in the form of Hill's now committed four brigades. He had restored order in his center, where his once broken brigades could now add weight to his counterattack. And finally, he could order Ewell's division to advance and turn the Union force's left flank.

In short, Jackson was now in command of the situation to the extent of being able to make a force counterattack that might overwhelm Banks' corps. The big question at this pivotal point: could Jackson then follow up a successful counterattack by mounting a pursuit that would assure the destruction of Banks' force?

JACKSON ORGANIZES A PURSUIT: BANKS MANAGES A WITHDRAWAL

Jackson must have seemed omnipresent to his subordinate commanders as he tried to make his presence felt everywhere, giving orders to gather his force for an organized pursuit. It also seemed that he had lost none of his energy or offensive spirit after his ordeal in personally rallying his troops. After putting Hill in charge of spearheading the pursuit, he had turned his attention to other urgent matters: seeing that Ewell got his division driving forward in a continued effort to get around Banks' left flank and cut off any of the Union force's withdrawal, and getting all the artillery he could moving forward to support the pursuing infantry.

Several factors combined, however, to limit Jackson's capability of carrying out a Napoleonic pursuit that would destroy his enemy. First of all, he had no assembled major cavalry force to fall upon and cut up a defeated enemy. Several cavalry regiments had arrived on the field after the battle, but they were few in numbers and lacked an overall command, so that they could be discounted. Second, it was already growing dark (sunset was about 7:00 P.M.) and Jackson was well aware of the difficulties that go with mounting any night operation, even when well planned and organized. Third, the Orange–Culpeper highway, which had figured so prominently in the battle, while not essential to the advance of Jackson's infantry, was needed for the forward movement of Confederate artillery batteries. This was because the banks of the north fork of Cedar Run were too steep to permit the off-road passage of the guns, especially after nightfall—a factor about which Jackson, the former artilleryman, needed no counsel. Lastly, the August heat had not appreciably diminished (the thermometer still read eighty-six degrees an hour after sunset), so much so that its effects on the troops continued to be acutely felt and added to their fatigue after the marching and fighting of the day.

Yet, in spite of all the difficulties Jackson's drive, in tandem with Hill's leadership, managed to mount increasing pressure on Banks' lacerated brigades. Hill had even managed to press forward with his leading brigade for as much as a mile and a half beyond Cedar Run after nightfall, until his vanguard encountered resistance in some woods to its front. At that point Jackson reluctantly called a halt long enough for advance artillery to shell the woods. After dislodging the enemy troops, the advance was resumed, only to encounter a repeat performance with increased resistance. This time Jackson ordered forward Pegram's battery, supported by Hill's leading brigade, to drive off the enemy. Instead of a scampering enemy, Pegram was greeted by the fire of three Union batteries. Pegram was drawn into an artillery exchange that lasted for nearly an hour, after which he was forced to displace his battery in order to save his men and guns. By this time it was after 11:00 P.M. and even Jackson had to concede that the action of the day was over, since the exhausted troops couldn't be counted on to advance another 100 yards. Jackson himself was so physically and mentally exhausted that his staff had to seek out a farmhouse for a night's rest for their chief. But there was no such place to be found; every house was filled with wounded awaiting a surgeon's care. Finally, as Freeman noted, "Presently in the moonlight he [Jackson] observed by the roadside a grass plot that seemed to invite sleep. He drew rein and announced that he would go no farther. A long coat was spread for him. He threw himself down on his stomach, and when someone offered him food, he muttered: 'No, I want rest, nothing but rest.' In a moment he was slumbering."[37]

From Banks' viewpoint, his troops had fought a praiseworthy action throughout the whole afternoon, and now their conduct in falling back under intense enemy pressure was no less creditable. How much credit Banks deserves for an orderly withdrawal—and how much should go to the troops and their regimental and brigade officers—may be arguable, but the fact remains that the Union regiments did not break and lose their unit integrity when the whole II Corps was counterattacked in its front and on both flanks. That is not to say that Banks' brigades executed a parade ground rearward maneuver, far from it. There were plenty of casualties (which included prisoners taken by the enemy), frequently broken ranks, and all the disorder that goes with troops trying to move to rear positions while under continuous fire. Yet both infantry and artillery units managed to hold off their attackers and still fall back in orderly enough fashion to take up a succession of rearward positions. Gordon's brigade deserves special mention for covering the corps right flank by fending off attack after attack by Hill's brigades. In Gordon's own words, "From the edge of the wood across the wheatfield, not over four hundred yards, the long lines of the enemy, who, having now advanced into clear ground, opened upon us a heavy fire, which was responded to. . . . The woods opposite us must have been literally packed with Rebels, and they must have extended far beyond our right to have enabled even one third of the [their] men to get to the front."[38] Eventually Gordon's brigade—after a succession of fallbacks, rallies, and regrouping—was relieved, on Pope's order, by General Tower of Ricketts' division. It was Ricketts' division, belatedly arriving after 7:00 P.M., which allowed most of Banks' troops to pass through to the rear, where they were eventually assembled. It was also Ricketts' artillery that had taken Pegram's battery under fire and Ricketts' supporting infantry that had caused Jackson to decide that his worn-out men could no longer attempt any kind of pursuit.

The battle was over. Jackson was clearly unable to continue a pursuit, and Banks' II Corps had been taken out of action, relieved by Ricketts' division and late-arriving units of Sigel's corps. The immediate outcome of the battle would be seen on the following day, 10 August, when Jackson would be confronting the concentration of Pope's newly arrived forces.

CHAPTER 8

What Happened at Cedar Mountain?

Because attention has been focused on Cedar Mountain for the purpose of observing the art of command in action, the immediate outcome of the battle—indeed its place in Civil War history—may be dealt with summarily. The bare facts were that both sides remained in a mutual standoff through 10–11 August, maintaining a truce while the wounded were recovered, the dead buried, and forces were regrouped. Jackson remained in control of the battlefield while Pope continued the concentration of his army until it was clear to Jackson that he was outnumbered to the extent that his present position was dangerously untenable. Accordingly, he withdrew his corps to his base at Gordonsville, from whence he had launched his intended strike against Pope on 7 August. The Cedar Mountain phase of the campaign was over. This leaves us to deal with our relevant question: what happened before and during Cedar Mountain that can provide insight into the ways that Jackson and Banks exercised command?

In both a military and a personal sense the one factor that remains uppermost in the mind of any commander is his mission. Its constant presence is as much a part of his being as the act of breathing—and as inescapable. So, while the mission is an obvious starting point for examining the command actions of the two opponents, the contrast in the way each received and evaluated his mission becomes not only interesting but essential to understanding what happened at Cedar Mountain. Jackson, it will be recalled, got his mission from Lee in the form of letters which were the equivalent, in today's military doctrine, of "mission type orders," orders that give the commander flexibility of action by telling him *what* to do, but not *how* to do it. Considering the close command relationship between Lee and Jackson, it was entirely appropriate that the latter then became free to determine what course of action he would take to accomplish his mission. Such freedom of action, in this case, placed Jackson in the de facto status of independent command, the only other time in his wartime career (the other being his Valley Campaign) that he would be in such a position. And, as history has shown, Jackson was at his professional best when acting on his own.

Banks, in contrast, as one of three of Pope's corps commanders, received his mission directly from his army commander, just as he would any other order or directive. Exactly how Banks carried out Pope's orders at Cedar Mountain then becomes a matter of primary interest because of the obvious effects on his command actions.

When Jackson had received Lee's letter of 7 August (wherein he had assured Jackson of his confidence in his ability to act independently: "Being on the spot you must determine what force to operate against"), he had already decided on "what force to operate against." That being so, he had already formed his concept of the operation, which was based on striking Pope's forward elements around Culpeper before Pope could concentrate the rest of his army in that area. As has been seen, two unforeseen obstacles cropped up that were to frustrate Jackson's intended strike-and-destroy operation. The first was the incredibly slow advance of his three divisions on 8 August, the day before the enemy was encountered in force. The other was Pope's moving Banks' corps forward on the same day in order to block the advance of any major enemy force in his direction. What can be seen now as an inevitable result was the meeting of the opposing forces at Cedar Mountain.

In order to compare the command methods of the opposing commanders it would be helpful to heed the classic advice of Aristotle that the whole of a work should have a beginning, a middle, and an end. With that in mind, Cedar Mountain may be summarized as follows:

- *The beginning*—advance guard actions and the initial deployments of both sides
- *The middle*—Banks' attacks, Jackson's near disaster and recovery
- *The end*—Jackson's counterattack, Banks' retrograde actions, Jackson's pursuit

THE BEGINNING

Once Jackson had become aware of an enemy blocking force (but with no knowledge of its real strength) he wasted no time in arriving at a course of action, namely, either to sweep aside any light resistance or to envelop and destroy his enemy, using a preponderance of force. When he found that he would have to take the latter course of action, he gave orders to his two division commanders, Ewell and Winder, to make the necessary deployments. Up to this time one would probably not take issue with Jackson's actions or reactions. There are two points, however, that now deserve attention because they impacted critically on the course of events. One unexplained factor was Jackson's apparent conviction that the main enemy force lay to the right (east) of the Orange–Culpeper highway. That part of his estimate of the situation, in all probability, caused him to pay inadequate attention to his left flank. As Freeman noted, "This plan [Jackson's battle plan] assumed that all the Federal forces were East of the Culpeper Road. So far as the records show, Jackson did not reconnoiter the wooded country West of the road, nor did he order any reconnaissance by the brigade commanders sent to the left."[39] That piece of negligence was to cost him dearly when his left and center forces came under an unexpectedly overpowering attack. The other point concerns Jackson's orders to his division commanders in the opening stage of the engagement. We know that Jackson and Ewell studied a map of the area while they conferred (near end of Chapter 5), so it is certain that Ewell got his orders at the time. In Winder's case, however, the details of Jackson's orders are not known (Freeman, Vol. 2, 26n), but it is certain that Winder, as narrated, did not have the time or opportunity before his mortal wounding to pass on to Taliaferro, his successor in command, his division mission and plan. As for A. P. Hill, the evidence shows that all he knew, before the action unfolded, was that his division, as corps reserve, was to move forward, ready to support Winder and to send a brigade to reinforce Early. Of any overall force plan he knew nothing. In effect, Jackson's orders to his division commanders were at best fragmentary and at worst too sketchy. In fairness to Jackson, however, one should note that the lack of planning time and combat intelligence that exert pressure on a commander in the opening phase of a meeting engagement could have hindered him from giving detailed orders to his commanders. Moreover, one can never discount that part of Jackson's nature that seemed to underlie all his command relationships—his reticence, even secretiveness, that kept him from sharing his plans with his subordinates.

To sum up Jackson's exercise of command in the beginning phase of Cedar Mountain: As an independent commander, he surveyed the situation, made his evaluation of it, formed his battle plan, and put it into execution. His decisions and subsequent actions were both timely and sound, flawed only by his faulty estimate of his enemy's situation and consequent inattention to his left flank elements—and possibly by incomplete orders to his subordinate commanders.

When comparing Banks' methods with Jackson's, one should bear in mind the contrast between their command positions. Jackson, due to his unique relationship with Lee, was relatively free to exercise command of an independent corps. Banks, on the other side of the coin, was only one of three corps commanders under Pope, an army commander who preached command initiative—and practiced highly centralized control. A case in point was the command relationship between Banks and Pope that was manifested when Banks rode forward from Culpeper to "assume command of all forces in the front." In order to keep Banks on a leash Pope had sent forward Brigadier General Roberts, his chief of staff, to designate the ground on which Banks was to deploy his force. For a higher commander to tell a subordinate leader how to deploy his own troops could be an unthinkable affront to a professional soldier, but in Banks' case the amateur general seems to have accepted the intrusion into his command prerogatives. Yet it does seem strange that Banks would have taken offense at Roberts' remark to the effect that "there must be no backing out this day" while not being offended at being told how to manage his own affairs on his own ground.

At any rate, Banks did proceed to deploy his two divisions as already described. He then had General Williams move Crawford's brigade forward far enough to occupy the woods on the edge of the wheat field. From that point on, Banks appears to have taken full charge of his situation without further interference by Roberts or Pope. His next move, as skirmishers and artillery went into action, was to order forward two regiments, one from the right (from Williams' division) and one from the left (from Augur's division), as he informed Pope in his message at 4:50 P.M. Whether this initiative was meant merely to drive off enemy skirmishers or to develop the situation across the front is not clear. On the other hand, what Banks intended next has been evidenced in his subsequent orders. How he had to contend with the most critical decision of his command career has already been recounted. It is unquestionably clear that he would not wait for his old enemy to take the initiative. He would attack first. What the results of his attack were, from a command perspective, remains to be seen in the next phase of the engagement.

THE MIDDLE

The greater part of historians' criticism of Cedar Mountain (hard to come by considering the relative unimportance of the battle in comparison to the so-called decisive or great battles of the war) has centered upon Banks' offensive action, and rightly so. However, the search for insight into command methods and the reasoning of the man behind them demands closer examination of the *tactical* factors involved. In the first place, it is easier to appreciate the form of Banks' attacks if they are seen from his viewpoint as made by brigades. He had four (after discounting Greene's weak brigade, which was left behind to secure the left flank) and he used three, leaving Gordon's brigade in a supporting role. He launched the three brigades, three-fourths of his combat power, in direct frontal attacks. This was done without adequate reconnaissance and without a real plan of maneuver. The fact that Crawford's brigade attack succeeded in enveloping the enemy's left flank and raising hell in general cannot be credited to Banks' plans. There were no such plans. Indeed, as we have seen, the success of that attack was entirely fortuitous.

Another tactical factor is the nature of an attack, once the forces have been designated, the orders given, and the enemy has been engaged. From that point on, the capability of the commander to influence the course of battle can be compared to the actions of an engineer who has opened the floodgates of a dam. He cannot close the floodgates to cut off the torrent he has unleashed. He is only capable of opening other gates to increase the flow—if other gates are available. But in no way can he stop the flood he has released, nor can he change its direction. That was Banks' situation after his three brigades had been committed to their attacks. He had opened all his floodgates because he had no reserves to commit, nor were any forthcoming in time to exploit any success of his attacks. In the case of army reserves that might have aided Banks, the command prospects of Pope and Banks became intertwined. The former's transcribed orders to the latter included the assurance that "you will be reenforced from here," an assurance that could not have been realized. Then too it will be remembered that those orders also included the phrase "deploy his [Banks'] skirmishers if the enemy approaches and attack him immediately as soon as he approaches." Much has been made by historians of Pope's *evident* intent that he expected Banks merely to thwart any significant enemy approach action and to hold his ground until he could be reinforced. But history is made up of actions, not intentions; this is a good place to recall the axiom attributed to Napoleon: if an order can be misunderstood, it will be misunderstood. In sum, three things resulted from Banks' reception of Pope's orders. First, Banks chose to make a command decision to attack, based in part on his interpretation of an ambiguously worded order. Second, Banks launched his attacks knowing that there were no reserves available to exploit a major attack by his force. Third, the attacks succeeded initially, in all probability beyond Banks' expectations. To determine why those attacks were at first so successful it is essential that one see the reasons—from the Confederate side.

Crawford's brigade attack struck, in rapid succession, the Confederate brigades of Garnett, Ronald, and A. G. Taliaferro. Regimental-size units of the three brigades were thrown into confusion, and the resulting panic spread rapidly, threatening the turning and even destruction of Jackson's entire left. The threat reached such proportions that Jackson had to intervene personally to rally the tide of fleeing troops in an attempt to restore order. It became evident that he was forced to take such an action if he was to recover and renew his planned attack. Not so evident was his negligence in securing his left flank, which, in turn, was the cause of his being surprised. And surprised he was in the military sense, since his enemy had struck him at an unexpected time and place. It was a case of the surpriser being surprised or, as the British historian David Chandler might have put it, a case of the biter bit. That Jackson made a dramatic and timely recovery in no way condones the fact that he was caught with his guard down—and that the subsequent rallying could not have been accomplished without the efforts of the brigade and regimental officers.

It must be said, however, that the near disaster on the Confederate left cannot be laid entirely at Jackson's door when one looks beyond his command responsibility. The unfortunate facts are that the Union attacks hit the Confederate left and center at the exact time that the change of command of Winder's division was still up in the air, due to Winder's mortal wounding and his successor Taliaferro's desperate attempts to determine the situation and piece things together. All of this was compounded by brigade and regimental units being out of contact and trying to organize their attack in the midst of a dense woods. Needless to say, Crawford's attack—assisted by those of Geary's and Prince's brigades—was as much a bonanza to Banks as it was a shock to Jackson, a shock from which he was quick to recover.

A brilliant facet of Jackson's modus operandi was his seeming ability to make a ubiquitous presence felt throughout his forward elements wherever danger threatened or inspiration was needed to get things moving. That quality was clearly manifest during and following his rallying of his broken forces at Cedar Mountain. Certainly, as pointed out, the rallying was—had to be—carried out by regimental officers, but it was Jackson's charismatic genius that inspired the rally, and it had to be Jackson who personally directed the reorganization of both his engaged and reserve forces to get a timely counterattack under way. That he did so, including spurring on leaders like Hill and Branch along the way, has already been demonstrated. Once he had made his presence felt, recovery, reorganization, and counterattack merged as though a skilled hand had rejoined the pieces of a jigsaw puzzle which had fallen on the floor.

THE END

There can be no question that Jackson reorganized his combat power and turned it into an effective counterattacking force. Jackson's exact verbal orders (written orders were obviously out of the question at critical times like these) and how he gave them have not been recorded, but it is certain that the leadership of the now committed reserve forces in the left and center was given to the capable A. P. Hill. On the right of Jackson's corps, one can be sure that orders were also given to Ewell to move his brigades forward to try to outflank the Union brigades on Banks' left, which had already lost their attacking capability and were falling back under pressure. How much Ewell actually accomplished in his counterattacking and pursuit roles has never been made clear—and that unanswered question raises others concerning the part that Ewell's division played throughout the battle, questions that will be addressed in this summation.

Looking at the situation after Jackson had mounted his counterattack, one notes several salient points. That Jackson was becoming the victor was clearly evidenced by the fact that he had swept his enemy off the battlefield and was driving him back under mounting pressure. The record also shows, however, that Jackson was never able to bring an overwhelming force to bear that would *destroy* that enemy, that is, to shatter Banks' withdrawing brigades so that they could no longer be considered a fighting force. Moreover, Banks' regiments, however severely mauled and crippled, did not lose their colors—as they would have had they been overrun and wiped out—nor did the Union artillery lose their guns or have them put out of action. In fact, the Union batteries, though continually displacing to rear positions, did a fine job of covering the withdrawal of many infantry regiments.

In any event, Jackson did manage to turn counterattack into pursuit, though at best the pursuit never amounted to more than continued pressure on a defeated enemy. In fact, Colonel Andrews, whose 2nd Massachusetts took 34 percent casualties during Jackson's counterattack, went so far as to record that "the pursuit by the enemy was very feeble."[40] Whether Andrews could have spoken for the whole of Banks' force would be arguable, but we do know that eventually the pursuit had to be called off, mainly due to the exhaustion of the troops and the inherent difficulties that go with trying to carry out an unplanned night operation. The difficulties that Jackson had to contend with have been described; all that might be added would be to say that if Jackson's drive and offensive spirit could not have enabled an all-out destructive pursuit, then it was just not possible under the prevailing conditions.

Of all the aspects of command that have been observed—mission evaluation, combat intelligence, decisions, orders, supervision of operations—the one that most demands attention at the end of Cedar Mountain is the commander's mission. Ironically, such a refocus becomes more interesting when it reveals that neither commander had accomplished his mission in the operation. In Jackson's case, he had set himself a deduced mission, namely, to upset Pope's strategy by striking an exposed part of his army at Culpeper before Pope could concentrate the bulk of his force to counter the strike. After Cedar Mountain and after the opposing forces had withdrawn from the area— Pope toward the north and Jackson to Gordonsville, behind the Rapidan River—it became clear that Jackson had failed in his deduced mission: he had not destroyed an exposed part of Pope's army, nor had he even gotten to Culpeper. In Banks' case, he had apparently tried to exceed his *assigned* mission, but his all-out offensive actions had failed; moreover, he had not succeeded in blocking an enemy force until Pope could bring a preponderance of force to bear on the battle.

Probably the next most important element of command after the mission would be that of "the warrior able to control events," as Jomini puts it in the epigraph to this part of this book. Clearly Banks relinquished control of events after he had committed three-fourths of his combat power to the attack, without reserves to reinforce it. After his attack ground to a halt, his exhausted brigades were powerless to do anything except fall back against an overpowering counterattack. From that point on, Banks' only attempt at control was to see that the remnants of his corps could be withdrawn to safety behind Pope's late-arriving "reinforcements."

Jackson appears to have fared no better in the matter of exercising control.

Consider the judgement of Douglas Southall Freeman, the Southerner whose
appraisal of Lee's lieutenants continues to serve as a model for balancing
insight against fairness: "At Cedar Mountain, though he outnumbered his adversary two to one, he [Jackson] did not utilize anything like his entire force.
Nor did he dominate the field. Except for a hand in rallying the center after
it broke, Jackson had small part in the critical operations of the day."[41] Another
aspect of control concerns the employment of Ewell's division during the
height of the battle. The record clearly shows that Ewell's two uncommitted
brigades sat out the battle on the slopes of Cedar Mountain like spectators on
the fifty-yard line at a football game. The reason has been advanced that had
Ewell's brigades been committed to an attack against Banks' left they would
have been exposed to the cross fire of Confederate artillery firing against
Banks' infantry and artillery. Such a rationale can be dismissed out of hand,
even when one takes into account that cease-fire orders to the artillery would
have had to be sent by mounted messenger; there was plenty of time for even
that kind of communications to be effective. In fact, instead of letting Ewell's
brigades sit idly by, Jackson was capable of launching them in a Napoleonic
attaque débordante, a powerful thrust against Banks' exposed left flank—and
at a critical time when such an action could well have turned the tide of battle.

The prospect of applying an example of Napoleonic tactics in a Civil War
situation calls to mind the reality that Jackson was one of the more likely—
or most likely—of the Confederacy's generals to have been capable of doing
so. And as the history of the war shows, Cedar Mountain may have presented
him with his last opportunity to use a lesson from Napoleonic warfare. That
Jackson had studied Napoleon's campaigns has been made clear by Colonel
G. F. R. Henderson, the first and most perceptive of Jackson's military biographers, in his observations of Jackson's prewar career when he was a professor at Virginia Military Institute: "In the well-stocked library of the Institute
he found every opportunity of increasing his professional knowledge. He was
an untiring reader, and he read to learn. The wars of Napoleon were his
constant study. He was an enthusiastic admirer of his genius; the swiftness,
the daring, and the energy of his movements appealed to his every instinct."[42]
How far Jackson was able to pursue those studies in his later, wartime career,
indeed if such a pursuit was really needed, remains doubtful, despite the
persistent myth that he carried a copy of Napoleon's Maxims in his saddlebags
for his ready reference. Freeman has dispelled that part of the myth which
assumes that Jackson really referred to the book: "Jackson put the volume
[Napoleon's *Maxims of War*, which Jeb Stuart had given him as a gift] carefully
with his personal baggage, but neither then nor thereafter, so far as the pages
indicate, did he ever read it."[43] Freeman confirmed the fact when, in 1907,
he went to the trouble of examining the copy in the Confederate Museum at
Richmond.

Even when the possibility of Stonewall Jackson's missed opportunities is
set aside, Cedar Mountain continues to present two phenomena for reflection.

The battle and that part of the campaign leading to it may have been the last occasion where a skilled commander could have used Napoleonic models as guides for gaining a decided advantage in maneuver warfare in the early years of the war. Beyond that possibility, however, the battle shows us a certainty: a skilled professional met a courageous amateur, and the professional came within a razor's edge of disaster, saved by strong reserves and the rashness of his opponent, who had attacked without them.

PART THREE

CHICKAMAUGA: LOST COMMAND, LOST VICTORY

There is a tide in the affairs of men,
Which, taken at the flood, leads on to fortune;
Omitted, all the voyage of their life
Is bound in shallows and in miseries.
— Shakespeare, *Julius Caesar*, IV, iii.

CHAPTER 9

Rosecrans and His Chickamauga Campaign

This is the story of two men, opposed in war, each of whose human frailties eventually compromised his ability to command. The result—one lost his command, the other lost a victory. The former, William Starke Rosecrans, Major General, United States Volunteers, commanded the Army of the Cumberland; the other, General Braxton Bragg, Confederate States Army, commanded the Army of Tennessee. Before their stories can be told it would be helpful to take into account the national strategies which guided each commander in developing his plan of campaign.

The basic aims at the heart of each side's national strategy are simply stated. In order for the North to restore the Union it had to subjugate the South to its will. The South, since it did not have the means to subjugate its opponent, had to resist the North until it could be forced to recognize the Confederacy as a separate nation. This meant that the North, with its superior industrial and manpower strength, could afford to take the strategical offensive and continue to invade the South. The South, though forced on the strategical defensive as a nation, used its armies to strike back offensively and even invade the North when the opportunity was presented. Unfortunately for both sides in the earlier years of the war, their national strategies were flawed because each lost sight of what should have been its basic aim—to destroy its opponent's will to fight. Instead, their objectives in the early stages were based on such strategies as capturing or defending Richmond, in the illusory expectation that the other side would then give up the contest. It was only after a long and bloody series of indecisive battles that the Union was forced to realize that a combination of military strategies—eventually carried out by Grant and Sherman—aimed directly at destroying the Confederacy's armies and its people's will to fight was the only way to win the war.

William S. Rosecrans

With the prolonged and attrited struggle that ensued came the realization that both national strategies, in having to deal with two theaters of war, eastern and western (see Map 9.1), would be guided by geography instead of political boundaries or places. Thus the two theaters were defined primarily by the great chain of the Appalachians, which meant that the western flank of the Confederacy should be turned by Union armies seizing and exploiting the vital axis of Chattanooga–Atlanta. The appreciation of these realities had begun to dawn on the Union's national strategy team—Lincoln, his secretary of war Stanton, and his general-in-chief Halleck—by the summer of 1863, when the strategic importance of Chattanooga–Atlanta was beginning to gain recognition.

In the opening days of that year Rosecrans and Bragg had fought the battle of Stones River (also known as Murfreesboro, especially in the South), one of the war's bloodiest slugfests, which had resulted in Bragg withdrawing the Army of Tennessee southward toward Tullahoma while Rosecrans was consolidating the positions of his Army of the Cumberland around Murfreesboro. The two armies continued to confront each other in those areas for almost six months, but the reason for the apparent stalemate was not lethargy on the part of either commander. Bragg was fully aware that, in his strategic defensive role, he had to take every measure to ensure that his enemy would not capture Chattanooga. That vital railroad junction was not only the link to Atlanta but also the strategic gateway which, if lost, would lay open the heart of the Confederacy to invasion. But Bragg was equally aware that he was outnumbered by his enemy, in great part due to the higher priority for troops having to be sent to reinforce Vicksburg against Grant's offensive. Hence, his mission as he saw it at the time was to rely on cavalry raids against his opponent's communications until he could again build up his forces and resume the offensive.

Rosecrans, though equally aware of the importance of seizing Chattanooga, saw fit to remain in place because, in his words, "the winter rains made the country roads impassable for large military operations. . . . Meanwhile we hardened our cavalry, drilled our infantry, fortified Nashville and Murfreesboro for secondary depots, and arranged our plans for the coming campaign upon the opening of the roads, which were expected to be good by the 1st of May, 1863."[44] Unfortunately for Rosecrans, two members of Lincoln's strategic triumvirate didn't share Rosecrans' carefully laid plans for the next phase of the campaign. Stanton and Halleck became increasingly impatient with what they saw as a relaxed army commander stalling for time until he was good and ready to move. The basic thrust of the strategy they envisaged at the time entailed a simultaneous advance of Rosecrans' Army of the Cumberland and General Burnside's army from his Department of the Ohio to sweep the Confederate forces out of middle Tennessee.

There were, as one might expect, two sides to the story of Rosecrans' delayed operation. On the Washington side of the picture, one sees Halleck, the

Map 9.1

Courtesy Martin L. Wilkerson.

THE TWO THEATERS OF WAR

SCALE IN MILES

89

military operative of the strategy team, trying to control operations from a desk in faraway Washington, relying on the telegraph to transmit plans and orders for every major strategic move. The hard fact of the matter was that Halleck—and the rest of the team—had not yet devised a workable overall strategy that they would entrust to a *single* theater commander to implement in the field.

Rosecrans, on the other hand, was the commander on the ground who could see a road network on the map transformed overnight by rains into quagmires that were obstacles to infantry marches and impossible for the movement of artillery and wagon trains. But the difficulties of the rugged, mountainous terrain were, in Rosecrans' view, only a part of the larger strategic picture. As he saw the picture, there were two major problems that had to be solved before he should move against Bragg. First there was the logistical problem, involving the building of fortified supply bases that were invulnerable against cavalry raids, and organizing and expanding his supply wagon trains (he argued that he needed over 40,000 animals and some 10,000 wagons as the minimum required to support an army of over 50,000 men in hostile territory which, until summer, was barren of any kind of forage); also it was necessary to wait until the corn and other crops were ripe enough for forage. The other problem that he envisaged, far more open to argument, was that "we must not drive Bragg out of middle Tennessee until it shall be too late for his command to reinforce Johnston's [General Joseph E. Johnston's forces operating against Grant in his Vicksburg campaign]."

The latter argument failed to hold water with Halleck & Company, who continued to urge Rosecrans to get up and get moving. The disagreement resulted in a continuing tussle of telegrams between Washington and Rosecrans' headquarters, with Halleck increasingly impatient and Rosecrans increasingly obstinate. Finally, on 2 June the latter received the following telegraphic threat: "If you can do nothing yourself, a portion of your troops must be sent to Grant's relief."

Even then Rosecrans waited three weeks to finalize his plans for carrying out the opening phase of his operation to oust Bragg from Tennessee. In spite of his proclaimed reluctance to move against that gentleman, Rosecrans had arrived at a concept of operation which was to prove both simple and workable on the ground. When Bragg had moved his army's central elements to Tullahoma, he had entrenched one corps around Shelbyville and the other similarly around Wartrace, with cavalry securing both flanks and outposts in the mountain passes throughout the area (see Map 9.2). Rosecrans planned to maneuver against Bragg and force him to face being cut off from his base at Chattanooga. He had a well-conceived strategy, and it worked.

For all his seeming delaying, Rosecrans showed that he could be as swift in execution as he was meticulous in planning. His plan was based on deception and rapid maneuver. Starting on 26 June, he used Stanley's cavalry corps and Granger's reserve corps to swing around Bragg's left flank near Shelbyville

Map 9.2

MURFREESBORO

BRADYVILLE

McMINNVILLE

FAIRFIELD

WARTRACE

SHELBYVILLE

MANCHESTER

TULLAHOMA

Elk River

DECHERD

WINCHESTER

FAYETTEVILLE

SALEM

Sequatchie River

WALDON'S RIDGE

ANDERSON'S

TENNESSEE
ALABAMA

BRIDGEPORT

SHELLMOUND

Brown's Fy.

CHATTANOOGA

CHICKAMAUGA STA.

ROSSVILLE

McFarland's Gap

RINGGOLD

STEVENSON

RACCOON MOUNTAIN

TRENTON

LEE and GORDON'S MILLS

POND SPRING

Caperton's Fy.

CHARLESTON R. R.

BELLEFONTE

Tennessee River

Steven's Gap

Chattooga

MISSIONARY MT.

Dug Gap

LAFAYETTE

GEORGIA

ROCKY FACE RIDGE

MEMPHIS and

SAND MOUNTAIN

LOOKOUT MOUNTAIN

PIGEON MOUNTAIN

VALLEY HEAD

LOOKOUT

TAYLOR'S RIDGE

SUMMERVILLE

Winston's Gap

ALPINE

AREA OF OPERATIONS
TENN.–GEORGIA–ALABAMA

5   0   5   10   15

SCALE IN MILES

N

Courtesy Martin L. Wilkerson.

and deceive Bragg into believing that to be the Union main attack. At the
same time the real Union main effort, made by the other three corps of the
Army of the Cumberland, poured through the mountain gaps to envelop
Bragg's right flank. In spite of all of Rosecrans' worries about rains and rough
country roads both maneuvers succeeded. There were indeed heavy rains and
muddy roads plus stiff resistance in the defended passes. But despite it all,
Rosecrans' corps had accomplished their missions and were concentrating
their united strength around Manchester by 30 June. In four days Rosecrans
had not only deceived Bragg but had forced him to pull back all of his forces
into what could be called the "Tullahoma Pocket."

But Rosecrans had finished only the opening phase of his operation. Without pause he continued to outmaneuver Bragg. He moved swiftly to try to get
enough of his main force behind Bragg to seize the crossings over the Elk
River. Had this part of Rosecrans' maneuvers succeeded, Bragg would have
been trapped and cut off from his base at Chattanooga. Though the trap was
not sprung (Bragg was well aware of the dangers of maintaining defensive
positions with the Elk River at his back), Bragg was forced back across the
river. Rosecrans' forces, however, had moved so rapidly that Bragg was left
with no time to defend the river line, and he continued to withdraw all the
way to Chattanooga. By 4 July Bragg had completed his withdrawal across
the Tennessee River, and Rosecrans had halted his army corps along a line,
McMinnville–Manchester–Decherd–Fayetteville. Here he halted and began
preparations for his next moves. When he took stock of his accomplishments
to this point, he could believe that he may have even satisfied Washington.
In nine days he had continued to outmaneuver Bragg, forcing him out of
middle Tennessee, driving him across the Tennessee River and back into
Chattanooga—all with a loss of only 560 casualties to the Union army.[45]

If, at this pause in Rosecrans' operations, his mastery of strategy has been
made clear, one should look even further back if he is to be given full credit
for his abilities. Earlier, when Rosecrans had conceived his overall plan of
campaign, he had asked General Burnside, commanding the Department of
the Ohio, to "arrange for his forces to cooperate with ours [Rosecrans' Army
of the Cumberland] for the relief of East Tennessee." Burnside did cooperate
by sending his second-in-command, Major General Hartsuff, to hear at first
hand Rosecrans' plans. When Hartsuff arrived at Rosecrans' headquarters, his
host sat him down and took him into his confidence: "I explained to Hartsuff
my plan, the details of which I gave to no other." The details, typifying the
author's meticulous style of planning, were laid out in six clearly defined steps,
following each other in logical progression. In essence, Rosecrans—ever
mindful of Bragg's concern for protecting his rear and lines of communication—intended to cross the Tennessee River, turn Bragg out of Chattanooga,
get his army between Chattanooga and Bragg, and "fight him, if possible, on
ground of our own choosing, and if not, upon such ground as we can."[46] Steps
in the plan also envisioned Burnside's cooperating by advancing on Rosecrans'

left and thereby securing that flank while diverting Bragg's attention to the
north of Chattanooga and away from Rosecrans' forces crossing the Tennessee.
Also typical of Rosecrans' strategical vision was his concern that the main
thrust of his campaign should be timed to ensure that his next moves against
Bragg would demand the latter's full attention and thus prevent him from
sending any of his forces to reinforce the Confederate forces operating against
Grant at Vicksburg.

After General Hartsuff returned to Burnside's headquarters at Cincinnati,
it was not long until Rosecrans was assured of Burnside's cooperation in the
next phase of his campaign. This happy news, however, was soon offset by a
resumption of pressure from Washington. The pressure was renewed in the
same way and for the same reason that it had been applied during the winter
and spring. In Rosecrans' view, Stanton and Halleck were taking the same
old line: yes, you have accomplished much, but there is so much yet to be
done and so little time in which to do it that you have got to get moving—
now. In effect, Rosecrans had to agree with the first part of the Stanton–
Halleck line; it was the "get moving now" part that caused him to get his back
up. What faraway Washington saw as the obstinate unwillingness of an army
commander to carry out his part of a national strategy, Rosecrans saw as the
inability of the high command to recognize reality, the reality of logistics and
geography. The ultimate reality was that both Washington and Rosecrans had
logic on their side. Both saw Chattanooga as the key to the strategic outflank-
ing of the Appalachians and the doorway to the Deep South. With the railroad
hub of Chattanooga in their hands, Union armies would be free to liberate
Unionist sympathizers in east Tennessee (one of Lincoln's cherished hopes)
and, more important in the strategic sense, to split the South, eventually striking at the heart of the Confederacy itself. Conversely, with Chattanooga still
in Confederate hands, Union forces had no hope of invading and conquering
the Deep South. In the minds of Lincoln, Stanton, and Halleck those strategic
facts of life overrode all other questions of strategy; moreover, time was of the
essence in carrying out the national aims. In their view, time had become a
critical factor since 4 July, when the twin victories of Gettysburg and Vicksburg had made possible a strategic momentum that had to be maintained at
all costs; and a primary cost was that the Army of the Cumberland continue
its advance against Bragg—even if its commander declared it unready to
move.

While Rosecrans was fully aware of the importance of taking Chattanooga
and defeating Bragg, he nevertheless saw that he would be unable to accomplish that mission unless his army could survive in a region that was hostile
in every sense. Not only did he have to contend with an enemy army on its
own ground, but the terrain presented logistical problems that had to be
solved before he could even start to move his army and carry out his strategy.
He had made a thorough terrain study that showed him only too clearly what
lay at the heart of his problems. Before his forces could reach the Tennessee

River they had to cross the Cumberland Mountains, made up of rugged, ridges covered with scrub oak, and having few streams and even fewer roads. The roads were rough trails, barely useable by wagon trains, that zigzagged their way through a few gaps. The terrain east of the river was of a similar nature: a series of sharp, mountainous ridges and deep valleys running parallel to the Tennessee. In military terms these ridges and valleys constituted cross-compartments, obstacles perpendicular to a strategic advance—in contrast to avenues of approach, which facilitate an advance against one's enemy. Moreover, the series of cross-compartments supported only scattered and isolated farms scratched out of sparse soil to raise subsistence crops of corn and wheat. It was this forbidding scarcity of potential forage that concerned Rosecrans as much as the rugged terrain. He had to depend on his wagon trains, made up of thousands of draft animals, to transport the sustenance for his army of over 50,000 men: "Our trains must carry twenty days' rations and ammunition enough for two great battles. We have not trains to carry anything beyond this, and hence feed for our animals must be obtained from the coming corn crop of the country into which we are going, or our campaign will be a failure."[47] Looking even further back to his sources of supply, his lifeline was the Nashville and Chattanooga Railway, which had to be repaired all the way from Tullahoma to Stevenson and Bridgeport on the Tennessee River before those so essential wagon trains could move east of the river. And not only must that vital railway be repaired, it had to be protected from the forays of Confederate cavalry, which outnumbered Rosecrans' weaker cavalry force. Since the Army of the Cumberland couldn't afford detachments to provide the protection, its commander had to scratch for ways to find reinforcements to do the job. He took the step—inconceivable to a modern-day military commander—of obtaining the support of the governors of Pennsylvania, Massachusetts, and Illinois to reenlist seven regiments of veterans which would join the Army of the Cumberland as mounted infantry, provided that the federal government would fund the project.

Rosecrans submitted the proposal and request for the funding in a letter to Secretary Stanton, along with an explanation showing "how very important would be the services of such a body of men in guarding the long and exposed line of our communications, soon to be lengthened by our advance to Chattanooga, . . . [and] that every such mounted man in that move would give us three infantry men at the front." The letter was hand-carried to Stanton by Major General Lovell Rousseau, who was stunned by the reaction of the secretary of war: "I would rather you would come to ask the command of the Army of the Cumberland, than to ask reenforcements for General Rosecrans. He shall not have another damned man." Stanton's caustic reaction not only assured Rosecrans that federal funding for the project was at an end, but convinced him that Stanton was openly hostile to him and that his performance as an army commander would never escape the scrutiny of the secretary of war. His apprehension in that regard would be borne out in the days that followed during the next phase of his campaign.

It would be misleading, however, to think of Rosecrans as giving way to an apprehension that was tantamount to fear. It wasn't a part of his nature. He was a complicated man whose character requires insight to make him credible to an observer in our times. But insight is hard to come by, as his biographer, William M. Lamers, has complained: his was a "popular image distorted with error, an unfriendly caricature" because, in great part, his public history was written by enemies, including such prominent figures as the secretary of war, his assistant secretary, Charles A. Dana, and even Grant himself.[48] In fairness, it can be said that sometimes the "enemies" may have been created by Rosecrans himself. In any case, it would be enlightening to take an overview of his life in order to gain a clearer insight into his character.

William Starke Rosecrans came from solid German and Dutch stock, his forebears having first settled in the Wyoming Valley of Pennsylvania, then relocating in Delaware County, Ohio. His father Crandell was originally a farmer who had moved up to make a living from real estate and the income from his country store. William could have been seen as the ideal son of a solid, middle-class father; he was not only intelligent beyond his years but hardworking and eager to learn both from books and down-to-earth experience. By the time he was fourteen he had gotten all the schooling available in the county and had gone on to keeping his father's books and collecting bills. At fifteen he had become the head clerk in another store and might have settled into the retail business had he not hired out in his off time to drive Lawyer T. W. Barkley to Columbus. During the long drive and their ensuing long talk, Barkley had become so impressed with the boy that he told him, "Your conversation has been so intelligent that I strongly urge you to get more education." Young Rosecrans really didn't need a lot of urging; he had already become so fascinated with mathematics and scientific subjects that he longed to go to college, but his family couldn't afford the expense at the time. But an ideal solution was at hand. West Point appealed to him not only for the four-year curriculum that offered math, engineering, and history—his favorite subjects—but the promise of a military career as well. So the youthful Rosecrans went all-out in pursuit of the required appointment. He so impressed his congressman, Alexander Harper, in an interview that Harper decided to nominate Rosecrans instead of his own son, for whom he had been holding back the appointment. After sending the required papers to Harper he waited for three and a half months without getting a reply. Chafing at the bit, the impatient Rosecrans applied directly to Secretary of War Joel R. Poinsett, who eventually made the appointment himself. Finally, in June 1838 the eighteen-year-old cadet-to-be arrived at the boat landing at West Point. He was one of 112 plebes in the incoming class of 1842.

West Point in the late 1830s, contrary to popular conception, was anything but a military college preparing future generals for war by giving them a thorough schooling in the strategic and tactical principles required to guide them in conducting campaigns and winning battles. Actually the curriculum was devoted principally to engineering, mathematics, and the natural sciences (in that order); and, as James L. Morrison's studies have revealed, "71 per cent of the total number of classroom hours in the four-year program was devoted to these three subjects, compared to 29 per cent for all the others, including military tactics. . . . The capstone of the academic program was Professor Dennis H. Mahan's Civil and Military Engineering and the Science of War which all First Classmen [the senior class] studied daily. . . . The science of war which followed [all the civil and military engineering classes] was only nine hours in length."[49] Dr. Morrison, a West Point graduate and later a faculty member of the Military Academy, concluded that "it seems highly unlikely that one nine-hour period out of an entire four-year program would so impress a student that it would continue to govern his thinking years later."[50] Why then, one may ask, if West Point was truly a *military* academy, all the emphasis on engineering and math?

It appears that there are several answers to the question. First, as Dr. Morrison has also pointed out, West Point was a child of the Army's Corps of Engineers and, accordingly, the superintendent was an officer of that branch; moreover, the chief of engineers in the War Department was charged with staff supervision of the academy. Second, one should remain aware that the academy was dedicated to graduating educated gentlemen who would become officers in *all* branches of the army, and the proven way to make them think and reason in the real world was to ground them in engineering, math, and the sciences. Then too, it is important to bear in mind the daily regimen of strict military discipline and training that was designed, then as now, to transform boys into men. Yet, "all the other" subjects—academic as well as training in "minor tactics," which amounted to strict adherence to the drill manuals—were small potatoes compared to the cadets' constant awareness that their class standing and future assignment to their branch of the army depended primarily on their proficiency in engineering and math. It followed then that the first choices of branch of service for the graduating cadets went by class standing—and those choices went almost invariably to the "scientific corps": first the Engineers, then the Topographical Engineers, then the Ordnance Corps. Finally, after all the coveted first selections, came the line—the combat arms and the other branches of the army. How did raw young Rosecrans fit into this framework of cadet life?

The short answer is—very well. A deeper look reveals that the boy Rosecrans, so precocious in mathematics and its basic applications, became an ideal cadet who came to excel in all the scientific subjects. He also adapted well to cadet life, though his brother cadets at first thought him almost a recluse because of the time he spent alone at his studies. That image, however, changed with time as they began to see him as the "brilliant Rosy," who could not only be sociable when he wanted to be, but even charming, fun-loving and a fellow who was "good at everything and who talked 'interestingly, daily, fast, his imagination racing.' "[51] His roommate was James Longstreet, who was no role model when it came to academics, but who was later dubbed the handsomest man in his class at the same time that Rosecrans was considered the most studious. There is an inescapable irony in noting that the two roommates were fated to meet as generals on the field of Chickamauga, with one becoming a prime instrument in the defeat of the other.

Among Rosy's other classmates were John Pope, Abner Doubleday (the inventor-to-be of baseball), George H. Thomas, William T. Sherman, and Ulysses S. Grant. The last-named was a fresh new plebe in the summer of 1839 when he encountered the cadet officer of the day under circumstances that neither would have chosen. Rosecrans, while making his rounds as O.D., found the naive plebe standing guard over a pump in the yard. Grant explained, "I've orders to stand here until after the next call." Rosecrans, taking pity on the duped recruit, ordered him to return to barracks, douse his lights, and get some sleep. But a confused Grant persisted, "But how do I know that you're not playing a trick on me too?" "See my chevrons. I'm officer of the day."[52] The two future generals had met for the first time; whether the meeting was to affect any future relationship remains an open question.

There is no question, however, about Rosecrans' progress in his studies and his class standing. After the June 1840 examinations he ranked third highest in his class, and in the following year he stood fifth in class rankings and was promoted to cadet lieutenant, ranking second out of eighteen cadet officers in that grade, a top honor at the time. Yet, the studious youth who was proving a leader in an institution where leadership was regarded as the Holy Grail had another serious side. He had been raised in a staunch Methodist family and had remained deeply religious, in an America that held religion as a high social standard. But young William held even higher standards in his devotion to religion. At some time during his cadet career he was converted to Catholicism. Actually, "Rosecrans moved by slow degrees toward his new faith. He accepted it over strong parental objection before his graduation from West Point."[53] He was to remain deeply devoted to his faith throughout the rest of his life.

In his final academy year as a first classman, his future was to be influenced by a powerful worldly factor in the form of Dennis Hart Mahan, the awesome professor of civil and military engineering and the science of war. In the fall of 1841, Rosecrans was enrolled in Mahan's engineering classes, and later became one of the selected few to be accepted in Mahan's "Napoleon Club." Founded by Mahan, an admirer of the emperor, the club was actually an after-duty-hours series of informal "seminars" whereby Mahan hoped to expose a gifted few to the higher principles of strategy that had been so short-changed (as brought out in Dr. Morrison's findings) in the curriculum. Yet it is impossible to determine to what extent Mahan was able to bridge the gap—for even a tiny cadre of selectees—between a nine-hour class and a four-year program through the sessions of the Napoleon Club. Even so, in Rosecrans' case, his biographer was no doubt on firm ground when he found that "it is clear that Mahan fired Rosecrans' interest in strategy and made him a lifelong student of the campaigns not only of Napoleon, but also of Frederick the Great."[54] Whether the master personally took Rosecrans under his wing may be doubted, but it is certain that Mahan did exert a very real influence on Rosecrans' military career.

Finally, after "the brilliant class of 1842" had made its graduation parade on the Plain, Rosecrans was one of the seven (out of a class of fifty-one) to be commissioned a second lieutenant in the Corps of Engineers, the final proof of his achievements at the Military Academy. Yet, while it may have been interesting to follow Rosecrans' performance as an outstanding cadet, it is far more important to take note of what had happened to the green adolescent who had stepped off the boat landing in June of 1838. West Point had not only taken a boy in his formative years and turned him into a man; more significantly, it had molded a youthful intelligence into an "engineer's mind," perhaps the most important of all the factors that were to shape Rosecrans' character and career as a commander.

His first assignment as an engineer officer was to aid in repairing the seacoast fortifications at Fortress Monroe in Virginia. His main interest, however, was to gain a professorship back at his alma mater, and in the summer of 1843 he was accepted to teach engineering in Mahan's department. Not only had he gotten the career appointment he so desired, but he took on another big responsibility as well. In August of that year he was married to Ann Eliza Hegeman, the daughter of a New York City judge. After four years of academic duty at West Point, he was assigned to engineer duties at the Washington Navy Yard. Following that and during the next ten years of routine duty assignments, mostly in New England, he missed being one of the thirty-eight members of his class who saw combat service in the Mexican War. A less significant but interesting one of his "misses" happened after the war in 1851 when Rosecrans applied for the professorship in tactics and natural philosophy at the Virginia Military Institute. The appointment, however, went to a native Virginian, one Thomas J. Jackson.

During his nearly twelve years of military service, Rosecrans and his wife had become increasingly unhappy with his military career. In all that time he had been promoted only once and now had four children to raise, and worse— as the couple had concluded—a resourceful mind was going to waste facing a dreary and unpromising future. Finally, in April 1854 he resigned from the army, as had so many fellow officers in the prewar years, and went on to pursue a mixture of business and professional enterprises in which he became increasingly successful, mostly in his native Ohio. After turning his mind to experiment and inventions, he foresaw a breakthrough in the production of refining coal oil, and he became the head of a firm and its plant in Cincinnati. He had been working by himself in the plant laboratory on an experimental product when a safety lamp exploded, set the building ablaze, and burned him terribly. With his clothes on fire, his flesh seared, he managed to put out the flames by himself, save the plant, and then walk a mile and a half to his home. Needless to say, wife and doctors, after treating his burns, got him to bed, where his life hung in the balance for the first months of the next year and a half. He came through the ordeal, due in great part to his determination, but was left with burn scars over his body and several on his face, most of which were later covered by his beard, except for one on his forehead that remained visible for years.

By the time he was back on his feet and working to get his business back on track, the news of Fort Sumter reached Cincinnati, and Ohio's political leaders were looking for military professionals who could organize and train the militia volunteers. Rosecrans answered the call, first by serving as drill-master of the local "Marion Rifles." Soon, however, his abilities were put into real service, first as chief engineer of Ohio, then as colonel of the 23rd Ohio Volunteer Infantry. That command was cut short by his recognition as general officer material when he was appointed a brigadier general in the regular army and called to head a brigade by McClellan, who was then commanding in Ohio and preparing for his first campaign. Rosecrans led his brigade into his introduction to war as a combat commander under McClellan, who had the mission of invading western Virginia to drive rebel forces out of the region and "liberate" its people, who were mainly loyal to the Union. Rosecrans distinguished himself at the battle of Rich Mountain—the first real engagement of the Civil War—in July 1861, when his brigade outflanked and encircled a Confederate force which was forced to surrender. The minor victory (the Confederate command under Lieutenant Colonel John Pegram totaled only 553 officers and men) was publicized out of all proportion by the Northern press, which was keenly aware of the public's need for any military success after the disaster at Bull Run. McClellan's reputation was made as a national figure and Rosecrans too was on his way to higher command.

September of the following year found Rosecrans commanding the left wing of Grant's forces near Corinth, Mississippi, the command to which he had been promoted to succeed General John Pope, who had been called east to command the new Army of Virginia. When Grant took the offensive to strike at Confederate general Sterling Price's army at Iuka, Rosecrans was directed to maneuver around Price's south flank and cut him off, while Grant sent General Ord eastward to keep Price fixed in place. On 19 September, when within two miles of Iuka, Rosecrans was attacked by Price's left wing. In the fierce little battle that ensued, Rosecrans beat off the attack, costing the enemy twice as many casualties as his loss of 780. Price, learning of Ord's advance, withdrew, and Rosecrans and Ord returned to Corinth.

On 3 October the combined forces of Van Dorn and Price (Van Dorn in command) attacked Rosecrans' force of 23,000 at Corinth. Although the opposing forces were almost equal in strength, the Confederates succeeded in driving back Rosecrans' exterior lines, but on the following day Rosecrans counterattacked and decisively defeated his enemy. Van Dorn was driven back to Holly Springs, and Rosecrans followed, but was unable to force Van Dorn into another engagement. Rosecrans' reward was a promotion to major general of volunteers and a reassignment to replace Buell, who had failed to defeat Bragg or drive him out of Kentucky and Tennessee. Rosecrans relieved Buell in early November and reorganized the Union forces into the Army of the Cumberland, with a total strength of 47,000, divided between three army corps.

For most of the months of November and December Rosecrans and Bragg faced off while organizing their forces and preparing to take the offensive. The weeks of preparation so irked the high commands of both sides that the two commanders were continually prodded to take the field. In late December Rosecrans moved against Bragg, and the two armies met on Stones River at Murfreesboro. Both commanders took the offensive, each having planned to envelop his opponent's right flank. On the first day, 31 December 1862, Bragg's attack almost carried the day, but his initial success was spoiled by his failure to exploit his reserves in a decisive stroke. Because both sides were fighting astride Stones River, the shifting of reserves at critical times became the dominant feature of a battle that was distinguished further by the heavy losses sustained by each side. After Rosecrans was forced on the defensive he showed himself at his best, shifting and reorganizing his corps and divisions so effectively that every Confederate attack—too often made in piecemeal fashion—was beaten off with heavy casualties. Bragg's last major attack on 2 January suffered such a bloody repulse that he pulled back and that night started his forces in retreat toward Tullahoma, thirty-six miles to the south. Tactically it could be termed a drawn battle, but since Bragg had retreated such a distance, the Northern press could trumpet it as a strategic victory. Actually it was one of the bloodiest and hardest fought battles of the whole war, Rosecrans having taken a total loss of 31 percent against Bragg's casualties of 33 percent. Cold statistics such as these, however, only begin to indicate the time-and-again failure of Civil War generalship to attain decisive results, along with the attendant shock to the morale of their surviving soldiers who had fought alongside the dead and wounded.

As we have already seen, Rosecrans redeemed his tactical impasse at Stones River by his brilliantly conceived and executed strategical maneuvers that resulted in forcing Bragg to withdraw finally across the Tennessee River and into the key center of Chattanooga. At this point it would be helpful to take a further look and see the forty-four-year-old army commander as his staff and others saw him in the late summer of 1863.

He was of medium build, erect in posture, carrying himself well, both in the saddle and in personal contacts with his officers. His dark hair was beginning to show tinges of gray above a high forehead which tended to look white against his generally ruddy complexion. His features, most of which were covered by his heavy beard, were distinguished by his long Roman nose and were usually outlined by his peculiar habit of wearing his broad-brimmed felt hat tilted back on his head until the brim rested on his collar. Prominent too were his clear, gray eyes which never seemed to rest, shifting swiftly from one person to another as he talked to a group. He had another habit which he seemed to have shared—unconsciously, to be sure—with Grant. In the field he always had a cigar in his mouth, and even if it had gone unlit he continued to hold it between his teeth, removing it only to give an order or ask a question.

He was neat in his personal appearance, a careful but unshowy dresser who demanded the same of his staff, who made an impressive array on formal occasions such as reviews and inspections, where the group was always preceded by an escort with his two-star flag. His personal neatness and sense of order was mirrored in his relations with his staff and the daily running of army headquarters. After the briefest hours of sleep he was up and by 8:00 A.M. was taking his morning devotions with his chaplain-priest. A short breakfast followed; then the day's routine of reports, staff briefings, and issuing of orders lasted until 2:00 P.M. At that time he mounted his horse and led his staff on his round of inspections of camps and visits to subordinate commanders. These rounds continued uninterrupted (Rosecrans took no time for lunch, having only two meals a day) until 4:00 P.M., when a combination lunch-dinner with his staff ended that part of the headquarters day. The informal meal was a pleasant interlude, enlivened by good conversation led by the commander's lively interests and remarks. After a short break to enjoy a cigar and a quick reading of the newspapers, it was back to work, through sundown and on through the night. He then conducted the business of army headquarters, with interruptions allowed only to introduce shifts of his attention to reports, court-martial reviews, administrative decisions, and dictating of a voluminous correspondence, all the endless details that went with the running of an army. His attention to detail never wavered. He was the very devil of a work tyrant; his boundless energy wore down two shifts of staff officers every night, much in the same fashion that Napoleon was noted for driving sets of secretaries to exhaustion. His only diversion seemed to be his delight in map study, in which he excelled, even having invented a photographic process for duplicating maps which he had distributed to subordinate headquarters. By midnight, the day's business taken care of, he relaxed in the company of grateful staff officers who could then relax in an atmosphere "not unlike college 'bull sessions' [where] the commanding general was blithe, facetious, happy, almost charming."[55] These lively interchanges invariably lasted until at least 2:00 A.M., since the commander never retired before that time. In fact, in the field Rosecrans was known to go for days at a time with little or no sleep. During his hours of relaxation he was a witty conversationalist, never ceasing to impress his staff, particularly the junior officers, with his penetrating comments on historical and literary topics. In both fields he was notably impressive in his criticisms

of authors of the classics. Yet his urbane conversational style, as several observers have noted, seems to have been offset by another characteristic. When
addressing a large assembly of troops he often embarrassed his staff by stammering—almost stuttering at times.

This curious drawback, however, seems not to have been noticed by his
troops, who were devoted to "Old Rosy," especially for the ways in which he
became esteemed for his dedication to their welfare. Few Union army commanders seemed to have gained the universal trust, even a kind of father-son
relationship, that Rosecrans had with his soldiers. In general, he shared a
confidence in his leadership with junior officers and soldiers throughout the
army. The same confidence in his style of leadership might have been equally
shared by his staff and higher-level subordinates had it not been for a shortcoming that was unknown to the troops—his tendency to lose control of his
temper when he became angry, most often at an officer who had failed to
execute one of his orders. On such an occasion, he could become upset, even
at the very time when he should have shown restraint. Then, despite his
religious disposition, he could explode in profanity, shouting and stammering,
seeming momentarily to lose all control. On one occasion, while in camp, he
found that a brigade commander, John Beatty, had failed to execute an order
from army headquarters. When called on the carpet in front of Rosecrans,
Beatty tried to explain that he thought that the order had been intended for
another, namely Brigadier General Samuel Beatty, who commanded a brigade
in another division. The apparent confusion and Beatty's attempt at explanation served only to trigger Rosecrans' notorious temper. "Why in hell and
damnation didn't you mount your horse and come to headquarters to inquire?"
Rosecrans bellowed, as his irritation boiled into a rage. He went on—in front
of General Garfield, the army chief of staff, and other staff officers—to hu-
miliate Beatty with such violent language that the latter recorded in his diary
that he had been publicly exposed to language that was "ungentlemanly, abu-
sive and insulting" to the degree that "for an instant I was tempted to strike
him." But Beatty exhibited the restraint that his army commander had clearly
lacked, and he turned and left the room. Later, when the two met on the drill
field, Rosecrans greeted Beatty cheerfully, apparently indicating that the incident was closed.[56] Needless to say, the harm had been done, and the memory
of the incident continued to stick with those who had witnessed the scene
and those who had heard about it. Indeed, the case may well have served as
an omen of a similar one that would take place on the battlefield.

Unfortunately, this shortness of temper was not confined to the "chewing
out" of a hapless subordinate. It extended to Rosecrans' relations with higher
authority, especially when he thought that his command prerogatives were
being invaded, as on the occasions that General Halleck or Secretary of War
Stanton had "interfered with" his plan of campaign by ordering him into what
he considered premature action. It appears that Rosecrans' testiness with both
subordinates and superiors had deeper roots than mere irritation and subse-

quent loss of temper. His energetic drive, when combined with his orderly engineer's mind and its systematic organization of detail, simply could not brook interference when he was bent on putting a plan into execution. Then the brilliant strategist seemed transformed into a temperamental tyrant who could turn on the offender with a vengeance. Yet this remarkable man's character contained another trait that not only followed an outburst of temper, but seemed to carry a reverse image of it. After a brief interval, once his anger had cooled, he tended to thrust aside any recollection of his display of temper and would act toward the injured party as though the incident had never occurred, just as he had demonstrated on his encounter with Beatty. This odd combination of display of temper and its seeming absolution couldn't help but serve him ill, especially during the Chickamauga campaign.

To recapitulate Rosecrans' campaign at this point, it will be recalled that by 4 July 1863 he had succeeded in outmaneuvering Bragg between Tullahoma and the Tennessee River, thus forcing Bragg to withdraw across the river. As a result, with Bragg's army apparently redeploying east of the river to cover the vital strategic link of Chattanooga–Atlanta, Rosecrans could move to implement the next phase of his strategy. In essence, his plan envisioned crossing the Tennessee, initially with the three forward corps of his army, and turning Bragg out of Chattanooga by cutting his communications with Atlanta. To get his corps across the unfordable Tennessee, he was counting on Burnside's Army of the Ohio to cover his left flank by advancing on Knoxville, and on elements of Grant's forces from Mississippi to cover his right flank. Among Rosecrans' major concerns were deceiving Bragg about the Union army's river-crossing sites and how to take on Bragg in a major battle when and where that became necessary.

As recounted, Rosecrans had made detailed terrain and logistical studies in preparation for carrying out the next phase of his campaign east of the Tennessee River. His preparations for carrying out that phase now became the focus of a renewed hassle with Washington: the high command wanted no delay in the resumption of Rosecrans' successful operations that had driven Bragg out of Tennessee—and, more importantly, they wished to maintain the momentum resulting from the Gettysburg and Vicksburg victories or the precious time would pass when the Union could strike the Confederacy to its knees. In view of the strategic urgency, on 4 August Halleck sent Rosecrans a direct order: "Your forces must move forward without delay. You will daily report the movement of each corps till you cross the Tennessee River."

To the short-tempered Rosecrans this was more than interference with his operations; it was a slap in the face, probably with the knowledge or connivance of a hostile Stanton. Here was an army commander up to his ears in restoring a vital railroad line, clearing mountain roads, pushing to establish essential supply dumps, assembling and training a pontoon bridge train in secrecy, accumulating ammunition for two major battles, preparing thousands of wagons and draft animals for the vital supply trains that would enable the

Figure 9.1
Rosecrans' Army of the Cumberland

Courtesy Martin L. Wilkerson.

army to operate far from its supply bases beyond the Tennessee—all the preparations required to move an army over three mountain ranges, cross an unfordable river, and move to outmaneuver and defeat a wily enemy on his own ground. All this, and then being ordered to report all his plans and actions to "Old Brains" at his desk in Washington! It was more than this army commander could stand. Rosecrans fired off a telegram that ended with a demand to know of the general-in-chief "if your order is intended to take away my discretion as to the time and manner of moving my troops." Halleck's response was clear and to the point: "The orders for the advance of your army, and that it be reported daily, are peremptory."[57]

Rosecrans took the reply as a challenge. He called together his chief of staff and his five corps commanders (see Figure 9.1) Thomas, Crittenden, McCook, Stanley (the cavalry corps), and Granger (the reserve corps) at his headquarters at Winchester Springs, and after reiterating the main points of his concept of the upcoming operation, read them the telegram he intended to send to Halleck. The message ended, "If, therefore, the movement which I propose can not be regarded as obedience to your orders, I respectfully request a modification of it or to be relieved from the command." Then, having gained the assent of his commanders, Rosecrans sent off the telegram. The cumulative effects of it—too detailed to relate here—could be summed up as one would expect—negatively electric. However, after the president had caused the dust to settle, he restored calm all around, and sent Rosecrans a letter, fatherly in tone, which smoothed ruffled feathers and, in effect, put the army commander back in the saddle to conduct his campaign as planned. So finally, on 16 August a prepared Rosecrans set his corps in motion.

A look at Map 9.3 shows that Rosecrans had advanced his three forward corps (McCook's XX Corps, Thomas' XIV Corps, Crittenden's XXI Corps) on a broad front. There were at least two reasons for his maneuver. For the first we can be certain; the other may be controversial. First, advancing his corps in such a manner allowed the corps commanders to avoid revealing their actual crossing sites until the last moment; meanwhile the enemy could be deceived about the real sites until it was too late for him to take preventive action. The other reason becomes apparent after a second glance at the map. The picture of the three corps moving independently over such a wide area brings to mind an application of Napoleon's *bataillon carré* system. We know that Rosecrans had studied Napoleonic strategy under Mahan and on his own. Moreover, Rosecrans made reference to those methods in the opening sentence of his own story of his campaign: "I avail myself of the opportunity to perpetuate testimony concerning the strategy and *grand tactics* [italics added] of that wonderful campaign . . . in which the battle of Chickamauga was an inevitable incident."[58] Yet it may be argued that this conception of employing a variation of a *bataillon carré* may be countered by the fact that the rugged, mountainous terrain would impede mutual support between corps; also, the corps commanders would need to have experience, or at least training, in the employment of such a system for it to work, and history shows no evidence of Rosecrans' commanders having the requisite experience or training.

In any case, major elements of the Army of the Cumberland had reached the Tennessee by 20 August, and by 29 August the pontoon bridge train was laying the crossing bridge at Caperston's Ferry. In only four and a half hours the pontoon engineers had completed laying the bridge, and the lead elements of McCook's XX Corps were crossing the river and heading toward their first objective at Valley Head. Thomas' XIV Corps followed, crossing at three sites: Caperston's, Bridgeport, and Shellmound; then it moved on its first objective at Trenton. Crittenden's XXI Corps moved east, then converged southward and crossed at Shellmound, heading toward Chattanooga, the critical objective which, when secured, would assure that Bragg had been turned out of that strategic center.

All of these successful moves had been made possible by careful planning,

Map 9.3

ROSECRANS' RIVER CROSSING
& PLAN OF MANEUVER

SCALE IN MILES

Courtesy Martin L. Wilkerson.

rapid movement, and well-laid deceptive measures. From the start Rosecrans had planned to deceive Bragg into thinking that the Union forces would make their main effort against Chattanooga by crossing the river above the city and coming down on it from the north. Deception was aided in this regard by carefully staged demonstrations by a three-brigade force of Crittenden's along the river to the north of Chattanooga and by a shelling of the city from across the river, a cannonade which lasted until 1 September. In the end, it was apparent that Bragg had been fooled, realizing only too late that Rosecrans had gotten major forces across the Tennessee *south* of Chattanooga and, what was equally dangerous, that they were moving eastward with the obvious intent of cutting him off from his communications with Atlanta.

By 8 September it was clear to Rosecrans that Bragg had avoided entrapment and was giving up Chattanooga. On the following day Crittenden's leading division entered the city. Now came a pivotal stage in Rosecrans' campaign, one in which intelligence of the enemy was to play a critical role; therefore, he had to rely heavily on his cavalry's reconnaissance capability. Unfortunately, not only was that arm weaker in strength than his opponent's, its quality was significantly lower. While Rosecrans was understandably concerned about screening his army's flanks, he badly needed the information that could come from cavalry reconnaissance. Once across the river he was employing most of Stanley's cavalry corps to cover McCook's corps and the wide-open flank to the south. The only remaining cavalry brigade (plus a mounted infantry brigade) was covering Crittenden's corps on the north. As a result, Thomas' corps in the center had to move on its objectives without cavalry cover. Though Rosecrans chose to accept that risk, he had to face the fact that not only was Thomas' corps moving without a cavalry screen, the army commander was being denied essential information from that corps' front in his army's center. It appears (from our invaluable hindsight vantage point) that the resulting lack of strategic/tactical intelligence led Rosecrans to draw a fateful, erroneous conclusion: Bragg, having abandoned Chattanooga, was indeed withdrawing the whole of his outmaneuvered army toward Dalton and possibly toward Atlanta.

Rosecrans' conclusion was aided, albeit unwittingly, by interrogations of deserters whose "reports" appeared to agree that Bragg's demoralized army was in full retreat toward Dalton. As will be seen, a retrograde move was the last thing in Bragg's mind. The deserters were carefully primed agents who were all too willing to unload their false information about the Confederate army's withdrawal. In retrospect it would seem that Rosecrans and his staff should have exercised more care in their analyses of this source of intelligence. One of the staff later wrote, "Whether he [the deserter] told the truth or a lie, he was almost equally sure to deceive. He was sometimes a real deserter and sometimes a mock deserter. In either case he was sure to be loaded."[59]

As a consequence of his interpretation of his tactical intelligence, by 9–10 September Rosecrans was pushing his still widely dispersed corps in what amounted to the strategic pursuit of the retreating Confederate forces. On the right (south) McCook was directed to press forward toward Alpine and to employ his cavalry aggressively in a thrust to cut the railroad at Resaca. Crittenden on the left (north), after seizing Chattanooga, was to head southeastward through Ringgold in his continued advance. Thomas, in the center, was to continue pushing forward toward Lafayette. In fact the advance of Thomas' leading division, Negley's, now served to stir up all sorts of activity on the part of the Confederates. Negley had been advanced by Thomas, without the cover of a cavalry screen, through Stevens' Gap to a position near Dug Gap on the far (east) side of McLemore's Cove, actually a long valley formed by West Chickamauga Creek, which ran between Missionary Ridge on the west and Pigeon Mountain on the east. Once in position in the cove Negley could cover the advance of Thomas' other divisions coming toward Dug Gap. However, all of the concerned Union commanders—Negley, Thomas, and Rosecrans—were unaware that the division was about to become the victim of a trap in McLemore's Cove.

During the next several days (9–18 September), while his three corps were continuing to move, Rosecrans was becoming increasingly exposed to intelligence that must have shown him that he had not only been deluding himself in regard to the precipitate retreat of Bragg's forces, he had also dispersed his three corps to such an extent that several of his major elements could be attacked in detail before he could concentrate the bulk of his army. The scary case in point was Negley's division, which, once it was realized that it was in danger of entrapment, was hurriedly withdrawn. This narrow escape and concurrent events finally convinced Rosecrans of his errors. In his words he began to concentrate his forces (see Map 9.4):

By the 12th I found that the enemy was concentrating behind Pigeon Mountain near Lafayette. When Crittenden's reconnaissance in force, of the 12th and 13th, showed the rest of Bragg's retiring columns near the Chickamauga, I instantly ordered him to move westward within supporting distance of Thomas as speedily and secretly as possible. At the same time orders were dispatched to McCook to join Thomas . . . with the utmost celerity.[60]

Another significant development, resulting from Crittenden's maneuvering of his corps, was his moving Wood's division to Lee and Gordon's Mills while his other two divisions were moving toward Reed's Bridge. When Crittenden's reconnaissance sources (and Rosecrans' orders) convinced him that he should concentrate his corps, he moved his other two divisions to the vicinity of Wood's position. Even before the other two divisions were moving toward him, Wood had informed Rosecrans, late on 10 September, that the enemy was massing large forces to the east of his front.

By the night of 17–18 September Rosecrans had moved his three corps within supporting distance of each other: McCook near Stevens' Gap, Thomas

Map 9.4

Courtesy Martin L. Wilkerson.

centered around Pond Spring, and Crittenden in the vicinity of Lee and Gordon's Mills. Of equal importance to Rosecrans' moves is his state of mind at this point. His later account of the campaign and his official reports at the time disclose an army commander whose spirit of the offensive, once the driving force behind his plan of campaign and the aggressive maneuvering of his forces, had shifted to that of a commander intent on positioning his forces to ward off an attack by an enemy who now threatened to overturn his offensive strategy. What we have been observing is a sequence of transformations: once across the river, the chess master became the hunter in pursuit of his quarry; but when the hunter sighted his target he fired and missed, only to find that his prey had turned and was hunting *him*; now the hunter was hastily trying to reload before his erstwhile quarry could come bounding out of hiding to charge him. Thus, in a certain sense Rosecrans was no longer acting but reacting. Indeed his enemy was now one who had become even more dangerous because the whereabouts of his preponderance of force—and its movements—could only be presumed. Again, Rosecrans' own words give us an insight into his reactions:

At last, on the 18th, McCook's corps came within reach of the enemy, who was then moving through gaps in the Pigeon Mountain to attack us. Over the tree-tops we saw clouds of dust moving toward our left. Bragg wanted to get between us and Chattanooga. We had no time to lose.[61]

Then followed his account of his movement orders, which directed the closer concentration of his forces on Thomas' corps, which was moved to the northeast to positions across the Ringgold Road and the more westward roads leading to Chattanooga. At the same time, "Crittenden and McCook were to follow *when the enemy's plan developed* [italics added]." Those five words say all that is needed about the army commander's state of mind on the eve of battle.

CHAPTER 10

Braxton Bragg, Confederate Strategy, and the Tactical Offensive

If Rosecrans had believed that Bragg had withdrawn from the Chattanooga area to regroup his forces instead of retreating toward Dalton and Atlanta he would have been right. If he had believed that Bragg was about to attack as a result of a tactical decision based on a strategy of Bragg's own making, Rosecrans would have been both right and wrong. To understand what underlay Bragg's aims it is necessary to look back to the roots of a Confederate national strategy that had brought him to this confrontation with Rosecrans' now concentrating army.

By the summer of 1863, following the twin disasters of Gettysburg and Vicksburg, it would scarcely seem surprising to a late–twentieth-century observer if the South's leadership had adopted a strategy that would gain time to tighten up the Confederacy's defenses while arousing the national will to resist renewed invasions of their land. In actuality, a defensive strategy was far from the minds—and strong urgings—of the most influential of the South's military and political voices. And those voices were anything but a cacophony of demands; they came instead from a widespread network of factions or blocs, the most prominent of which was the so-called western concentration bloc. This informal group, gaining in influence since the fall of 1862, had the ear of James A. Seddon, the secretary of war, and was listened to by President Davis himself. Although composed of a diversity of individual interests—political, social, financial, and military—the members were united in one common lobby: to reinforce an army in the west which could then exploit a strategic thrust that would split asunder the Union armies and destroy them and any Northern hopes for further invasion of the South. If that reinforcement meant taking forces from Lee in Virginia, so be it, especially in mid-1863 when Union forces, east and west, seemed to be resting on their laurels

Braxton Bragg

and showing no signs of moving to carry out a unified thrust against new strategic objectives. The most influential of all the voices in the western concentration bloc was that of General Pierre Gustave Toutant Beauregard. The Creole general, though speaking at the time from a nonstrategic command position in Charleston, carried a name that was not only a household word throughout the South but one which carried weight in high circles. He had been a national figure ever since that astounding victory at First Manassas, and what was more, many of the higher-level commanders had served with or under him since that time. A colorful, if at times flamboyant, figure, he had been a professional soldier, even a protégé of Mahan's at West Point, as well as a disciple of Napoleon and Jomini and the author of works that were respected in antebellum military thought. During the war his advice on strategic matters was often sought (when it wasn't, it was offered anyway), and though some of his proposals reached the scale of the grandiose and unattainable, he did consistently recognize and advocate the use of two strategic instruments in which his vision was above that of most of his peers. He continued to push for the joint employment of the telegraph and the railroads for the rapid concentration of forces to exploit strategic mobility. In a more specific sense, in the words of the scholars Hattaway and Jones, "He became both the strategist and the publicist of the western concentration bloc, not only because of his extensive overlapping contacts but because he perceived the Tennessee and Kentucky area as the Union's weak point and he wished to direct a surprise Confederate concentration against Rosecrans's army."[62] Of equal importance, in his correspondence with Bragg, Beauregard found that the commander of the Army of Tennessee was in full agreement with him on that score. Bragg, however, began to have second thoughts when he reflected on how lacking in troop strength his army was to take the offensive against Rosecrans. During the same period (before Rosecrans launched his offensive in June 1863), Davis became convinced that a western concentration and offensive could be undertaken, and Cooper, his adjutant general, even urged him to direct Bragg to take the offensive. Davis, the former professional soldier and federal secretary of war, rejected the recommendation in keeping with his policy of making suggestions rather than giving orders to his commanders in the field. Consequently, for a while the proposal for a western concentration and offensive lay in abeyance, destined to be resurrected when Rosecrans succeeded in threatening both Bragg's army and the Chattanooga gateway to the heart of the Deep South. Then, after mid-August, other developments combined to force a decision on the Confederacy's taking the offensive in the west.

First, when Burnside moved his army to cooperate with Rosecrans' plan of campaign, Bragg became alarmed enough to use his newly extended authority to direct General Simon B. Buckner to move his corps to join his forces near Chattanooga, thus abandoning Knoxville to Burnside, who was now moving into east Tennessee from Kentucky. Bragg's orders meant not only that he had begun a concentration of force on his own, but also that he had, by giving up Knoxville, lost the important direct railroad link between Richmond and Chattanooga, the consequences of which will be seen. Second, on 21 August, the same day that he directed Buckner to join him, Bragg made an urgent request of General Joseph E. Johnston for reinforcements. Bragg's request was now backed up by Richmond, and on the following day Johnston started moving half of the infantry (9,000 men) of his small army by rail through Alabama toward Chattanooga. Another development which was to bear directly on the question of a western offensive was Davis' calling Lee to Richmond in late August to advise him on matters relating to national strategy. During more than a week of conferences Lee was at first understandably reluctant (as one of several department commanders) to assent to reinforcing Bragg with troops from the Army of Northern Virginia. But as he began to see things from Davis' national perspective and realized that the Union had weakened Meade's forces (facing Lee's army), he went along with the president's inclination to reinforce Bragg—that inclination no doubt due in no small part to lobbying from the western concentration bloc. The final decision was to send Longstreet's corps of two divisions by rail to the Chattanooga area. Though Lee ordered the rail reinforcement upon his return to his army headquarters, the movement was doomed to be slowed by Burnside's cutting the Richmond–Chattanooga railway link. As a result Longstreet's overall rail mileage was almost doubled: "Instead of traveling 500 miles directly to Chattanooga, the reinforcements took a circuitous path through North and South Carolina and Georgia, a distance stretching nearly 1,000 miles over ten different rickety railroads. Despite enormous difficulties, the first of Longstreet's men reached Bragg in ten days, and half the force arrived in eleven."[63] As will be seen, that first detachment arrived in the nick of time to be committed to action.

Now the picture of the western concentration can be seen in its entirety (see Map 10.1). Buckner had already moved from the northeast to join Bragg. Johnston's reinforcement was moving from the southwest toward the Chattanooga area. Longstreet's two divisions were coming from the east via the roundabout route just described. In spite of its apparent piecemeal commitments the Confederates' railway strategy was a surprising success, both in the rapidity of its execution and the secrecy that managed to conceal its troop movements from Union intelligence—until it was too late for the high command in Washington or its commanders in the field to react effectively. Taken all in all, it was no less than a master stroke of strategic surprise, one that Bragg might exploit to achieve a victory in the west. Two questions then emerge: How well equipped was Bragg to handle this bonanza? Would he be capable of achieving a victory that would turn the tide of the war to offset the Union successes at Gettysburg and Vicksburg?

The answer to the first question lies in two closely related fields—Bragg's relations with his subordinate commanders and his own character. In the first

Map 10.1

CONFEDERATE STRATEGIC CONCENTRATION

Courtesy Martin L. Wilkerson.

place, the Army of Tennessee was as unlike Lee's Army of Northern Virginia as one could imagine. The raw iron that made up Lee's forces had been forged in the heat of battles into a sword that was instantly responsive to the hand of its master. In the west, though the same raw metals were there—Tennessee mountaineers, rugged farm boys from Alabama and Georgia, tough volunteers from Mississippi and Louisiana—they had never become forged into one resilient weapon, in spite of the spirited toughness of the soldiers and their officers. Though the army had fought through its share of brutal battles, it had also suffered a series of changed commanders, lost and recovered elements, and reorganizations that had left it without the *esprit de corps* that it deserved. Then, after its terrible bloodletting at Murfreesboro, the Army of Tennessee was badly in need of a leader who could breathe life into it and make it the force that the Confederacy so badly needed in the west. What it got instead was Braxton Bragg, the same commander who had dragged it back in retreat after retreat following the confused combats of Perryville and Murfreesboro. In the six months of inactivity after the latter the army did recover its physical well-being thanks to Bragg's administrative skills and rigid enforcement of discipline. At the highest command levels, however, a cancerous tumor was eating away at the base of the army's brain.

A major cause of the tumor was one of the factions that made up the aforementioned western concentration bloc, one that historians have labeled the anti-Bragg bloc. This clique was composed mainly of corps and division commanders within the Army of Tennessee who shared a distrust of Bragg's generalship and a combined fear and loathing of his tendency to blame operational failures on his subordinates. In its formative stage the faction might have been called a cabal, though later its activities—confined to confidential exchanges and correspondence with political leaders, the secretary of war, and Jefferson Davis himself—never assumed the form of an outright conspiracy. As will be seen, however, the relations between Bragg and his unhappy commanders eventually came to an open break. Among the more prominent dissidents were two corps commanders, Generals Leonidas Polk and William J. Hardee, as well as two division commanders, Generals John C. Breckinridge and Patrick R. Cleburne. There were others of equivalent or lesser rank, though it should be made clear that the term "anti-Bragg bloc" held true only within the Army of Tennessee and did not include other officers, inside or outside that army, who simply disliked Bragg. Also deserving emphasis is the fact that the anti-Bragg bloc was essentially a faction or clique, though its informal nature in no way made it less of a powerful force, a force that came close to removing Bragg from command.

Following the retreat from Murfreesboro and through the winter and spring of 1863, the festering resentment of Bragg by the bloc had broken out into open quarrels between Bragg and senior members of the bloc. In great part the break was brought about by Bragg's growing distrust of his generals, like Polk and Hardee, and by his suspicious nature. The clashes between personalities became so intense and prolonged that an observer could not help but note that Bragg was waging war on two fronts—against Rosecrans as well as the Confederate generals who wanted him ousted from command. Matters came to a head after Bragg came under caustic criticism in the press regarding his alleged mishandling of his operations that had led to the botched battles of Perryville and Murfreesboro and particularly the retreat following the latter. The general tone of most of the press's criticism pointed toward the charge that Bragg had lost the confidence of his commanders and that of the army in general. The fuel that fired Bragg's anger came after he learned from other sources that rumors were flying that he was about to be replaced by another of his generals or even by Beauregard. All this spurred Bragg into taking steps that were as unprecedented as they were to prove damaging to his command relationships.

By 10 January Bragg had decided to put matters directly to his own staff, evidently to use those officers as a sounding board to determine whether or not the rumors and criticism were unfounded and what action might be indicated on his part. To his surprise and chagrin the staff, having conferred in private, returned a consensus that he should relinquish command. Far from being humbled, on the following day Bragg decided to challenge once and for all the chief dissidents and either gain their support or make them lay their cards on the table. He sent a circular letter to his corps and division commanders asking them, in effect, to acquit him of the charge that he had gone against their wishes in ordering the retreat from Murfreesboro and thereby to solicit their support in opposition to the wave of criticism in the press. The circular might have had the effect that Bragg was seeking, had he not made the mistake of ending the letter as follows: "I desire that you will consult your subordinate commanders and be candid with me. . . . I shall retire without regret if I find I have lost the good opinion of my generals, upon whom I have ever relied as upon a foundation of rock." The historian Shelby Foote in his distinguished narrative history has summed up the impact of the letter on its addressees: "This last was what opened the floodgates. . . . his closing statement that he would retire if he found that he had lost their good opinion presented the generals with a once-in-a-lifetime opportunity, which they did not neglect."[64] Hardee, for example, replied immediately that he and his division commanders, Breckinridge and Cleburne, were of one mind—that he should resign. Polk was away on leave and in his absence his two division commanders merely acknowledged (presumably awaiting Polk's return) that Bragg had followed the advice of his commanders in withdrawing after Murfreesboro. When Polk, a widely known opponent of Bragg and a leader in wishing Bragg ousted, returned, he replied to the circular asking, in effect, whether Bragg wanted to know who had counseled the retreat or whether the army commander wanted to know if he had lost the confidence of the army. It would seem that, after a subsequent exchange of letters, the two generals were content to let the matter rest. A little later, however, when Polk learned that Hardee and his generals thought that he had sidestepped the issue, Polk wrote directly to his good friend Jefferson Davis and attached to his letter copies of all the correspondence between him and Bragg, including a copy of the latter's circular. Parts of Polk's cover letter included his opinion (and that of his senior commanders) that Bragg be transferred to Richmond and that the command of the Army of Tennessee go to General Joseph E. Johnston. President Davis, who was aware of the existence of the anti-Bragg bloc, sent Johnston to Bragg's headquarters at Tullahoma in late January to determine "whether he had so far lost the confidence of the army as to impair his usefulness in his present position. . . . by conversation with General Bragg and others of his command, to decide what the best interests of the service require, and to give me the advice I need at this juncture."[65]

Johnston, who was the de facto commander of the western theater, carried out his directed visit, but with mental reservations. He was well aware that Davis and others really wanted him to take personal command of the Army of Tennessee, but there were very strong opposing feelings that tugged at his heart. First, he continued to hold Bragg's generalship in high regard. Second, a corollary of the first, how could he—personally present in Bragg's own headquarters—make an unbiased investigation of his host's fitness and then make public findings that would include the recommendation that he himself be appointed to replace Bragg as army commander? The result of Johnston's observations (and the tug-of-war with his conscience) was the closing of his letter to Davis: "I am sure that you will agree with me that the part I have borne in this investigation would render it inconsistent with my personal honor to occupy that position. . . . General Bragg should not be removed."

With that, one would assume the matter closed. Davis and Seddon, however, took a different view of the matter. It would seem that by now the president and his secretary of war had made up their minds that indeed Johnston should take over command of the Army of Tennessee, and on 9 March Davis ordered Johnston to take command and Bragg to report to Richmond for reassignment. But fate intervened for Bragg in the form of two unpredictable happenings. Bragg's wife came down with typhoid fever so dangerous that it threatened her life, and Bragg was constantly at her bedside. About the same time Johnston had to take to his bed with a flare-up of the wounds that had removed him from command at the start of the Seven Days Battles. A third influence then intervened in the form of another visitor to Bragg's headquarters. On 12 March Davis sent his military aide, Colonel William P. Johnston, to Bragg's headquarters to check on matters. The upshot of these seemingly unrelated events was that the two patients soon recovered, and Colonel Johnston returned a report that skirted around the dissension within the army command while otherwise giving Bragg a favorable report. The result was that the Davis administration apparently decided to treat the whole affair as a series of misunderstandings; Bragg would remain in command and matters would be patched over. The real outcome, however, was that though the government had put the lid on the pot, the contents continued to stew and could boil over when the lid was removed. Meanwhile the rank and file of the army remained (most fortunately for their country) unaware of the controversy involving their higher commanders and went about their duties as might be expected. All that is not to say, however, that the dissident generals had forgotten—or forgiven—their grievances. On the contrary, the basic distrust of their chief was in reality intensified and dissension and dissonance continued, even though subdued, right through the spring and summer, interrupted finally by the intervention of another general named Rosecrans. Before our story can be taken up at that point, however, one should look into the other cause of the contention between Bragg and the disaffected generals—the inside and outside of Bragg's own character—for that is the only way that one can begin to understand this most complicated of all the Confederacy's generals.

To begin at the beginning, Braxton Bragg was born and bred a Southern gentleman, even though his family may not have been one of the 15,000 plantation owners who made up the so-called aristocracy that the American public nowadays associates with *Gone with the Wind* and other novels and movies of that genre. Braxton's father, Thomas, was a contractor and builder who could count among his accomplishments the reconstruction of the state capitol at Raleigh, North Carolina, after it had burned down in 1830. His mother was Margaret Crossland Bragg, a lady noted for her energy and intelligence, qualities she managed to pass on to Braxton, who was one of twelve children, six sons and six daughters. Braxton was born in Warrenton, North Carolina, in

1817 and was educated at the academy there. The academy had an excellent reputation, one that must have been deserved, for of all the Bragg children who attended, John went on to become a member of Congress and a state supreme court judge. Another older brother, Thomas, took up the law, was elected governor and later a U.S. senator, and finally was appointed attorney general of the Confederate States. After Braxton had graduated from the academy, he applied for and got an appointment to West Point from General M. T. Hawkins, his congressman from the Warrenton district. He arrived at West Point on 1 July 1833 to become a member of the class of 1837.

The boy Bragg was hardly two months past his sixteenth birthday; there were only two boys younger in a class that numbered eighty-five. His youthfulness, however, proved to be more of an incentive than a handicap, for at the end of his plebe year Bragg rated fifteenth in his class. His progress in his class standing was as progressive as it was outstanding. At the end of his second year he stood number eleven out of the surviving seventy-five. In his third year he was number seven out of fifty-eight, and he graduated fifth in a class of fifty. Among his classmates were general officer material, Union and Confederate, such as John Sedgwick, John C. Pemberton, Jubal A. Early, and Joseph Hooker. The last-named has left us insight into the young Bragg's character when he wrote an appraisal of Bragg for the Annual of the Association of Graduates in the eighth reunion of the class in 1877. Skipping over flowery phraseology ("the minds of all of his countrymen who admire and sympathize with magnificent achievements, for which that officer deservedly held a conspicuous position in the public estimation"), one can find insightful observations: "tall, ungainly in his gait. . . . [Feeling] free to express his opinion on all occasions and all subjects, utterly regardless of its influence on himself, he appeared to be conscious of his own rectitude, and therefore free in approving or condemning the acts of others. To those who enjoyed his more intimate acquaintance this harshness of character disappeared, and he appeared to them a genial, generous, brave and clever companion. To others of his associates he sometimes appeared brusque even to rudeness."[66] Those frank insights, written by a classmate who also became an army commander, tell one a great deal about how Bragg's double-sided personality could have had such varying impressions on his peers.

Among his class Bragg ranked second in tactics, seventh in artillery, and fifth in engineering and the science of war; the last two, it will be recalled, were Mahan's chief subjects. When he left West Point in 1837 Bragg left behind him a top record, if not one of distinction; and he was remembered by his classmates as "equal, if not superior, to any member of their class." Upon graduation he was assigned as a second lieutenant to the 3rd Artillery Regiment, and so Bragg found himself—like so many other brand-new shave-tails—no longer a high-ranking first classman and cadet officer, but the lowest of the low among regimental officers. His first duties were the ordinary garrison chores at Fortress Monroe, where Bragg remained for only seven months. In February 1838 he was reassigned, along with his artillery company, to Fort Marion at St. Augustine, Florida. The Seminole War was grinding down toward its end, and in the few antiguerrilla operations that were still going on, there was little if any need for artillery support. As a result, Bragg saw no combat action during his tour of duty.

What he did see was that the military environment in Florida in the 1830s was anything but a land of bright sun and tropical beaches. Inland the country seemed to consist of murky swamps, mosquitoes, and fevers that struck down the hardy as quickly as the weak. Unfortunately for Lieutenant Bragg he was to find himself counted among the latter as far as his health was concerned. It was there that the first of the illnesses that were to dog him all his life dragged him down. In the spring of 1838 he was so sick that he was given three months sick leave to go home and recuperate. Though his recovery was complete enough for him to return to duty, that illness could have been a sign that his body would not always keep up with his mind's dedication to his military service.

Following his return to duty and subsequent service in Florida, Bragg was transferred, along with the regimental headquarters, to Fort Moultrie on the sandbar called Sullivan's Island in the harbor of Charleston, South Carolina. Among his messmates were three future Union generals: Lieutenants George H. Thomas, J. F. Reynolds, and William T. Sherman. The last was to become not only a comrade but a good friend of Bragg's throughout their prewar careers. Their assignment with the 3rd Artillery at Fort Moultrie was to last almost three years. Garrison duty on a sandbar in Charleston harbor might be the deadliest bore in any lieutenant's career if all his off duty hours were spent in watching the surf breaking on the beach or gawking at cotton ships dumping their ballasts in the harbor, where Captain Bowman of the army engineers was supervising the raising of the foundations of what would become Fort Sumter. Fortunately for Bragg and his fellow officers they were welcomed in Charleston society, then one of the South's highest social centers. So, between the rounds of balls, cotillions, teas, and other social affairs, time rolled along smoothly for the young officers, broken only by the tedium of drill and routine garrison duties, which have their way of interrupting the social life of lieutenants in peacetime. Bragg's garrison routine, however, didn't always roll along so smoothly when it came to getting along with his superiors, for he was anything but a brownnosing junior officer. It seems that his tendency to expect perfection—presumably in others as well as himself—was not limited to his brother officers, but extended to his superiors. Bragg's regimental commander, Colonel William Gates, was to prove no exception. Gates couldn't help but notice that, for some unknown reason, Lieutenant Bragg was speaking to him only in the line of duty, an unacceptable breach of the customs of the service. Instead of calling the upstart on the carpet as a thick-skinned C.O. would have done, Gates chose to break the ice in a gentlemanly manner. One evening at the post officers' club, Gates encountered Bragg as the latter was coming in the door.

"Lieutenant Bragg, a glass of wine with you, Sir!"

The reply: "Colonel Gates, if you order me to drink a glass of wine with you, I shall have to do it." An officer today couldn't help but wonder how Gates would have recalled the incident when it came to writing a certain part of the lieutenant's efficiency report.

Not long after the incident had passed into regimental memories something happened to intervene in both the social life and careers of Bragg and all his companions: the outbreak of war between Mexico and the United States took them to new assignments. Bragg, Sherman, and Thomas went to join General Zachary Taylor's army, which, when built up with regiments of volunteers, invaded northern Mexico. Bragg's gallant conduct at Fort Brown and Monterrey quickly won him brevet promotions. But it was his key role in the battle of Buena Vista that brought him not only recognition of his professional qualities but even national fame. The battle became imminent when Santa Anna, the Mexican dictator-general, marched northward with an army of 14,000 with the intention of overwhelming Taylor's small army and clearing northern Mexico of the invaders. When Taylor learned of Santa Anna's approach he took up a defensive position with his 4,800 men across a defile about eight miles south of Saltillo. Although Santa Anna's force of 14,000 was still trying to recover from its hardships and losses, its commander attacked on 22 February 1847, driving in Taylor's outposts. On the following day he attacked Taylor's main body in what became the complicated and confused battle of Buena Vista. The regular army batteries of Major J. M. Washington and Captains Sherman and Bragg were to play decisive roles in holding off and eventually defeating the repeated attacks of Mexican infantry and cavalry. On the morning of the 23rd, one of the heaviest Mexican thrusts so threatened the Indiana and Arkansas volunteer regiments that they broke and fled. Bragg later wrote of this part of the action, "[I] kept up my fire until I observed our left flank turned, and the enemy rapidly gaining our rear. . . . Two whole regiments Indiana & Arkansas ran [after] the first fire and none returned." Bragg, seeing his opportunity, limbered up and went into a new firing position, unlimbering on the far side of a ravine on the attacking enemy's flank where he was joined by Sherman's guns. In Taylor's own report of this part of the action, "The 2d Kentucky Regiment and a section of artillery under Captain Bragg . . . arrived at a most opportune moment. . . . The batteries of Captains Sherman and Bragg . . . did much execution . . . particularly upon the masses which had gained our rear." And in Braggs' words, "So destructive was our fire that the enemy column was divided, and a large portion of it retreated, leaving those in front . . . totally cut off."[67] Throughout the morning and into the afternoon Santa Anna made repeated attempts to turn the American left, and then made thrusts against its center. During the shifting focus of action Bragg was limbering and unlimbering, in and out of one firing position after another, all the while delivering fire effective enough to turn back an attack. His three guns fired an average of 250 rounds, a phenomenal expenditure of ammunition for the muzzle-loading "Napoleons" of the day. By early afternoon Bragg's cannoneers and drivers were wearing down and the horses were so tired that they could only be made to move at a walk.

At this critical juncture, Colonel Jefferson Davis had arrived at the American center with his regiment of Mississippi volunteers. Davis deployed his regiment and advanced ahead of the artillery—Bragg had had the foresight to move into position to bolster up the center—to check the coming Mexican main attack. Davis at the head of his regiment took a wound in the foot but remained in the saddle. The next enemy volleys, however, not only stopped the attack but forced Davis' men to withdraw, leaving Bragg's guns exposed to the now advancing Mexican attack. It was at this critical point that Braxton Bragg was about to become a national hero. The story that was to be repeated by a news-hungry public (perhaps originating in the *New Orleans Daily Delta*) held that Taylor had uttered the famous line, "a little more grape, Captain Bragg."

There are several good reasons that the kind of exhortation from "Old Rough and Ready" would have been more like "double-shot your guns and give 'em hell, Bragg." In the first place, Bragg himself would later, when in good humor and relating the story to friends, say that the latter version was the right one. Moreover, Bragg needed no such order. Here was a professional hard at work who had already given the fire commands to load with canister. Then, in the words of Lew Wallace, the Civil War general and author of *Ben Hur*, who was there at Buena Vista as a lieutenant in the 1st Indiana, "When he [Bragg] wheeled his guns into battery, the enemy was within a few yards of their muzzles and at first he [the enemy] gave ground as the pieces recoiled." After the second and third rounds from Bragg's guns the enemy did more than give ground. Davis' Mississippians had rallied, and now joined by Kentucky, Illinois, and Indiana regiments, were adding volleys of musketry to Bragg's volleys of canister. The combined fire from front and flank was more than the Mexican infantry could stand, and after severe losses, Santa Anna's men broke and fled in wild disorder. Buena Vista was won, Santa Anna was finished in northern Mexico, and Bragg—already recommended to brevet major for meritorious service at Monterrey—was again recommended for promotion, this time to brevet lieutenant colonel.

After one gets past the kudos and military glories of the incredible American victory at Buena Vista—the defenders, against three-to-one odds, utterly defeated the attackers—it seems more pertinent to us, as detached observers, to find whether there were tactical lessons to be learned from the battle. Even more pertinently, what did Bragg himself learn that would profit him in command positions during the Civil War?

Perhaps not the lessons that some have surmised. While it is true that Bragg undoubtedly took advantage of the opportunity to survey the battlefield and relive his experiences, some of his conclusions may have been misleading in regard to lessons that might have been applied in the Civil War. In the first place, Bragg had to be keenly aware that it was the mobility of the light artillery that enabled it to get to the right place at the right time and play a decisive role in the battle. Later reflection, however, would have led him to realize that if (a big if) the American force had had sufficient artillery units continuously in support of the same infantry formations there would have been no need for artillery batteries to be galloping from one firing position to another to provide the needed support. Indeed such a lesson was learned on Civil War battlefields like Malvern Hill and Gettysburg where the defense employed prepositioned artillery with deadly effect. Secondly, Bragg's observations also led him to infer that artillery had accounted for "nine-tenths of the killed and wounded," a conclusion that may have been misleading in the light of the yet-to-come impact of *rifle* firepower in the defense, though that tactical clout was, of course, one that Bragg could not have then experienced, since Mexican War infantry were armed mainly with the smoothbore musket.

In any case, the foregoing may be thought of as intellectual baggage that Bragg, in coming home from the war, could have stored in his mental attic, when compared to a certainty that Bragg would always carry in his mental wallet. The certainty was founded on his contempt for the behavior of volunteer infantry who had broken and run, at times even on the first exchange of fire with the Mexicans. In Bragg's mind, and those of other West Pointers, when one compared the conduct of the volunteer militia to that of regular infantry (which Taylor didn't have at Buena Vista), the former were as unreliable in battle as they were dangerous to a commander's purposes. The intensity of Bragg's conclusions in this regard were clearly expressed in a letter that Bragg later wrote to Cump Sherman: "And yet that [Buena Vista] was a volunteer victory!! If any action in the whole war, Cump, proves the inefficiency of Vols. that is the one."[68] What is important here is not Bragg's inference that regular artillery saved the day at Buena Vista when the volunteers almost lost it, but the certainty that it was the *lack of discipline* that lay at the heart of the problem of the volunteers' disgraceful behavior. It was the keen awareness of the necessity to instill discipline in his troops that was to permeate Bragg's character all his life, and it was the relentless drive to achieve perfection in this regard that was to stamp him with the reputation of a harsh disciplinarian. And later it was the harsh part that was to separate him from other commanders in the minds of Civil War officers and soldiers. What was not apparent to others was how the need for discipline fitted into Bragg's nature. It was as much a part of him as the standards that he consistently applied to others: a person was either right or wrong, either competent or incompetent, careful or careless; therefore troops were either disciplined or they were undisciplined—and if the latter held true, the most stringent measures had to be taken to correct the fault. Unfortunately for Bragg's military image, his discipline was not administered with the "kindness, firmness and justice" advised in army regulations; it was dispensed more like punishment. Moreover, it was not accompanied with the warmth of soldierly understanding, nor was it backed up by a charisma like that of Stonewall Jackson, who could be a tough disciplinarian, but one whose strictness could be overlooked because he won his battles.

Though Taylor's victory had made him such a national hero that it would also make him president of the United States in the next election, it did nothing to change the government's strategy of throwing all its military weight behind Scott's campaign in central Mexico. What forces remained with Taylor were relegated to keeping order in northern Mexico. Since that territory remained quiet, the war had petered out for Bragg and his brother regulars, and they were content to return to the States for reassignment. "Content," however, until they had to settle in on small posts and take up garrison duties that were to become dull and duller in their isolated little worlds. Bragg's routine was no exception; he remained with his regiment, the 3rd Artillery, where he found that the aura of wartime fame, like that of so many wartime heroes, quickly disappeared. In Bragg's case, however, he was to find realization of a wish he had confided to only his closest comrades. Since he came from a middle-class family of twelve children, his army pay was his only income; his secret wish was to find a wife with money. In the year after the war more than his material hopes became real. He fell in love with, courted, and married Elisa Brooks Ellis, daughter of a wealthy Louisiana planter of Evergreen Plantation in Terrebonne Parish. She became his June bride in June 1849 when they were married at Evergreen.

Though Bragg might have realized a dream of becoming a man of independent means, the truth was that he was a bigamist of sorts, wedded to the woman of his dreams—and to the army. Elisa, it seems, went along with the affair, following him as an army wife, making do in less than comfortable garrison quarters and putting up with all the hardships of army life, an existence that was to last for over five years. Two months after their marriage, Bragg and his bride moved to Jefferson Barracks outside of St. Louis, where he took up his old command of Battery C, 3rd Artillery. Reassignments were to follow, to frontier posts like Fort Leavenworth, Kansas, and Fort Gibson in Indian Territory, where Bragg seems to have divided much of his time between his professional studies, writing essays, and squabbling with his superiors over matters which his brother officers thought of as "minutiae of the service." Finally, a minor difference soon grew to what Bragg considered a major dispute when he took on his friend Jefferson Davis, the secretary of war, over Bragg's pending transfer from Fort Gibson to Fort Washita. Though Bragg had accumulated a host of other annoyances, this disagreement seems to have been the one that forced him to make a career decision. On 3 January 1856 he resigned his commission and left the army. He deeply resented what he considered Davis' take-it-or-leave-it attitude in the matter, and expressed his resentment in a letter to Sherman when he referred to Davis as abandoning him at Fort Washita to "chase Indians with six-pounders."

Regrets or not, in exactly a month Bragg was in Louisiana fulfilling his dream of becoming an independent planter. In a letter of 3 February he was bringing Elisa up to date on his negotiations with a Mr. Shriver to buy "Leesburg," a 1,600–acre plantation near Thibodaux and not too far from Evergreen. The purchase was being made with Elisa's money, but according to custom and legalities Bragg would be the sole new owner. In his letter he explained, "Their terms are at a cash calculation about $145,000. $30,000 now, the balance at different amounts at from 1 to 8 years. . . . Negroes 104, 65 [field] hands. Mules, oxen, cows, sheep, implements, corn, hay, etc., plenty. After examining all I accepted the offer."[69] Two days later he wrote Elisa that the deal was closed.

The proud new owner renamed the plantation "Bivouac" (what a long-suffering Elisa thought of the name after five years in the army has not been recorded), and got down to the business of being a full-time farmer. And over the next four years he became a successful one. By the end of 1859 he could assess a net profit of $30,000, and in the following year his estate was valued at $120,000. By the measure of his times, Bragg was a wealthy planter, and successful enough to go into local politics. He was elected commissioner of public works for the second district of Louisiana, and during his term he managed to plan and implement a system of drainage that was to reclaim a great deal of land for farming. But after a year in office he was heartily tired of the deals, forced compromises, and political maneuvers needed to get things done; he was no doubt longing for the military, where an order was all that was required to convert a plan into action. Though coming out of his "retirement" to return to military life may not have occupied his thoughts at the time, the turn of events in 1860 would soon call it to mind.

With the certainty of war growing daily, Bragg was quick to offer his services to the governor of Louisiana, who immediately appointed him a colonel in the state militia and made him his military aide. In short order Bragg was promoted to major general in the militia, and on 23 February 1861 Jefferson Davis signed his commission as a brigadier general in the Confederate States Army. His first C.S.A. assignment was to command the forces being raised in the Pensacola–Mobile area. Operating from his headquarters at Pensacola Bragg soon came into his real metier, training troops and organizing forces. He did such an outstanding job that he attracted national attention—and that of Jefferson Davis. In September he was promoted to major general and given command of all the forces in Alabama and west Florida.

It wasn't long until Bragg perceived the fault in Davis' national strategy in deploying forces for coastal defense instead of concentrating them where they were badly needed to counter the invading Union armies in areas like Tennessee. Bragg expressed himself forcefully in letters to Richmond, where Davis soon recognized the wisdom of Bragg's advice, and in late February he

was ordered north to join General Albert Sidney Johnston, who was planning
to concentrate Confederate forces around Corinth, Mississippi. "At this time
Bragg was one of the highest-rated generals in the Confederacy. Almost everyone seemed to have a good opinion of him, and even Jefferson Davis was
coming to rank him nearly equal to Albert Sidney Johnston."[70] Johnston himself so highly regarded Bragg's abilities that he gave him command of one of
his corps and also made him his pro tem chief of staff. Bragg soon showed
Johnston that he had made wise appointments, for he proved to be an invaluable asset in both roles, particularly in organizing the far-flung forces that
Johnston was concentrating to take the offensive against the then divided
forces of Grant and Buell.

By late March 1862 Johnston had become increasingly aware that he would
have to strike Grant's six divisions, encamped around Pittsburg Landing on
the Tennessee River, before the united forces of Grant and Buell (75,000)
could attack his army of 40,000 at Corinth. On 2 April Johnston gave his orders
to march, and by the evening of the 5th his army was deployed to attack in
what was to become the battle of Shiloh. The army that he had deployed in
the dense Tennessee woods was probably one of the most ill trained and
poorly organized that the South had ever massed for a major battle. Despite
the organizing abilities of Bragg and the tactical skill of Hardee, there simply
had not been enough time to correct all the glaring deficiencies before the
twenty-five-mile march from Corinth. To make matters really worse, Johnston's three corps were deployed in a manner—thanks to Beauregard's
bumbling handiwork—which became a recipe for disaster. Instead of each
corps massing in its own zone for the attack, the three were strung out, one
behind the other, in parallel fashion that was sure to see their units becoming
intermixed in the heat of battle, so that all tactical control would be lost when
it was most needed.

By some fluke of fortune, Grant's divisions were as tactically unprepared as
their enemy, having set up camp in a bend of the river without field fortifications or even adequate outposts. Thus, by some miracle of fate, Johnston's
attacking army actually achieved tactical surprise. The whooping Confederate
infantry at first swept all before them, capturing guns and thousands of prisoners. A great part of the Confederate success on the first day was due to
Bragg's vigorous command actions, particularly on the right, where his personal supervision kept up the momentum of the attack. But after severe losses,
the battered Union divisions—with units often as mixed up as their enemy's—
fell back and managed to hold until nightfall. During the fierce fighting, Johnston, up front where he should not have been, was mortally wounded. Then
two command actions were to change things on both sides: Beauregard assumed command after Johnston's fall, and Grant arrived late in the day to
take charge and revive his half-beaten forces until Buell's rapidly approaching
army could link up with him.

On the next day Grant's iron will and calming leadership had so reinforced his army's will to fight that the Union forces, reinforced by Buell's fresh troops, counterattacked and drove back the exhausted Confederates. Despite Bragg's brilliant performance on the first day, he and the other corps commanders reluctantly had to follow Beauregard's orders to withdraw and take up a dismal retrograde march back to Corinth. The near victory and its disheartening aftermath, accompanied by the loss of the irreplaceable Johnston, called for a high-level command shake-up. Under the circumstances Bragg stood out as the most valuable candidate for the command; he had already been promoted to full general, to rank from 12 April. The promotion placed him at the top of the Confederacy's military hierarchy. There were few others ever to attain the same rank: Samuel Cooper, Joseph E. Johnston, Robert E. Lee, P. G. T. Beauregard, Edmund Kirby-Smith, and Albert Sidney Johnston. For this and other reasons, including Bragg's outstanding performance at Shiloh and Beauregard's mishandling of matters in the same battle, on 27 June Bragg relieved Beauregard and took command of the Army of Tennessee. From that date on, one cannot fail to compare Bragg's notable performance as a corps commander with his functioning as an army commander.

On 20 July Bragg met with Major General Kirby-Smith, then commanding the Department of East Tennessee, in a command conference at Knoxville. During their talks Bragg learned of the threatened Union capture of Chattanooga as well as Kirby-Smith's proposal that Bragg strike into mid-Tennessee and save the situation. The idea so intrigued Bragg that he conceived a strategic plan that was as bold as it was grand in concept. He would take his army of two corps (30,000 strong) and, in a strategic turning movement, "gain the enemy's rear, cutting off his supplies and dividing his forces so as to encounter them in detail." Meanwhile, Kirby-Smith with his force of 18,000 would turn the Union forces at Cumberland Gap, advance westward into Kentucky, and march to join forces with Bragg.

The overall scheme, almost Napoleonic in concept, not only lacked a Napoleon to carry it out, but also lacked two fundamental aspects: a defined final objective (that of meeting and defeating the main Union force), and unity of command (because Bragg did not command Kirby-Smith's department). Moreover, the plan had no real military objective since it was really founded on the idea of invading Kentucky in the somewhat nebulous hope that its citizens would rise up and take that border state into the Confederacy. Thus Bragg's "invasion" was actually a gigantic raid with political overtones, its marches dependent in part on seizing and using key sections of the railroad network. In regard to Bragg's generalship, the campaign was intended to show Bragg's critics and the public that his talents were not limited to his recognized skills as an organizer and trainer of troops, but that he also possessed superior qualities as a strategist and logistician.

In late August Bragg moved, and by 17 September had captured Munfordville, Kentucky, thus placing his army between Buell's Union army and its base at Louisville. At this point a disciple of Napoleon would have grasped a double opportunity: to attack Buell while his forces were divided, or to seize Buell's base at Louisville, then maneuver in Buell's rear and force him to fight on his enemy's terms. Bragg did neither. His fears overcame his chance to exploit his opportunity; he feared that he was not strong enough to attack Buell's exposed army and he felt that he couldn't afford to let slip a political goal, that of taking the state capital, Frankfort, and installing a Confederate governor. He chose the latter course of action, thus in effect letting the role of raider take the place of the commander dealing with matters of strategy. It was a fateful decision, for when Bragg marched to Frankfort, Buell fell back to Louisville, incorporated reinforcements into his army, and prepared to drive Bragg back into Tennessee.

In the meantime Kirby-Smith had defeated a green, unprepared Union force at Richmond, Kentucky, and moved on to occupy Lexington. By this time, however, Buell was on the move and by 1 October was marching to the southeast with widely dispersed forces (totaling 60,000) against Bragg's army of 22,500, then at Bardstown. Bragg, in part misled by faulty intelligence, misjudged the overall situation and sent a detachment eastward to link up with Kirby-Smith, leaving a main force of only 16,000 at Perryville. The battle that was fought there on 8 October took on the character of a meeting engagement for which neither major commander was prepared, both having dispersed forces that couldn't arrive in time to affect the action. Thus the battle of Perryville, though a fiercely fought local action, became a tactically drawn battle, with Union losses of over 4,200 killed, wounded, and missing, compared to a total Confederate loss of nearly 3,400. That night Bragg, knowing that his small army would be greatly outnumbered, started withdrawing into Tennessee.

If Bragg the strategist had continued to show his generalship after he had taken Munfordville instead of yielding to his political aspirations, his original strategy might have succeeded. The historian Archer Jones has aptly summarized Bragg's performance: "The Kentucky campaign showed that Bragg, the brilliant strategist and organizer and administrator, did not perform well when operating close to the enemy. He often failed to understand the situation and his judgment became unreliable."[71] Another way of looking at Bragg's shortcoming as an army commander would be to say that he failed to exploit his strategic maneuvers with tactical decisiveness, a failing that was to cost him dearly in coming campaigns.

In any way of assessing it, Bragg's Kentucky campaign was an unqualified flop. It had failed to bring Kentucky into the Confederacy: there were no signs of public demonstrations for joining the South and no rush of volunteers to enlist, with over 15,000 stands of arms for volunteers remaining unissued. Bragg had to admit in his gloomy report to his government, "I regret to say that we are sadly disappointed in the want of action by our friends in Kentucky. We have so far received no accession to this army."[72]

Bragg's immediate withdrawal after Perryville did nothing to diminish his generals' (and the army's) perception of a commander who had suffered near defeat and subsequent retreat due to his own ineptitude. The perception continued to grow, adding fuel to the fires of resentment that smoldered in the minds of the generals of the anti-Bragg bloc, which, as we have seen, became more and more active in the following spring and summer. Bragg's retreat after Perryville took his army all the way back to Murfreesboro in central Tennessee, where this recounting took up the story of Rosecrans and Bragg with their first major encounter in the battle of Stones River at the end of 1862. Before we return to the coming confrontation of the two commanders on the eve of Chickamauga, it would be helpful to see how Braxton Bragg's personal history had contributed to the image of Bragg, the army commander.

Over the years Bragg's high standards of performance in his military duties had hardened into a model of perfection that calls to mind the story of Procrustes in Greek mythology, the tyrant who made his captives fit his bed, either by stretching them if they were too short or by lopping off legs if they were too long. In Bragg's case the perfectionist lacked one essential quality: the modeler didn't always fit his own model, and that missing quality seems to lie at the heart of Bragg's difficulties with his subordinates. He failed to recognize the fact that they were human with human shortcomings which should be taken into account when they didn't measure up or the fault corrected by tactful counsel. To make matters worse, when there were recriminations following failures like those in the Perryville or Murfreesboro operations, Bragg tended to blame the failures on his subordinates. In the minds of his generals that was the unforgivable act of a commander who in the final analysis is responsible for *everything his command does or fails to do*. Hence the gap of misunderstandings between Bragg and many of his generals couldn't help but widen, since neither side would try to communicate with the other.

On a brighter part of the portrait, Bragg's personal courage was unquestionable. He had stood alongside Zachary Taylor as a national hero after Buena Vista, and there can be little doubt that his moment in the sun must have reinforced his self-esteem, a most forgivable foible in any man. To add to his reputation as a professional soldier and the outstanding artillerist in the antebellum army, his administrative skills as a Confederate commander were as admired as they were widely known. In spite of his reputation as an unforgiving disciplinarian, his genius for training troops and organizing fighting forces was universally recognized by both subordinates and superiors. When given time and latitude he unfailingly turned out a corps or army that was unmatched in the Confederate service for efficiency and standards of performance. He was also a commander who constantly looked out for the health of his command in assuring that his same high standards were followed in the sanitary measures of troop units in camp and in the field. In the fields of logistics and staff management he created innovations that were models of effectiveness. At the outset of his Kentucky campaign, in order to outmaneuver his opponent Buell, he conceived and executed a logistical marvel when he "secretly moved 35,000 men by six rail lines on an almost 800–mile circuitous route south through Mobile to get in front of Buell at Chattanooga." Earlier when he took command of the Army of Mississippi, he directed each corps to augment its headquarters with a "company of cavalry of not less than fifty effective men assigned to their headquarters to act as escort and couriers."[73] The augmentation was not a security measure, but a very real improvement in staff communications with subordinate commanders and staffs that would prove an invaluable command asset.

In addition to his administrative genius Bragg had few peers in the grasp of strategy and its application on the highest military level. It was mainly his concept of rapid concentration followed by a swift and aggressive offense that had made possible the tactical surprise of Grant's army at Shiloh. Unfortunately, as demonstrated in his Kentucky campaign, he somehow lost his aggressiveness in failing to exploit a strategic success at the exact time that he should have mustered all his energies to follow it through. He was like a boxer who has his opponent on the ropes, then suddenly backs off, as though the man would obligingly collapse at his feet. A fatal flaw like this, combined with his poor health, made him the wrong choice for field command. Because of his other outstanding capabilities he would have performed superbly as the army's inspector general or the president's chief of staff in an advisory role like that of Halleck's later relationship with Lincoln. In such a high position, if Jefferson Davis had realized it early in the war, his qualities of intelligence, patriotism, and diligence—when combined with his administrative skills and strategical insight—could have been of immeasurable value to the Confederacy.

There can be little doubt that good health and energy have been essential attributes in the makeup of any general who has been successful in applying an art of command. "When General Grant was asked what he thought were the qualities that most sustained him throughout his Civil War campaigns, he replied that health and energy should head the list. In his words they gave him 'the power to endure anything.' "[74] Good health was certainly a prerequisite to Bragg's effectiveness as an army commander, but his bad health continued to handicap him throughout his military career. Among the ailments that contributed to (or were a part of) the stress that seemed to torment him at critical times were migraines, rheumatism, boils, and dyspepsia, or severe indigestion. One of the patent medicines of the day that Bragg kept on hand was calomel, a purgative whose continued use "caused severe gastrointestinal irritation (Bragg's dyspepsia?) and central nervous systems of lethargy or restlessness."[75] In the same study of Bragg's contribution to the Confederacy's defeat, the historian Grady McWhiney has pointed out perceptively, "Illness hampered Bragg all his life; it was as much a part of him as ambition, worry, dissatisfaction, and contentiousness. His various sicknesses, which became more pronounced as his responsibilities increased, seem to have been partly psychosomatic, for they frequently occurred when he was despondent or frustrated. Too ambitious to be satisfied with himself or with others, he sought perfection, and was disappointed when he failed to find or achieve it. Authoritarian himself, he nevertheless resented his superiors' authority. Yet Bragg won and held the friendship and admiration of some of the army's best minds, despite his cantankerousness. He represented an unusual combination of potentially dangerous eccentricities and high ability."[76] It would seem that the state of Bragg's health was reflected in his personal appearance, as an observer, Lieutenant Colonel Fremantle of the British army, noted when visiting Bragg at his headquarters at Tullahoma: "He is very thin; he stoops, and has a sickly, cadaverous, haggard appearance, rather plain features, bushy black eyebrows which unite in a tuft at the top of his nose, and a stubby iron-grey beard; but his eyes are bright and piercing. He has the reputation of being a rigid disciplinarian, and of shooting freely for insubordination. I understand he is rather unpopular on this account, and also by reason of his occasional acerbity of manner."[77] Fremantle's observation is noteworthy, not only for revealing the connection between Bragg's health and his appearance, but also for the picture that Bragg, the commander, presented to his officers and men in the Chickamauga campaign. And in the end, the combination of "potentially dangerous eccentricities and high ability" that McWhiney has perceived reached its zenith during the later phases of the campaign, especially when Bragg's poor health affected his ability to act decisively in correcting the tactical failures of subordinate commanders, or in his failing to take aggressive command action when it was so badly needed to follow up a successful maneuver of his own. It is to those maneuvers—Bragg's operations from 8 to 18 September which led Rosecrans to a series of urgent reactions—that we should redirect our attention.

It was after Rosecrans' successful river crossings and the subsequent movements of his three corps that Bragg's intelligence sources (mainly Forrest's and Wheeler's cavalry screens) gave him barely enough information to form an estimate of what his enemy was about. Bragg's combination of strategic sense and limited combat intelligence told him that Rosecrans was seeking to accomplish one or both of two objectives: (1) to gain Bragg's rear or to outflank him and turn the Army of Tennessee out of its positions east of the Tennessee River; then (2) perhaps to attack Bragg on ground favorable to Rosecrans once he could reunite his widely separated forces. It was those "widely separated forces" that caught Bragg's strategic eye. He was well aware that the overall situation—the compartmented mountainous terrain (see Map 10.2), Rosecrans' scattered corps, and the new reinforcements still arriving (the strategic concentration of Confederate forces already recounted)—wouldn't allow him to strike at Rosecrans' forces with the whole of the Army of Tennessee, still in the process of regrouping. But an alternative course of action was within his powers. He had sufficient force to enable him to cut off major elements of

Map 10.2

Courtesy Martin L. Wilkerson.

Rosecrans' separated corps (as much as twenty miles apart in rugged terrain) and destroy them in detail.

It would be unrealistic to assume that Bragg immediately seized the opportunity to act out a Napoleonic concept and regroup his forces to destroy his divided enemy with a series of decisive actions. What really happened was that Bragg had made a painful decision to evacuate Chattanooga and march toward Rome to reorganize and prepare to meet Rosecrans with a stronger and more compact army. After his columns were moving south on 8 September, Bragg was trying to piece together bits of information that would enable him to ascertain the actual movements of Rosecran's three corps. By midnight of 9 September, Bragg had learned enough to see that advance elements of Thomas' corps, numbering between 4,000 and 8,000 infantry, had entered McLemore's Cove that morning and were moving toward Dug Gap. That night of 9–10 September Bragg decided to halt his march toward Rome and strike at the enemy force in the Cove. He called Major General Thomas C. Hindman to his temporary headquarters at Lee and Gordon's Mills, and after a command conference sketched out his plan. Hindman would take his division (of Polk's corps) and move into the Cove from the north while Cleburne's division of Hill's corps (Lieutenant General D. H. Hill had just arrived from Virginia to take over command of the corps from the replaced Hardee) would move through Dug Gap to attack the enemy from the east. Accordingly, orders were sent to Hill, but the orders, like Hindman's, were incomplete and vaguely worded—characteristic of most of Bragg's orders of the next few days. If Bragg were to seize the advantage over his enemy's dispersed forces, he would have to strike rapidly and decisively. The success of such an operation demanded two critical components: bold force commanders capable of acting independently and clearly defined missions in simply stated orders. Neither factor would be evident in the next two days.

Bragg took up an observation post on Pigeon Mountain on the morning of 10 September to observe how his plan would be carried out. "It was, as one of his officers described it, an opportunity 'which comes to most generals only in their dreams.' "[78] In the early morning of 10 September, however, Hindman had already begun to demonstrate a lack of boldness and independent judgement. He marched only as far as Pond Spring, waiting there in bivouac while sending forward scouts to locate the enemy. Hill, though a senior commander with combat experience in the Army of Northern Virginia, was to show Bragg that he was no more dependable in this operation than was Hindman. For reasons of his own he failed to press forward Cleburne's division to attack through Dug Gap, having sent a message to Hindman saying that Cleburne had been ordered to Dug Gap and that if the enemy attacked Cleburne, Hindman should attack the enemy's rear. So Hindman waited, as he tried to explain to Bragg later, for Hill to attack, since the latter's message led him to believe that he should wait for Cleburne's action *before* he should attack. In the meantime the Union commander had deployed a lead regiment and driven off the Confederate cavalry covering Cleburne's advance. Then Hindman learned from civilians that a large Union force was hurrying to reinforce the force in McLemore's Cove (actually Baird's division sent by Thomas to the support of Negley's division). This information and lack of further word from Hill added to Hindman's hesitation. Consequently each of Bragg's force commanders held back, waiting for the other to act, while an impatient Bragg "paced back and forth in his anxiety, dug his spurs into the ground, smote the air, hoped and despaired."[79] The confusion was complicated by the Union commander's actions when he realized his danger and deployed his division to defend against attacks from the north and east while preparing to receive reinforcements. When Hindman learned of the coming linkup of the enemy's forces he began to take counsel of his fears in a council of war with his subordinate commanders.

In the meantime Bragg, worried about the lack of action on the part of

Hindman and Hill, directed Buckner to send a force from his corps to reinforce Hindman. By 1:30 P.M. of 10 September Hill had started Cleburne's
division through Dug Gap, and by 5:00 P.M. Buckner had joined Hindman
about four miles north of a crossroads below Pond Spring. By this time it was
evident that Bragg should have been present at the front to see in person that
his plan was being executed. Instead he was at his new command post at
Lafayette, where he had moved on the night of 10 September. On that same
night he ordered Hindman, Buckner, and Hill to coordinate an attack in
McLemore's Cove. Again, Bragg's orders were discretionary in nature, resulting in more councils of war at subordinates' headquarters where it was
voted to hold off obeying Bragg's orders until "more information was received," thus proving two of Napoleon's dicta—councils of war do not fight
and if a commander's orders can be disobeyed, they will be disobeyed. And
again, due to Bragg's verbal orders (which were subsequently misconstrued,
whether purposely or not isn't clear), Hindman timidly advanced only a couple
of miles, while Cleburne sent forward couriers to inform him when Hindman's
guns were heard, so that he could then move to attack. But no guns were
heard because Hindman had retreated northward on the next morning (11
September) in alarm when he heard that the Union forces in the Cove had
been increased to 15,000 (actually only about 8,000 were there at the time).
Later Hindman reversed his march after learning of the actual strength of the
enemy, but not until 5:00 P.M. did he again advance—thirteen hours after
receiving Bragg's original order! While Hindman was vacillating, Bragg had
joined Hill and Cleburne at Dug Gap, only to pace back and forth in renewed
frustration. Finally, after Cleburne had advanced, only to encounter a Union
rear guard, Bragg rode forward and met Hindman at the crossroads in the
Cove about 6:00 P.M. The enemy had disappeared, withdrawing safely to Stevens' Gap. A furious Bragg gave Hindman the dressing-down he deserved,
but it was obviously too late to do anything but order the troops back to their
previous positions.

When Bragg returned to his command post at Lafayette on the evening of
11 September, he ascertained from reliable reports from Forrest that Crittenden's corps was still separated from the rest of Rosecrans' army. He was quick
to realize that here was the chance to recoup the opportunity so disastrously
lost at McLemore's Cove. During 12 September he firmed up his plan to
attack Crittenden, especially Wood's exposed division now near Lee and Gordon's Mills. On the same day he directed Polk to take his corps and Walker's
and attack Crittenden early on 13 September. On the night of 12–13 September, however, things were already beginning to go awry: at 11:00 P.M. Bragg
received a message from Polk saying that Crittenden had concentrated his
divisions and that it was impossible for Polk to attack under the conditions.
About midnight, despite two previous directives to attack, Bragg sent another
vaguely worded order—more permissive than imperative—including the
amazing clause that "he hoped that Polk would not maintain the defensive

'unless the enemy attacks early.' "[80] Bragg did assure Polk, however, that he would personally lead Buckner's troops forward to support an attack.

On the morning of 13 September Bragg and his staff rode ahead of Buckner's lead division toward Polk's command post at Rock Spring Church. When he arrived to meet Polk about 9:00 A.M. Bragg learned that Polk had not even fully deployed his troops for an attack, despite the fact that the total attack force (including Buckner's two divisions) would outnumber the enemy's divisions by five against three. An angry Bragg got a reluctant Polk moving, albeit far too slowly under the circumstances, and an attack was mounted about midday. But it wasn't until 2:00 P.M. that Walker's corps was moving forward, and by midafternoon scouts reported that the roads in front of them were bare of Union troops. It soon became clear that Crittenden had escaped, just as cleanly as had Thomas' troops at McLemore's Cove. Twice in three days Bragg's opportunities to deal Rosecrans a defeat in detail had slipped away.

During the next five days (14–18 September) Bragg had to deal with the ever increasing problems that threatened to overwhelm this army commander who was on the verge of confronting his opponent in what was certain to become a major engagement. Not only was he being constantly bombarded with bits and pieces of information that he had to evaluate into a credible intelligence picture that he could act on, but at the same time he had to control at least three other vital components of command. Operationally he had to continue directing the maneuver of his major forces, his army corps. Logistically he had to see that those forces had been assigned feasible march routes and that their supplies were moving over the best means and routes available. And he had to assure that divisions and brigades were assigned places under the right commanders, in a workable command structure. The problem of organizing the Army of Tennessee for combat was not a simple paper-and-chart exercise; it was complicated by newly arriving brigades and divisions that had to join their corps while their commanders had to find their places in command structures that were physically on the move. Bragg's problem in this regard can be compared to the situation faced by a battleship captain who has to bring boatloads of his crew aboard and assign them battle stations while maneuvering his ship to engage the enemy. That is why the organization chart (see Figure 10.1) should be regarded as being in a state of change until the actual day of battle.

In the midst of the problems that were besetting him Bragg didn't fail to lose sight of the latest opportunity that would allow him to remain on the offensive and maneuver against a major part of Rosecran's forces. He saw that, in bringing major parts of his army north to attack Crittenden, he was getting into a position from which he could still attack and defeat part of his opponent's army while there was time to do so before he could react to prevent it. Moreover, if Bragg moved quickly and in the right direction, he could envelop Rosecrans' left (northern) flank while simultaneously cutting his ar-

Figure 10.1
Bragg's Army of Tennessee

Courtesy Martin L. Wilkerson.

my's communications with its new supply base at Chattanooga. The initial phases of Bragg's new operation have been summarized in his own words: "As soon as his movements [Rosecrans'] were sufficiently developed I marched on the 17th instant [17 September] from Lafayette to meet him, throwing my forces along the Chickamauga [West Chickamauga Creek] between him and my supplies at Ringgold. . . . Immediate measures were taken to place our trains and limited supplies in safe positions, when all our forces were concentrated along the Chickamauga, threatening the enemy in front."[81]

With his newly reorganized army concentrating to strike its enemy in its first all-out offensive of the campaign, Bragg was prepared to do far more than threaten Rosecrans. What was to follow would soon become one of the greatest battles of the war.

CHAPTER 11

The Battle of Chickamauga

Historians have referred to the ground over which the battle of Chickamauga was fought as generally rugged and tending to have had an influence on the actions of 18–20 September. These are understatements. The military effects of the terrain on the course of battle *at all command levels* can hardly be overemphasized. The effects were shared by both sides; the very nature of the terrain was equally hostile to both Union and Confederate operations. In their respective command evaluations of the area, it may be said that Bragg had the advantage. While Rosecrans was seeing the area for the first time, Bragg had known it years before, in his first year after graduating from West Point. In 1838, he had been stationed at a small post in the area while the army was overseeing the forced migration of the Cherokee Nation westward out of Georgia and North Carolina. His advantage was balanced to a degree, however, by the passage of a quarter century and Rosecrans' skill at map reading and terrain analysis.

THE TERRAIN

It would be helpful to appreciate the terrain from two perspectives: the general topography of the area and a close-up look at the actual ground over which the soldiers had to fight (see Map 11.1) In general terms, the battle was fought in an area about ten miles south of Chattanooga, on the floor of the valley that lay between Missionary Ridge on the west and Pigeon Mountain on the east. The battle area was bounded on the north by the Rossville–Ringgold Road, and on the south by Lee and Gordon's Mills. With the exception of the few major routes like the Lafayette Road, the roads were rutted dirt trails, barely useful for wagons and artillery. The road net was

Map 11.1

Courtesy Martin L. Wilkerson.

sparse, consisting mainly of roads leading to and from the bridges and fords that afforded crossings over West Chickamauga Creek, as well as connecting with the gaps in Pigeon Mountain and Missionary Ridge.

In more specific or tactical terms, the major actions were fought between Lafayette Road (running north from Lee and Gordon's Mills) on the west, and on the east by West Chickamauga Creek, hereafter referred to simply as the Chickamauga. The Chickamauga, actually more a small river than a creek, aptly fitted the definition of a military obstacle. Though it appeared sluggish and meandering, it was ten feet deep in parts and had many steep banks which not only made it uncrossable for artillery, cavalry, and compact formations of infantry but further limited their passage to "one of the five bridges or nine fords that offered access to the field of battle."[82] The Chickamauga, however, would pose a major problem to Bragg only in the event of a forced withdrawal, since the bulk of his major forces were engaged between Lafayette Road and the Chickamauga, after they had crossed the stream on the night of 18–19 September.

The real problem affecting combat at all levels was caused by the vegetation which covered the greater part of the region. Dense forests overlay the gently rolling ground, broken only by cleared farmsteads varying greatly in size and shape, planted mostly in corn or furnishing sparse pasture for cattle or hogs which were usually turned loose to forage in fields or forest. But it was the nature of the woods themselves that caused the military headaches. They were made up of "thickets, with a low growth of dogwood, scrub oak, cedar, and pine, matted with underbrush of blackberry briars, honeysuckle, poison oak and trumpet vine."[83] Thus it was the underbrush, interlaced between the trees, that became the real obstacle to the attacking Confederate infantry. Not only was visibility limited to a few feet or at most some fifty yards, but the individual soldier had to struggle forward, forcing his way through tangles of thickets and briars, making it impossible for him to keep his place in ranks. No longer could regiments march forward in shoulder-to-shoulder formations, halting on command to fire directed volleys, and continue to advance on order. Instead, the underbrush and trees broke up close-ordered formations and forced companies and regiments into loose skirmish lines where the Southern soldier often came into his own as an individual skirmisher. His enemy, on the other hand, could take cover—his dark blue uniform coat blending into the brushy cover—and fire defensively from behind trees, brush, or thrown-together breastworks of logs and earth. Thus, from a tactician's viewpoint, limited visibility so restricted fields of fire that controlled firepower was out of the question, as would be the execution of the planned maneuver of large units above the regimental level. If the statement sounds a bit stuffy, it might be said that the thick woods forced higher commanders to hope for the best and rely on supports and reserves once their brigades or divisions disappeared out of sight in the wilderness.

BRAGG COMMITS HIS FORCES, 18 SEPTEMBER

Braxton Bragg may have had his personal and military faults, but his decisions that had assured him of retaining the initiative on the offense were not among them. Undaunted by the rugged terrain (perhaps even aided by it) and the pressing demands of feeding newly arriving forces into his reorganizing army, he had decided in the early morning of 18 September to clarify his earlier orders to resume the offensive, this time intending to use most of his available strength. His resolve had been reinforced by the arrival that same morning of the first three brigades of Longstreet's corps. They would be commanded by Major General John B. Hood, the gallant and much-admired leader who still carried his left arm in a sling because of his wound at Gettysburg. Two more brigades were due to arrive on the 19th, to be followed by the last four and the artillery train on the 20th. Bragg lost no time in hurrying Hood into action. When his train pulled into Ringgold Station, Hood was met by a courier carrying Bragg's dispatch directing him to take over command of the right (northernmost) column from Brigadier General Bushrod Johnson, and seize Reed's Bridge to cross the Chickamauga. "Hood hurried to the freight car that held his horse. With his left arm in a sling, he mounted and held onto the reins with his right hand. Hood applied the spurs, and his horse leapt from the train and galloped out the Reed's Bridge road."[84]

Bragg's amended orders of the 18th spelled out his new plan to envelop Rosecrans' left (north) flank, which Bragg believed to be held only by Crittenden's unsupported corps. By so doing, Bragg expected to cut the routes to Rossville and McFarland's Gap, which would cut Rosecrans' communications with his new base at Chattanooga. He would then roll up Crittenden's corps from north to south, driving it back on other Union forces and destroy them in the valley that ended in McLemore's Cove on the south. Hence the Confederate main effort would initially be the envelopment on the north, in concert with frontal attacks by other major forces after they had crossed the Chickamauga. The main elements of Bragg's orders to his major commanders, in order from north to south, included the following:

- The northern "column" (Bushrod Johnson's division plus Hood's three brigades, the force now being commanded by Hood) to cross at or near Reed's Bridge, wheel to the left (south), and attack toward Lee and Gordon's Mills

- Walker's corps to cross the Chickamauga at Alexander's Bridge, join flanks with Hood, and attack southward in conjunction with Hood

- Buckner's corps to cross at Tedford's Ford and attack, pushing the enemy southward and away from the front of Polk's corps

- Polk's corps to cross at Lee and Gordon's Mills, or if meeting too much resistance, bear to the right and cross at Tedford's Ford or Dalton's Ford, and attack the enemy wherever encountered

- Hill's corps to cover the army's left flank, seal off any enemy force in McLemore's Cove, push the cavalry in his front to ascertain if enemy forces were moving toward Lee and Gordon's Mills, and, if such should be the case, to attack them in flank
- Wheeler's cavalry corps to screen the front, secure the gaps in Pigeon Mountain, and cover the army's left and rear; Forrest's cavalry corps to cover the right front and flank

While issuing those orders, Bragg was still unaware that Rosecrans had become alarmed at the prospect of being attacked while his corps were widely separated, and was in the process of moving Thomas' and McCook's corps to Crittenden's support. Accordingly, acting on Bragg's orders of 18 September, his force commanders moved forward on the same day, but their progress was delayed by the poor roads and then by unexpected resistance at two crossing points. Moreover, in his haste to issue amended orders at first light on the 18th, Bragg had made two errors in his march orders. He had failed to specify starting times for the various corps, and in the case of Buckner's and Walker's corps he had overlooked the fact that the two corps would initially have to use the same road in their approach to their respective crossing sites. The inevitable confusion that followed caused such a delay in the approach marches of the two corps that it was early afternoon before the resulting mess could be cleared up and the two forces could reach the Chickamauga.[85]

The first engagements of the coming battle, brought on by the unexpected and well-fought resistance of Union cavalry and mounted infantry, caused serious delays in the crossing of the Chickamauga by Hood's force and Walker's corps. On the north, Bushrod Johnson, leading Hood's forward division, had to deploy the leading elements of his division east of the approaches to Reed's Bridge in order to drive back Minty's cavalry brigade, which fought a skillful delaying action east of the Chickamauga. Minty's regiments actually succeeded in holding up Johnson until the Confederate infantry could assault the bridge just in time to prevent its destruction by the Union troopers, but it was 4:30 P.M. before Johnson's brigades were marching across the bridge. To the south, Liddell's division of Walker's corps ran into just as determined resistance, but of a different kind. Liddell's infantry was opposed by the Union mounted infantry brigade, commanded by Colonel John T. Wilder. Unknown to the approaching Confederates, Wilder's men were armed with Spencer repeating rifles, a breechloader whose magazine held seven rounds that could be fired in a matter of seconds. Wilder had equipped his brigade with the weapon at his personal expense—and at a terrible expense to his enemy. Compared to the slow, muzzle-loading rifles of the Confederate infantry, the firepower of Wilder's units caused the latter to believe that they were opposed by a regiment or a brigade instead of, as was frequently the case, a company of less than 100 men. As a result of the differences in firepower and Wilder's effective delaying maneuvers, the Union mounted infantry brigade and its one artillery battery held up a whole Confederate corps for at least five hours.

To sum up the execution of Bragg's orders: Walker, who had to base the maneuver of the rest of his corps on Liddell's unsuccessful attempt to seize Alexander's Bridge, had to cross the Chickamauga at Lambert's Ford. Meanwhile, Hood didn't succeed in crossing Reed's Bridge until late afternoon. However, both Hood and Walker did manage finally to get all their units across the stream and into bivouac during the night of 18–19 September. As for the other advancing Confederate corps, they had only reached the Chickamauga by dark of the same night. Bragg, though disappointed by the slowness of his corps and their subsequent failure to reach their objectives, was not about to abandon his plan to envelop Rosecrans' left. As far as he was concerned, his concept of the operation remained unchanged, and tomorrow he would continue to carry out his plan with the corps of Hood, Buckner, and Walker.

ROSECRANS ACTS AND REACTS ON 18 SEPTEMBER

It will be recalled that Rosecrans finally became convinced that his enemy had indeed concentrated his forces and was in the act of moving to get around his left and cut him off from Chattanooga. By the morning of 18 September, though unaware that the mass of Bragg's forces was already advancing on the crossings of the Chickamauga, Rosecrans had begun to receive reports indicating that there were elements of Confederate forces moving toward the stream. At 10:30 A.M. Wood's division of Crittenden's XXI Corps, positioned near Lee and Gordon's Mills, reported increasing numbers of enemy skirmishers advancing toward their outposts from across the Chickamauga. Then there were the reports of the delaying actions involving both Minty's and Wilder's brigades, solid evidence that those brigade commanders were having to deal with major enemy forces. When Rosecrans had been assured of the full commitment of Minty's brigade, in late morning he directed Brigadier General Steedman (temporarily in command of Major General Granger's reserve corps) to send a brigade to support Minty, but it was actually 3:30 in the afternoon before Colonel Daniel McCook started his detached brigade on the march toward Reed's Bridge and Minty's aid.

These actions and reports convinced Rosecrans that he was going to have to shift the bulk of his army northward to protect his communications with Chattanooga and, at the same time, prepare to deal with any westward threat directed toward his forces along the Lafayette Road and the roads west of it. Viewed in concept his general plan was simple; in execution it was bound to be more complicated, but one that Rosecrans and his corps commanders could handle—if the movements were completed before a major enemy thrust could interfere. In brief, Rosecrans' orders for his corps' movements of the 18th included the following:

- First, Crittenden to shift the XXI Corps divisions of Van Cleve and Palmer to the left (north) of Wood's division, which would continue to hold near Lee and Gordon's Mills
- Second, Thomas to move his XIV Corps northward, posting one division near Crawfish Springs to link up with Crittenden's right flank, moving his other three divisions behind and across Crittenden's rear, then to position them facing eastward, generally along the Lafayette Road, with his left north of Kelly Field
- Third, McCook to close up his XX Corps on Thomas' right and position enough force near Crawfish Springs to protect Crittenden's south flank, the remainder of his corps to act as army reserve
- Fourth, Mitchell's cavalry corps to cover the army's right (south) flank, screen the crossing sites on the south, and act on McCook's orders

In addition to their complexity, the orders were incomplete in the sense that they took for granted that the army's left would be covered by Granger's reserve corps, but that weak corps actually consisted of only three brigades, one of which had already been directed to support Minty's cavalry. Moreover, even if Granger's other two brigades were deployed to cover the roads leading from the bridges (Reed's and Dyer's) to Rossville, there would still exist a gap of at least a mile between Thomas' new left flank and Granger's nearest brigade. Fortunately for Rosecrans, the gap would not be discovered in time to be exploited by the Confederates. Unfortunately for Rosecrans, however, there were mixups in the transmission of corps marching orders and all sorts of unforeseen delays until divisions were on the move.

In Thomas' case only incomplete orders were received by midafternoon, and it was not until 10:30 that night that Thomas had matters straightened out with Rosecrans; by then his corps was forced to make a night march to reach its designated position areas. The march was to prove an ordeal at all levels. The night of 18–19 September was to turn chilly, with the temperature in the 40s; the roads rough and rutty; and there was all the confusion that goes with night marches. Rosecrans and Thomas were well aware of the conditions, and the two deliberated at some length whether to postpone the march until the next day, since neither commander wanted to face the prospect of fighting on the morrow with soldiers stumbling with fatigue. It was finally decided that the tactical urgency of having the corps in position to meet an enemy attack overrode all other considerations, and Thomas' corps would make the march as planned—and that night.

In the meantime, Rosecrans' combat intelligence showed him that Minty was being overpowered and was being forced rearward from Reed's Bridge, how far rearward no one could tell by late afternoon. Rosecrans directed Steedman to send a second brigade toward the bridge. Hence, by 5:00 P.M., not only did Steedman have the brigades of Colonels Dan McCook and John B. Mitchell on the road, but that of Brigadier General Walter C. Whitaker was already skirmishing with enemy cavalry west of the Chickamauga. So

Granger's corps would be stretched across a three-mile front, with no reserves left to deal with any major developments.[86]

The upshot of all the actions and marches was that by dawn on 19 September the Union and Confederate corps had reached the areas shown on Map 11.2, leaving the two army commanders yet to deal with the greatest battle that either would ever face.

19 SEPTEMBER: THE EFFECTS OF BRAGG'S ESTIMATES AND COMMAND ACTIONS ON MANEUVER AND ATTACK

In contrast to his intense activity in amending and issuing orders during the previous night, Bragg seemed almost tranquil on the night of 18–19 September. Tranquil not simply in the way that he seemed to accept the slowness of his commanders to move and carry out their missions on the 18th, but in the way that he treated planning and directing the army's operations for the coming day. He seemed unworried about the problems that had arisen and the obvious ones that had to be dealt with on the morrow. There were probably at least two reasons for his seeming unconcern. First, he appeared oblivious to the signs that "the Confederate command structure was faulty when the battle began." Consequently, "Bragg never brought his bulky force under control."[87] The reasons behind the condition have been recounted in treating the dissension among Bragg's generals and the mistrust that had arisen between them and their army commander. The mistrust and lack of rapport must have contributed strongly both to the slowness on the part of the generals and their failure to act decisively on their own at critical times.

The second factor can be laid to Bragg's inadequate intelligence, which led him to continue relying on his previous estimate of his enemy's situation. Specifically, his intelligence estimate continued to place Crittenden's corps on the left of Rosecrans' army, so that XXI Corps' left flank rested on Lee and Gordon's Mills; Thomas' corps appeared to be in the center around Crawfish Springs and Glass' Mill; and McCook's corps seemed to be on the south, in or beyond McLemore's Cove. Hence Bragg believed that he had already outflanked Rosecrans on the north, but was also dangerously unaware of the night march of Thomas' corps, which would end with him in positions that extended Rosecrans' left flank far northward. By the same token, he was equally ignorant of the moves of McCook's divisions, which would close his corps up on Crittenden's right. This unawareness was compounded by Bragg's rejection of a report from Martin's cavalry division that reconnaissance elements on Pigeon Mountain had observed dust clouds raised by columns of Union infantry marching northward out of McLemore's Cove toward Lee and Gordon's Mills. The end result of Bragg's faulty intelligence and his deductions was "evident in his [Bragg's] orders issued that night for the nineteenth. No general attack order was issued, but merely a series of vague instructions."[88]

The effects of such "instructions" could challenge the imagination of mili-

Map 11.2

Courtesy Martin L. Wilkerson.

tary observers. Though Buckner knew he was expected to advance his corps, he had no orders telling him to coordinate his moves with Hood. In fact the latter had sat down on a log outside his headquarters on the morning of the 19th, discussing with Walker the coordination of their force movements. Meanwhile Bragg had ridden forward from his command post at Lee's Tanyard to observe Cheatham's division crossing at Tedford's Ford to join Buckner across the Chickamauga. It was at that spot near the ford that a hurried messenger from Polk caught up with Bragg to inform him that reports had been confirmed indicating that columns of Union infantry had been marching northward, west of the Chickamauga, moving opposite Bragg's rightmost elements. Bragg apparently chose to ignore the warning, and merely sent Polk further instructions to wait until he heard Bragg begin to attack, and then to move his command toward Tedford's Ford as a general reserve. "As for his own plans, Bragg vaguely remarked that he was moving to attack the enemy where he could find him."[89] As it turned out, Polk wouldn't have to wait for the sounds of Bragg's forces engaging the enemy; instead the enemy was about to take the initiative in the matter of attacking.

As recounted, on the 18th Walker had been stalled on his crossing of the Chickamauga by the encounter of Liddell's division of his corps with the Spencer repeating rifles of Wilder's Union brigade at Alexander's Bridge. That engagement, due to Wilder's fierce delaying action, had eventually caused Walker to cross the Chickamauga at Lambert's Ford. That march and subsequent movements caused Walker's corps to end up on the morning of the 19th west of the stream but on the extreme right of Bragg's forces instead of in the center. But that situation was only the beginning of Walker's involvement with the enemy. His morning conference with Hood was interrupted by a message from his headquarters that units of his corps were under heavy attack from an unexpected quarter. Walker galloped back to his command post to find that the enemy attack was indeed a serious threat, so much so that his corps was in danger of being pushed back on the Chickamauga. In spite of the resistance that Walker mounted, his units had, by noon, been driven back almost a mile and a half. The Union threat was brought to a halt when Cheatham's division came up from the direction of Alexander's Bridge to attack the enemy in flank and hook up with Walker's left.

This was the real opening of the battle of the 19th, and it found Bragg unprepared to take decisive action to carry out the basic thrust of his original plan: to get around Rosecrans' left, cut him off from Chattanooga, and finish him off by attacking him simultaneously from flank and front. By noon Bragg's corps had been forced into a rough north-south line by the unexpected attack on Walker and by the movements of his other corps after they had crossed the Chickamauga. That line now consisted of Walker's corps on the right, Hood in the center, and Buckner on the left. With these unanticipated developments, Bragg was apparently faced with two courses of action if he were to keep his opponent on the defensive and unprepared to cope with Bragg's full force. He could throw the main strength of Hood and Buckner in a co-ordinated attack against what appeared to be Rosecrans' still-forming center, or he could reinforce Walker and continue to make a main effort on the north to turn Rosecrans' left. Bragg did neither. Instead he chose to send only Hind-man's division of Polk's corps to reinforce Walker, and gave Polk command of the forces on the Confederate right. Bragg's only other actions that fol-lowed—foretold by his incomplete "instructions" of that morning—consisted of piecemeal, frontal attacks. The attacks and the tough resistance they met were revealing that the main Union line extended for at least three miles, stretching roughly from Kelly field on the north to Lee and Gordon's Mills on the south. By 4:00 P.M. Hood had made a belated but all-out attack against what now appeared to be Rosecrans' center along the Lafayette Road. Here the fighting raged at its fiercest, both sides throwing every available regiment into the battle. Hood attacked with his own three brigades plus Bushrod John-son's division, and forced a penetration of the Union line across the Lafayette Road at Viniard's farm. He was thrown back by Thomas' fiercely resisting defenders and a counterattacking Union force thrown against his left flank from the south. Hood had to call off his exhausted and decimated brigades and withdraw back to the east. Bragg didn't witness this or any of the other engagements of the afternoon or early evening, having retired to his command post, where he remained, apparently unaware of the intense nature of the fighting in the center and on his right. He was, however, fully aware by 11:00 P.M. that he had his whole army across the Chickamauga, and fully alive to the fact that he needed a revised plan to continue the attack in the morning, though that demanded a full reorganization for combat of his force to enable it to execute any plan. It was the problem of reorganization that demanded his attention on the night of 19–20 September while he was anxiously awaiting the arrival of Longstreet and the rest of his corps.

19 SEPTEMBER: ROSECRANS MOVES TO FEND OFF CONFEDERATE ATTACKS

After considering Bragg's plans and orders to seize and hold the initiative, one would expect that the Confederates would have opened the battle on the 19th. On the contrary, it was one of Rosecrans' corps commanders, Thomas, who took the initiative and started the action that began to threaten the ex-ecution of Bragg's plan to turn Rosecrans' left. So it was Bragg's north flank (and his main attack in that area) that was threatened when the battle began.

It will be recalled that General Steedman (temporarily in command of Granger's reserve corps), following an order from Rosecrans, had sent Colonel Dan McCook's brigade to the support of Minty's cavalry. By 3:30 P.M. of the 18th McCook was on his way toward Reed's Bridge, and shortly after sundown his troops had captured several prisoners near a bend in the stream just south of the bridge. The next morning McCook encountered General Thomas, who was overseeing the march of Brannan's division of his corps into its battle positions. McCook reported to Thomas that a lone Confederate brigade was deploying near Jay's Mill, south of Reed's Bridge. According to McCook the enemy brigade (actually McNair's brigade of Bushrod Johnson's division) was isolated because McCook's troops had destroyed the bridge behind it. Since Thomas believed that the enemy brigade was the only Confederate force west of the Chickamauga, it seemed too tempting an opportunity to pass up. He directed Brigadier General John M. Brannan to take his division and develop the enemy force and destroy it. What Brannan first encountered was not a lone infantry brigade but elements of Forrest's cavalry screening the Confederate right and the front of Walker's advancing corps. Forrest, skirmishing and fighting dismounted actions, held off Brannan's two leading brigades until the lead elements of Walker's two divisions could get across the stream and deploy to relieve his troopers.

The actions turned into meeting engagements and eventually into a full-scale battle, with Walker's brigades having to repulse a Union attack involving both Brannan's and Baird's divisions of Thomas' corps. Thus the battle of Chickamauga on 19 September began on the north with Thomas taking the initiative, but as more forces became committed on both sides, the tempo of battle swept increasingly from north to south until it reached a crescendo that centered more and more on the divisions of Thomas' corps and the reinforcements from other corps that Rosecrans rushed to support Thomas. For Thomas, the battle that had begun with his aggressive action turned into one demanding all the defensive power that he—and Rosecrans—could muster, since he had to take on the preponderance of the Confederate attacks.

For Rosecrans the mounting intensity was revealed at first by sounds of battle coming from the north and by the reports that he was getting from Thomas and others. He was reported to be in good spirits that morning, no doubt relieved that the concentration of his forces and their deployment was proceeding satisfactorily. Besides, he was confident that the ever dependable Thomas would hold his own, and that the morale of his troops was excellent, despite the night marches that some units had endured. By noon, however, it had become apparent from the sounds of battle in the north that the focus of combat was going to be on Thomas, and Rosecrans moved his command post north to the Widow Glenn's house, about two miles south of Kelly field, where Thomas had first aimed the march of his corps. After Rosecrans had approved the location and spread out his maps, he explained to the Widow Glenn that she could be in danger and helped her and her two children into a wagon driven by a family slave; then he saw her off to safety at her father's farm near Pond Spring.

Unfortunately, the Widow Glenn's house, though located near the front, couldn't afford the army commander the view that he would have wished: "Unhappily the battlefield was not in the classic ideal of Gettysburg or Waterloo, with accommodating elevations and clearings. . . . Chickamauga was closer akin to the jungles of World War II warfare in the Pacific than the clean farmlands of Antietam and much of Gettysburg."[90] And even if Rosecrans could have observed much of the battlefield, he would have been too busy elsewhere that afternoon to take advantage of the view. His report of the battle of the 19th shows a commander increasingly occupied with evaluating combat intelligence, making on-the-spot decisions, and issuing orders that would commit fresh forces to the battle while shifting others from the corps of Crittenden and McCook to support elements of Thomas' corps. Hence some division commanders like Richard Johnson of McCook's corps and Palmer of Crittenden's corps found their commands fighting under Thomas' corps. However, one's understanding of the roles of the two army commanders throughout the battle is not served by a detailed recounting of the complicated division and brigade marches and their commitment to action. It is sufficient to say, in Rosecrans' case, that at day's end he was still very much in control of events on his side. His summary, understandably omitting dramatic accounts of the fierce fighting, would indicate that he was satisfied that he had completed the concentration of his forces, foiled the attacks of his enemy, and had maintained his army's communications with Chattanooga:

The roar of battle hushed in the darkness of night, and our troops, weary with a night of marching and a day of fighting, rested on their arms, having everywhere maintained their positions, developed the enemy, and gained thorough command of the Rossville and Dry Valley roads to Chattanooga, the great object of the battle of the 19th of September.[91]

THE NIGHT OF 19–20 SEPTEMBER: PREPARING FOR BATTLE

Bragg's Headquarters

Sometime during the early evening Bragg decided on a reorganization for combat that would affect all the higher levels of command. He summoned Polk to his command post near Tedford's Ford, where he and several other commanders arrived about 9:00 P.M. Seated at Bragg's campfire, Polk was given the details of the new organization and his mission. Bragg had decided to divide the army into two wings (see Figure 10.1). Polk would command the right wing: the wing would consist of Cheatham's division of his own corps; a new corps to be commanded by Lieutenant General Hill, made up of Cleburne's division and Breckinridge's division; and Walker's reserve corps, consisting of Walker's division and Liddell's division.

Longstreet, who was expected to arrive that evening, would command the left wing, which would include the following: Buckner's corps, made up of Stewart's division, Preston's division, and Hindman's division (to be detached from Polk's former corps); and Hood's corps, consisting of McLaws' division,

Bushrod Johnson's division, and Hood's own division, now commanded by Brigadier General Law.

The chart showing the new organization looks simple enough but these radical changes, *literally made overnight and in the middle of a battle*, were anything but a solution to Bragg's problems; in fact, they created new ones. The wing commanders were given no opportunity to confer with their corps commanders, and the latter were denied the chance to consult fully with their division and brigade commanders about their new roles in the coming action. Additionally, of the three lieutenant generals present, the two senior had been assigned command of two wings; yet the third, Lieutenant General Daniel Harvey Hill, had been given only the command of a made-up corps under Polk. This had been done in spite of Polk's suggestion that the army be divided into three wings, each under a lieutenant general, which could have been a workable solution. But Bragg ignored this suggestion. No full explanation has been given for Bragg's decision, but it has been suggested that he had been disgusted with Hill's failure to carry out his part of the plan to trap a Union division in McLemore's Cove, and so he was in effect punishing Hill by relegating him to a subordinate role, perhaps accentuated by his leaving it up to Polk to inform Hill of his new assignment.

Yet those were not the only effects of the overnight reorganization. Fundamental to a smoothly working command structure is the rapport between the commander and his subordinates. Bragg's changes were bound to increase the dissension among the generals and add to their distrust of a commander who, in their collective opinion, was out of touch with them—and reality. This ill will was compounded by Longstreet's late arrival at Bragg's command post about an hour before midnight. Longstreet's train had pulled into Catoosa Station at 2:00 in the afternoon of the 19th, and the general, his chief of staff, and another staff officer had to pace the platform for two hours until the next train arrived with their horses. In the meantime they were not met by any representative of Bragg's, surely an affront to the general who had left Lee to become the second in command of the Confederacy's largest army in the west. He could excuse Bragg's absence—the sounds of the afternoon's battle were clear signs of the demand for the army commander's presence on the field— but the absence of welcoming senior staff officers must have seemed inexcusable. Longstreet's state of mind was not improved by the long ride that his party had to make through late afternoon, early evening, and then through the darkness of night. As they had to find their unguided way over rough roads and through the dark forests, they suddenly came upon an outpost and a sentry's challenge. When one of the party got the sentry to give his brigade and division, the sentry had responded with their numerical designations. Longstreet, in his words, immediately caught on: "As Southern brigades were called for their commanders more than by their numbers, we concluded that these friends [the outpost] were the enemy. . . . it did not seem prudent to turn and ride back under the fire that would be opened on us, so I said, loudly, so that the guard could hear, "Let us ride down a little way to find a better crossing."[92] The party quickly escaped under cover of the trees in time to avoid a parting shot from the sentry, and found their way back onto a main road. After getting directions from a civilian, Longstreet finally found his way to Bragg's headquarters, where he found the army commander asleep in an ambulance to which he had retired after his session with Polk. When awakened, Bragg sat down with Longstreet for an hour's conference during which the latter was given a crude map, the composition of his wing's organization, orders for his mission, and a summary of "orders which Bragg had previously given other commanders for the attack in the morning." Shortly after, "exhausted from his travels, Longstreet made no effort to find his command or to communicate with Hood or Buckner that night. A few leafy branches were gathered together and covered with blankets for his comfort and that of his lieutenant colonels, and the trio was soon fast asleep."[93]

It is noteworthy that Polk and several other commanders had also been given only verbal orders, nor had Bragg's staff taken any action to coordinate the details of the new organization and missions with subordinate staffs during the night. Bragg's plan for resuming the attack in the morning was summarized in his after-action report: "Lieut. Gen'l Polk was ordered to assail the enemy on succession rapidly to the left. The left wing was to await the attack by the right, take it up promptly when made, and the whole line was then to be pushed vigorously and persistently against the enemy throughout its extent." Essentially, his concept of the operation remained basically unchanged, the main effort being to get around Rosecrans' north flank, between it and Chattanooga, meanwhile rolling back that flank into McLemore's Cove and destroying it there by the other Confederate attacks from the east. The main flaw in the plan was the lack of a massive force on Bragg's right which should have made the army's main effort. Furthermore, Bragg had given command of that attack to Polk, a man who not only shared a mutual animosity with Bragg but also one in whom Bragg could never place his full trust, facts that were to be brought out the next morning. There was a coincident flaw in Bragg's plan, one that would virtually supersede Bragg's concept of continuing a main effort on the north, and instead turn one of his frontal attacks on the south into a breakthrough that would be as smashing a success as it would be surprising to both attacker and defender. The "flaw"—a virtual blessing in disguise—was the massing of force in the center of Longstreet's zone due to Longstreet's forethought and tactical competence as well as the last-minute arrival on the field of the last of his brigades that could be rushed into the battle, still panting from their forced march following their hasty unloading from their railroad cars.

Exactly why Bragg's overall plan called for timing an army attack by its major elements, starting on the north and proceeding progressively southward, has never been fully explained. The best explanation may be found in Peter Cozzens' reasoning: "Because the heavy forest reduced visibility to something less than a regimental front, the advance could not be simultaneous; therefore, each brigade commander was to move only after the left flank of the unit to his right started forward."[94] For whatever reason, Bragg's attacks were to be launched under an ill-timed reorganization of his army and a plan that left its execution up to subordinate commanders who, for all practical purposes, had to take the battle in their own hands. Now it was becoming evident, as in past campaigns, that Bragg, the strategist, had done a masterful job up to the point of turning matters over to Bragg, the tactician. But typically the tactician was shying away from taking the reins of battle fully into his own hands after coming face to face with the enemy.

Rosecrans' Headquarters

On the same night and at the same time that Longstreet was arriving at Bragg's headquarters, Rosecrans' corps commanders were answering his summons to report to army headquarters. By 11:00 P.M. Thomas, Crittenden, McCook, and several division commanders had arrived at the Widow Glenn's house for a command conference that had three major items on the agenda. Rosecrans wanted his corps commanders' summaries of the day's events, as well as their estimates of the day's casualties. When those items had been covered, he wanted their advice as inputs for his decision-making process for continuing the next day's battle. Finally, he would issue his orders for each corps commander's preparations for battle and their missions for the day.

Brigadier General Garfield, the army chief of staff, passed around a map showing the last-reported positions of the divisions; this provided a basis for the discussion that followed. After agreements had been reached regarding the positions, Rosecrans was able to estimate that his line of battle now extended for a distance of some 3,500 yards, while the enemy's was estimated to be twice that length, some 7,000 yards. These estimates, though exaggerating Bragg's capabilities, gave credence to Rosecrans' evaluations that he had acted correctly in concentrating his forces and shortening his defensive line, and, moreover, assured him that the last two days' developments clearly exposed Bragg's intentions to get between his north flank and Chattanooga. Accordingly, Rosecrans' concept of the morrow's operations (which was coming out informally during the discussion) would be based on continuing a tightened-up defense that would assure his army's hold on the Lafayette Road and the Dry Valley Road behind it, which in turn would assure that his communications through McFarland's Gap and Rossville would be secure. Additionally, he wished to maintain as strong a reserve as possible east of Missionary Ridge, all showing clearly that the Army of the Cumberland would have to remain on the defensive—and dependent in great part on "what the enemy's plan developed." Outside of Rosecrans, the principal figure present was "Thomas [who] drowsed intermittently. Throughout the previous night he had not slept. Rosecrans spoke to him, and he straightened up, said, 'I would strengthen the left,' and slept again. To all suggestions that the left be reinforced, Rosecrans responded, 'Where are we going to take the troops from?' "[95] It would seem that Rosecrans eventually had to answer the question himself, which he proceeded to do when he issued his orders near the end of the session.

In contrast to Bragg's orders for the coming battle, Garfield had transformed Rosecrans' verbal directives into writing for each corps commander, which he then read aloud to the conferees, making sure that all questions were answered before the orders were handed out in final form. Essentially, the orders directed Thomas to hold in his present position, facing east with his line running from the McDonald house on the north, extending southward roughly parallel to the Lafayette Road as far as about the Poe farm. McCook was to shift the divisions of Sheridan and Davis northward to ensure that his line was closed up on Thomas' right. Crittenden would move the divisions of Van Cleve and Wood to positions behind Thomas' right. On the north Granger was ordered only to place his corps in army reserve where it could, on Rosecrans' order, support either McCook or Thomas. It was significant, as Cozzens has pointed out, that Thomas' orders closed with the following caution: "You will defend your position with the utmost stubbornness. *In case our army should be overwhelmed it will retire on Rossville and Chattanooga* [italics added]. Send your trains back to the latter place."[96] My italics continue to bring out Rosecrans' changed state of mind, pointed out earlier, after he became convinced that Bragg was concentrating his forces to take the offensive. Those were hardly the words to hearten a corps commander who was about to bear the brunt of an upcoming battle.

Once the orders were read and agreed on, Rosecrans followed his custom of socializing after business had been disposed of, though it challenges the imagination to picture a group of worn-out generals cheerfully chatting away, with the cares of the coming day uppermost in their minds. In any case, Rosecrans got McCook to "entertain" the gathering with a rendition of "The Hebrew Maiden's Lament," a long-popular song whose lyrics seem more appropriate to be accompanied by the bugle notes of "Taps" at graveside than the stirring notes of "Assembly" or the "Charge." Then too, one wonders if Thomas slept through McCook's closing line, "Bitter tears I shed for thee."[97]

When the conference broke up shortly after midnight, the commanders went their various ways. It is worth observing that the previously drowsy Thomas, once he had gotten back to his own command post, was not too sleepy to make sure of two things: first, that Negley's division would be moved (as approved by Rosecrans) to strengthen his corps' left flank; second, that his troops, especially in the Kelly field area, were constructing log breastworks for the next day's battle.

THE BATTLE OF 20 SEPTEMBER: INITIAL PHASES

Even before daylight Bragg and his staff had mounted and ridden forward where they could hear guns sounding assurance that the forces of Polk's wing were moving "to assail the enemy on our extreme right at day-dawn of the 20th." (For the disposition of forces on the morning of the 20th, see Map 11.3.) But there were no such sounds coming from the north—or anywhere else. How Bragg was beginning to feel, after long moments of silence, was expressed in his after-action report: "With increasing anxiety and disappoint- ment, I waited until after sunrise without hearing a gun, and at length dis- patched a staff officer to Lieutenant General Polk to ascertain the cause of the delay and urge him to a prompt and speedy movement." When the staff officer returned to his anxious commander, his report was to engender anything but a sigh of relief, for he stated that he had found Polk "at a farm house three miles from the line of his troops, about one hour after sunrise, sitting on the gallery reading a newspaper and waiting, as he said, for his breakfast." Bragg's reactions were first to let loose a "terrible exclamation" regarding Polk & Company, one that would never have reached the ears of a Southern lady; then to ride directly to Polk's headquarters to demand in person what was going on. Upon arrival he found that Polk had gone forward, leaving word: "Do tell General Bragg that my heart is overflowing with anxiety for the attack. Overflowing with anxiety, sir."[98] Bragg's thoughts at this news have not been recorded, but one would have no difficulty in surmising their gist. Bragg's side of his stormy relationship with Polk can be appreciated, at least in part, from a glimpse of the latter's background. Leonidas Polk was a fellow North Carolinian who had graduated from West Point in the class of 1827, but re- signed his commission only five months later to take up studies for a career in the Episcopalian ministry. By 1861 he had become bishop of the Southwest, living in New Orleans. His dedication to the cause of the South (as well as a close friendship with Jefferson Davis) got him an immediate commission in the Confederate army. "He had the distinction, rare if ever duplicated in the line, of jumping, after thirty-four years in civilian life, from brevet second lieutenant to major general."[99] Needless to say, Polk's qualifications for gen- eralship were not universally admired, least of all by Braxton Bragg. Now, about 8:00 A.M. and nearly two hours after the attacks had been ordered to begin, Bragg began to learn from several staff officers some of the causes for the delay.

Apparently the underlying fault was Hill's and so not really chargeable to the bishop-general. Hill had not only failed to accompany Polk to Bragg's headquarters the previous night, but had also failed to report to Polk that same night. Consequently, unlike Generals Walker and Cheatham, Hill had received neither orders nor any word of his role in the coming attack. To what degree Hill had been negligent in not taking the initiative, as a general officer would have been expected to, in seeking out his commander to ascertain the

Map 11.3

Courtesy Martin L. Wilkerson.

next day's mission is not clear. It is clear, however, that when he learned, from conferring with Breckinridge and Cleburne, of his corps' mission, he had still delayed, even when Bragg had ridden up to hear from an unconcerned Hill that he would soon be ready—after his two divisions had been issued their rations and ammunition, and thereafter taken up their attack positions. It would be interesting today to estimate how long it would have taken a George Patton to relieve Hill on the spot, had he been standing in Bragg's boots. What actually happened was that two North Carolinians, Bragg and Polk, were still unable to get their fellow statemate Hill to move his two divisions forward in the attack until 9:30 A.M., when Breckinridge moved out, followed fifteen minutes later by Cleburne on his left. Almost four hours had passed since the time set for the attack (sunrise was actually at 5:47 A.M.) on the far right. So, not only was the entire Confederate attack delayed, but the enemy was taking full advantage of four more hours of daylight to build or strengthen the breastworks across his front.

As it turned out, when Breckinridge's right flank brigade came up against enemy breastworks, it was repulsed by the fierce fire, but the other two brigades met only Union troops who had no such cover. The reason: Negley's leading brigade had arrived only a short time before, and had had no time to fell trees and build fieldworks; thus, the whooping Confederates nearly succeeded in overpowering their enemy. But Thomas soon had reinforcements, in the form of a brigade from Brannan and another from Van Cleve, pounding up to the rescue. The three Union brigades not only stopped the attackers in their tracks, but then counterattacked, throwing back the enemy and restoring the flank on the north.

Then it was Cleburne's turn, this time to come up against the formidable Yankee breastworks at Kelly field. Though his men made a series of gallant attacks, they were all repulsed by the sheer force of the defenders' firepower. Cheatham's attack that followed met with the same fierce resistance. Walker's two divisions were then committed at 10:45, so by 11:00 A.M. the bulk of the right wing had been committed to the attack. By then, it had become apparent that Bragg could no longer hope to crush the Union north flank, and he was now committed to trying to smash Rosecrans with the sheer force of massed attacks across the Confederate center and left. And so, by 11:30 A.M., it was to become Longstreet's battle if the attacking Army of Tennessee was going to succeed in wrenching the victory from a Union army whose firepower was proving to be as effective as its fighting spirit.

Whether Rosecrans slept better than Bragg after their respective middle-of-the-night conferences remains unknown, but it is certain that Rosecrans was up and ready for the day by 6:00 A.M. of the 20th. He heard mass, following his daily custom, and was off to ride the line of his army, trailed by his staff. While he had every good reason to see things for himself (as far as the woods and underbrush permitted), his command problems of the early morning were minor compared to Bragg's. In retrospect, yesterday's battle had not gone too badly, all things considered. While his army had suffered severely in casualties, he could be reasonably certain that his troops had inflicted even worse losses on their attacking enemy. Additionally, the divisions of Sheridan and Negley had not been committed to action, nor had Granger's reserve corps seen action as a fully engaged force. More important, two major outcomes of the battle were now evident: Bragg had failed to turn the northern flank, while Rosecrans had succeeded in shifting divisions to defend endangered points. The latter process was a ticklish business in the midst of a raging battle, in great part mitigated by the divisions of Bragg's right wing being launched in a series of uncoordinated attacks instead of a massed effort—a spectacle that would have turned Napoleon red with rage had a similar event occurred under his eye.

As Rosecrans and his staff rode northward his prime concern was to see that his line had been consolidated and was ready for the attacks that were sure to come at any time that morning; meanwhile, he was taking advantage of the time that Bragg was giving him by the delays of his generals. While en route, Rosecrans received a message from Thomas informing him that Negley's division, expected to strengthen the north flank, had not yet arrived. When Rosecrans met Thomas at the latter's command post at 6:30, the two rode out to make a hasty check of the northern end of the line near the left flank of Baird's division. There Rosecrans saw for himself that indeed Negley's division was needed to bolster that flank. The ever efficient Garfield was immediately busy sending orders to Negley to move without delay as well as a courier to McCook to inform him of Negley's orders and directing him to fill any gap left by his departure. At the same time, about 7:00 A.M., Rosecrans himself sent Captain Willard of his staff to guide Negley to his destination.

During his visit to Thomas, Rosecrans was assured of the former's confidence in his ability to hold his position against any attack, provided that he got the timely reinforcements he so badly needed. Rosecrans had concurred all along, being fully aware that Thomas' defense—so critical to the army's defensive mission—was already absorbing three-fifths of the army's combat power. Thomas would now have not only his own divisions (Baird, Brannan, Reynolds, and Negley), but also the divisions of Richard Johnson from McCook's corps and Palmer from Crittenden's corps. Thus the organization for combat for the 20th (after Negley had moved to rejoin Thomas' corps) was now in effect, due mainly to the shifting of divisions made during the battle of the previous day. This left McCook's corps with the divisions of Sheridan and Davis, and Crittenden's corps with the divisions of Van Cleve and Wood.

After Rosecrans parted company with Thomas, he rode on to check on Negley. He soon found that division in the act of forming into columns for its march northward. All of this may, at first glance, have indicated that the army commander's orders were being carried out. But—and it became an important "but"—it quickly became apparent to Rosecrans that Negley had pulled all three of his brigades out of line, while the rattle of rifle fire was also telling him that many of the division's skirmishers were still engaged with their enemy counterparts in the woods. At this point the army commander's notorious temper came into action, its effects falling on Negley: why in the world would he pull *all* his brigades out of line while their skirmishers were still engaged? He ordered the unfortunate division commander to put the brigades of Stanley and Sirwell back into line, meanwhile sending Captain Willard to start Beatty's brigade (which had been in reserve) on the march. When he had calmed down, Rosecrans sent word to Crittenden to send Wood's division forward to relieve Negley's brigades in the line—and time was of the essence, in order that the moves be completed before the enemy's impending attack struck in that sector.

Rosecrans rode on to find McCook about 8:00 A.M., and by then it was time for that corps commander to feel his chief's mounting displeasure. Why hadn't he personally seen to it that Negley had been pulled out of line and was marching northward? When McCook tried to explain that he was occupied with checking on the positioning of Sheridan's division, Rosecrans cut him short, telling him that his line was stretched too thin and that he must close it up by shifting it leftward. Then, without waiting for further words from McCook, Rosecrans rode back to see if Negley's two remaining brigades had been relieved, so that they could be hurried northward. To his disgust he found that Negley's brigades were still in line and that Wood's division, which by then should have relieved them, had halted and occupied a low ridge some distance to the rear. What had apparently happened, unknown to Rosecrans, was that Crittenden's order for Wood to relieve Negley had somehow been misconstrued, allowing Wood to halt where his division now stood.

By this time if Rosecrans' rising temper could have been shown graphically, it would have been seen approaching the boiling point. When he rode back to find Wood's troops halted on the ridge, the latter tried to explain that he had halted there because that was what he understood Crittenden's order to have intended. But Rosecrans' temper exploded, unleashing all the morning's frustrations on Wood. His voice rising, he is reported to have roared, "What is the meaning of this, sir? You have disobeyed my specific orders. By your damnable negligence you are endangering the safety of the entire army, and by God, I will not tolerate it. Move your division at once, as I have instructed, or the consequences will not be pleasant for yourself."[100] Whatever his exact words, their intent and impact were unmistakable. What makes the reprimand so noteworthy is not only its severity, but the fact that it was delivered in front of Wood's own staff. Obviously, Rosecrans' rage had overridden his reason in his failure to call Wood aside, to rebuke him in private and get him moving as directed. The immediate result was that Wood merely saluted, turned, and gave the orders for his troops to move forward.

Coincidentally, at about 9:30 A.M., as Wood's leading files trooped in to take over the breastworks from Negley's men, the ever increasing sounds of cannon and musketry could be heard coming from the north. No one was more acutely aware of their meaning than the army commander. Rosecrans was giving his full attention to assuring himself that his divisions were presenting a solid front to whatever attacks Bragg could now mount against them. So now the overriding question: just where would the attacks come?

THE BATTLE TAKES A CRITICAL TURN

Of the several unusual features of the battle of Chickamauga, none is more remarkable than the contrast between the handling of command and control by the commanders of the two wings of Bragg's army on the morning of the 20th. As related, matters in Polk's wing got only more confusing as time wore on, with friction between commanders resulting in all sorts of misunderstandings and delays that extended down through corps, division, and brigade levels. In Longstreet's wing, where one would have expected the "fog of war" to have overwhelmed a commander arriving in the middle of the night in strange territory, instead order became the rule of the day, extending from the wing commander down to every brigade. Following his midnight conference with Bragg and before he could take to his rough bed on the ground, Longstreet had given orders to find a soldier who knew the local area and could serve as his guide. One Tom Brotherton, who knew "every pig trail through the woods," reported to the new commander and did a masterful job of guiding "Old Pete" to all the commanders and units he would visit in the morning.

Lee's "old war horse," the stolid professional, wasted no time in familiarizing himself with the terrain, his major commanders, and their troop dispositions. Fortunately he was able to turn the time being consumed by delays in Polk's wing to his own advantage, managing to use every minute from daylight to 11:00 A.M. in learning the situation on the ground, making his plans, and giving his orders. Calmly and methodically he proceeded to organize his forces and form an attacking force in depth.

It was apparent that he must have had the lesson of Gettysburg uppermost in mind when he formed his forces for his attack (see Figure 11.1). Instead of aligning his divisions on a broad front he employed Hood's corps as the central mass, with its three divisions in depth, most with two brigades forward. Thus, Bushrod Johnson's division led the formation, followed next by Hood's old division, now commanded by Brigadier General Law; and third in depth was McLaws' division, composed of the brigades of Kershaw and Humphrey, which had just detrained and made a forced march to the field that morning. Attacking on the right of Hood's column of divisions was Stewart's division of Buckner's corps, and on Hood's left was Hindman's division, also of Buckner's corps. Preston's division was to follow on the extreme left, acting as wing reserve.

Figure 11.1
Longstreet's Attack Formations

HOOD'S CORPS

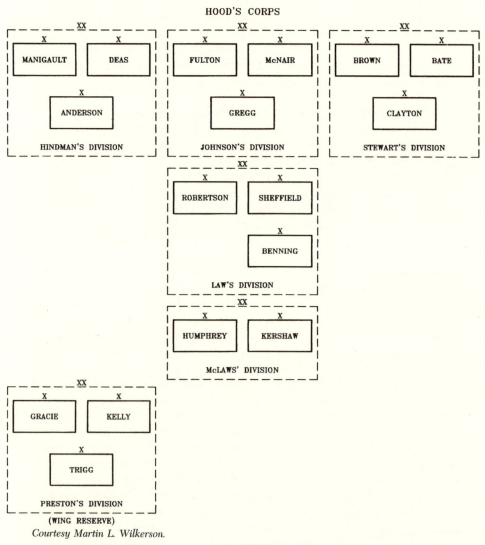

| XX |
| X | X |
| MANIGAULT | DEAS |
| X |
| ANDERSON |
| HINDMAN'S DIVISION |

| XX |
| X | X |
| FULTON | McNAIR |
| X |
| GREGG |
| JOHNSON'S DIVISION |

| XX |
| X | X |
| BROWN | BATE |
| X |
| CLAYTON |
| STEWART'S DIVISION |

| XX |
| X | X |
| ROBERTSON | SHEFFIELD |
| X |
| BENNING |
| LAW'S DIVISION |

| XX |
| X | X |
| HUMPHREY | KERSHAW |
| McLAWS' DIVISION |

| XX |
| X | X |
| GRACIE | KELLY |
| X |
| TRIGG |
| PRESTON'S DIVISION |
| (WING RESERVE) |

Courtesy Martin L. Wilkerson.

Unfortunately for Buckner, the three divisions of his corps (Stewart's, Hindman's, and Preston's) had been widely separated on the previous day by their commitments to battle; and now the integrity of his corps had to be sacrificed, since time and the press of events would not allow Longstreet the luxury of regrouping his wing's divisions to suit the former command structure. What Longstreet was able to do, however, was to assemble a main attack column of over 11,000 men on a front of less than half a mile, with its lead elements only a half mile east of the Lafayette Road—and pointed at that part of the Union line where Wood's division was completing its relief of Negley's division. Longstreet had also been able to take advantage of the thick wooded cover to move up and deploy his forces without being detected by Rosecrans' forces on the Union right. Although he could count on only forty-two guns for artillery support, "Old Pete" was not in the least dismayed because the thick woods severely reduced the effect of artillery fires and movement of the guns. Additionally, his infantry would achieve a measure of surprise without the kind of artillery preparation that had preceded his corps' attack at Gettysburg. By 11:00 A.M. he was able to send a message to Bragg "indicating that he believed he could break the enemy line if he advanced without waiting for Polk's attack."[101]

Before Longstreet could get a reply from Bragg a series of events intervened, events that would seem to have enabled the former to act without an answer to his recommendation. At some time in the late morning Bragg had become so overcome with disgust and frustration at the delays of Polk and his generals that he is said to have sent aides to the division commanders of the right wing, directing them to make their attacks as soon as they were ready. While it seems uncertain how and when such orders were received and executed, it is certain that Bragg did send orders directly to Major General Stewart of Buckner's corps to take his division into action. Though Stewart made a gallant effort his attack was stalled by the fierce resistance of Brannan's Union division. By this time Longstreet had become fully aware of the general failure of the right wing's piecemeal attacks as well as the necessity to attack before any more enemy forces in his front could be reinforced. Now the commitment of Stewart of his own wing sent a clear message to Longstreet that the time had come for action, and Longstreet was making final preparations for his attack.

Probably the busiest command post on either side on the morning of the 20th was that of Rosecrans at the Widow Glenn's house. From hours before sunrise until late morning, General Garfield and his assistants were constantly occupied in receiving messages, dispatching couriers, posting maps, writing orders, all the myriad activities that go with running an army headquarters in the midst of battle. Rosecrans lends an insight in his after-action report, referring to activities after he had returned from checking on his line, sometime after midmorning: "The battle, in the meanwhile, roared with increasing fury, and approached [i.e., increased] from the left to the center. Two aides arrived successively within a few minutes from General Thomas, asking for re-enforcements. . . . [another] message from General Thomas soon followed, that he was heavily pressed, Captain Kellogg, aide-de-camp, the bearer informing me at the same time that General Brannan [Brannan's division] was out of line, and General Reynolds' right was exposed. Orders were dispatched to General Wood to close up on Reynolds, and word was sent to General Thomas that he should be supported, even if it took away the whole corps of Critten-den and McCook."[102] The highly significant phrase "that General Brannan was out of line, and General Reynolds' right was exposed" becomes ominous in the light of what followed Captain Kellogg's report to Rosecrans. So many fateful events followed the warning that a close look at what led up to it—and what was set in motion by it—deserves closer attention.

Captain Sanford C. Kellogg had come up from the ranks, rising from a sergeancy in the 37th New York to an appointment as an aide-de-camp to General Thomas just before the Tullahoma phase of the campaign. As men-tioned in Rosecrans' report, Kellogg was delivering a message from Thomas requesting reinforcements, and had arrived about 10:30 A.M. There are varied accounts of the observations that Kellogg made en route, mainly the conclu-sion that he could not have seen Brannan's battle line—actually extending from Reynolds' "exposed right"—because of the thick woods that intervened between that line and the road along which he was riding at the time. It therefore appears best to rely on the account and findings of General John B. Turchin, who was not only a professional military observer but also the com-mander of the 3rd Brigade of Reynold's division during the battle:

Capt. Kellogg, an *aide-de-camp* of Gen. Thomas, coming to Gen. Rosecrans with another request for reenforcements for the left, reported at the same time that "Brannan's division was out of line, and that Reynolds' right was exposed." Galloping along the line and being in a hurry to reach Gen. Rosecrans, Kellogg stopped to hear the statement from Gen. Reynolds that his flank was in the air and exposed. Accepting it as a fact, Kellogg reported it to the general commanding. But there was no break in the line. . . . Brannan's division stood in line with King's brigade of Reynolds. Pressed so much with business, Rosecrans credited the report and ordered his *aide-de-camp* Maj. Bond to write that order to Wood, which proved so fatal to us.[103]

In a moment, more about the fatal order. It is important to note that author-ities agree that Rosecrans was understandably quite busy at the time, and moreover that Garfield also was occupied at the time with writing orders to Generals Sheridan and Davis. Yet it is questionable that Rosecrans should have been too busy to turn his attention to getting a full explanation from Kellogg in determining how and why such a dangerous gap could have existed in his army's line. In any case, it is clear that Rosecrans did turn to Major

Bond, *instead of Garfield*, and told him to write an order, which Bond composed and wrote in his own words:

Headquarters Department of Cumberland
September 20th—10:45 A.M.

Brigadier-General Wood, Commanding Division:

The general commanding directs that you close up on Reynolds as fast as possible, and support him. Respectfully, etc.

Frank S. Bond, Major and Aide-de-Camp.

Then, *without Rosecrans having read the order*, Bond labeled it "Gallop," gave it to Lieutenant Colonel Lyne Starling, and asked him to deliver it to General Wood. It took Starling only about five minutes ride to reach Wood, and he handed it to him personally at 10:55 A.M. Wood is reported to have read the order carefully and placed it in his pocket notebook. What happened—and didn't happen—in the next few minutes determined the outcome of the battle of Chickamauga. Brigadier General Thomas J. Wood was a thorough professional who had graduated fifth in his West Point class when Ulysses S. Grant (graduating thirty-eighth in his class) had been his roommate. He had served with distinction in the Mexican War, distinguishing himself at Buena Vista, and later became a lieutenant colonel of cavalry. At the start of the war he helped raise 40,000 Indiana volunteers, and soon rose to general officer rank. He commanded his division under Rosecrans at Stones River, where his was the only division that had steadily held its position in the Union center, solid proof of his moral courage. And, it is important to note, this was also the man who was still smarting from his humiliating chewing out in front of his own staff only a short time before.

What Wood could have done, as a professional soldier and a general officer, was to question the order, since his division's skirmishers had been hotly engaged to their immediate front and he knew that pulling his command out of line with an enemy attack imminent would create a highly dangerous situation (see Map 11.4). He also knew that the Widow Glenn's house was only 600 yards to his rear, and it would have taken him only five minutes to ride back to Rosecrans and voice his concern in person about such a questionable order.[104] What Wood did do, after pocketing the order, was to send immediate orders to his three brigade commanders, directing them to face their brigades about, march them to the rear, put them in march columns, march around the rear of Brannan's division, and move to occupy support positions in rear of Reynolds' division. While such a decision and the orders that followed it appear no less than incredible from a detached viewpoint, it can only be said for our immediate concern with the battle that, while Wood's orders were being executed, a gap of several hundred yards was being opened in the Union

Map 11.4

Courtesy Martin L. Wilkerson.

line at the very moment when it could be exploited by the advancing mass of Longstreet's divisions.

When Longstreet heard the sudden outbreak of firing to his right front, his apprehension was somewhat relieved after he learned that Bragg had sent orders directly to Stewart to attack with his division. Stifling his annoyance at the interference with his chain of command, Longstreet immediately sent for Generals Hood and Bushrod Johnson, and at 11:10 A.M. gave them the order to attack at once.

Johnson's lead brigades, Fulton's and McNair's, led out smartly, their advance through the thick woods taking them toward the Brotherton farm directly ahead. They took only ten minutes to reach and cross the Lafayette Road. What followed when Johnson's leading troops came upon the gap created by Wood's withdrawal has been related vividly by Shelby Foote: "As they surged across the dusty road and the open field beyond . . . they encountered galling fire from the left and right, where Hindman and Law [Stewart?] were hotly engaged, but almost none from directly ahead. Welcome though this was, they found it strange until they found out why. Entering the woods on the far side, they scrambled over the deserted breastworks and caught sight, dead ahead and still within easy reach, of the last of Wood's brigades in the act of carrying out the order to 'close up on and support' Reynolds. Yelling, the Confederates struck the vulnerable blue column flank and rear, sitting-duck fashion, and, as Johnson described the brief action, 'cast the shattered fragments to the right and left.' "[105] It seems that Bushrod Johnson was not only a superb leader but talented when it came to dramatizing the sudden success of his men after they had broken through the Union line: "The scene now presented was unspeakably grand. The resolute and impetuous charge, the rush of our heavy columns sweeping out from the shadow and gloom of the forest into the open fields flooded with sunlight, the glitter of arms, the onward dash of artillery and mounted men, the retreat of the foe, the shouts of the hosts of our army, the dust, the smoke, the noise of firearms—of whistling balls and grapeshot and of bursting shell—made a battle scene of unsurpassed grandeur."[106] In less dramatic terms Johnson's brigades were able to maintain the momentum of their attack until they had penetrated almost a mile beyond their first encounter. In forty-five minutes they had destroyed a Union brigade and captured nineteen guns and a large bag of prisoners. Remarkable as that breakthrough had been, it was being rivaled by the smashing success of Hindman's division on the left of Longstreet's attack. Hindman was reaping a stroke of good fortune that exceeded even Johnson's. His leading brigades, those of Deas and Manigault, followed closely by Anderson's, caught the divisions of both Davis and Sheridan in march column as they were moving north to close up and support Thomas. Coming on with the rebel yell, the Confederates struck Davis first, whose men got off only a few random shots before their columns were shattered. The fugitives fleeing rearward spread panic through Sheridan's marching brigades, which were swept away to min-

gle with the flood that now poured rearward and up the road toward Mc-
Farland's Gap. The overall result of the debacle was that, in the words of a
Union officer who observed the spectacle, "McCook's corps was wiped off the
field without any attempt at any real resistance." The scattered islands of
resistance that formed were swept away "like flecks of foam upon a river." As
Foote observed, McCook himself became one of those flecks, and Sheridan
and Davis were two more. In contrast to Johnson's dramatic description of
events Longstreet's accounting was a masterpiece of laconic summation: "As
we approached a second line [Davis' and Sheridan's divisions], Johnson's division happened to strike it while in the act of changing position of some of
the troops, charged upon and carried it, capturing some artillery, Hood's and
Hindman's troops pressing in close connection. This attack forced the parts
of the Twentieth and Twenty-first Corps from that part of the field, back over
Missionary Ridge, in disordered retreat, and part of Negley's division of the
Fourteenth Corps by the same impulsion."[107]

At some point during the disaster to the Union right, a Confederate shell
struck the Widow Glenn's house, setting it afire. As events had unfolded, it
no longer mattered to Rosecrans and his staff. They had taken to the field,
and now, at the height of the rout of the divisions of Davis and Sheridan,
were fully occupied in trying to halt and rally the flood of fugitives. Although
they had waded into the flood with drawn sabers, desperately trying to stop
the frenzied horde, they too became "flecks of foam" on the rushing river that
had carried away Davis, Sheridan, and McCook. By noon Rosecrans had given
up, and though he and Garfield and three others of his staff were no longer
carried on the crest of a torrent, they rode along with it toward McFarland's
Gap. When his party reached a fork in the Dry Valley Road—a fork that would
become more symbolic in the commander's decision than a physical feature
on the ground—Rosecrans says in his official report that after "hearing the
enemy's advancing musketry and cheers, I became doubtful whether the left
had held its ground, and started for Rossville. On consultation [with Garfield]
and reflection, however, I determined to send General Garfield there, while
I went to Chattanooga, to give orders for the security of the pontoon bridges
at Battle Creek and Bridgeport, and to make preliminary dispositions either
to forward ammunition and supplies, should we hold our ground, or to withdraw the troops into good position."[108] In his personal story of the battle,
written twenty-four years later, Rosecrans not surprisingly went into detail in
his version of the hurried conference that followed after they had halted at
the fateful fork. He states that he made clear to Garfield and Major Bond his
fears that Longstreet would exploit his success by capturing their supply trains
and then "he will turn the rear of our left [Thomas' embattled defense], seize
the gap at Rossville, and disperse us." He then went on to cite a series of six
detailed orders intended "to provide against what may happen." At this point
one can imagine Garfield's consternation in trying to cope with such a flood
of orders while trying to catch his breath, just after dismounting at the road-

side. Rosecrans must have realized his chief of staff's dismay, for he paused to ask, "General Garfield, can you not give these orders?" Garfield is related to have replied, "General, there are so many of them, I fear I might make some mistake; but I can go to General Thomas for you, see how things are, tell him what you will do, and report to you." Garfield's answer must have been convincing, for Rosecrans states that he then told Garfield, "Very well. I will take Major Bond and give the orders myself. *I will be in Chattanooga as soon as possible*" [italics added]. He went on to remind Garfield that the army had a telegraph station at Rossville from which reports could be sent to him; then the two went their separate ways.[109]

There is a great deal more behind the wording in the official report and Rosecrans' later version of events than merely showing Rosecrans, the logistician, taking over from Rosecrans, the tactician. One sees revealed behind the words the commander who has given up the battle, and, instead of going forward to lead his other corps and trying to save the rest of his embattled army, sends his chief of staff to find out what has happened and report back. Such a decision paints a sad picture indeed, though there have been substantial arguments defending Rosecrans' actions in the light of an understandable concern for saving *all* his forces in the face of the threat of a powerful enemy exploitation.

How greatly the combination of mental despair and physical stress may have influenced Rosecrans' thoughts and decisions by the time he and Garfield were conferring at the roadside can only be surmised. According to Tucker's sources, Rosecrans was "physically exhausted, broken in spirit, emotionally jarred and confused. Rosecrans had to be helped from his horse when he reached the house where department headquarters had been set up [the new army command post in Chattanooga]. . . . He sat with his head in his hands, as beaten and shattered as his right wing."[110] Though this description is based on the account of one observer (Captain Alfred L. Hough of General Negley's staff), it is not unreasonable to conclude that Rosecrans' decisions and actions, at those critical times after the collapse of his army's right, were not those of a commander who still had command of all his personal powers—or command of his forces that were still fully engaged with the enemy.

If Rosecrans was driven to despair after the collapse of his right, one might expect that Bragg would be overcome with joy at Longstreet's success and eager to shift forces to exploit the breakthrough by his left wing. Strange as it seems, something quite the opposite was to follow. When Longstreet realized the full extent of the results of his breakthrough, he was quick to perceive that the time had come to take advantage of the opportunity presented. As a skilled tactician, he knew what was expected of a commander under the circumstances—after all, the whole object of making a penetration was to create artificial flanks in the enemy's front, flanks that had to be enveloped in order to roll up the enemy's line and finish him off. With that realization uppermost in mind, Longstreet was eager to report to Bragg that the time had come to wheel his forces to the right and exploit his breakthrough. Since Longstreet had not heard from his army commander since midmorning, he wasted no time in complying with Bragg's summons to meet with him at 3:00 P.M. After describing the results of his breakthrough and the immediate steps he had taken on his own, Longstreet, in his own words, went on as follows: "I then offered as suggestion of the way to finish our work that he abandon the plan for battle by our right wing, or hold it in defence, draw off a force from that front . . . join them with the left wing, move swiftly down the Dry Valley road, pursue the retreating forces, [and] occupy the gaps of the Ridge behind the enemy standing before our right [Thomas' defensive positions]." Bragg's re-action to the recommendation must have taken Longstreet completely aback, as he went on to describe it: "He was disturbed by the failure of his plan and the severe repulse of his right wing, and was little prepared to hear sugges-tions from subordinates from other moves or progressive work. His words, as I recall them, were: 'There is not a man in the right wing who has any fight in him.' From accounts of his other operations I was prepared for halting work, but this, when the battle was at its tide and in partial success, was a little surprising. His humor, however, was such that his subordinate was at a loss for a reopening of the discussion. He did not wait, nor did he express approval or disapproval of the operations of the left wing, but rode for his head-quarters at Reed's Bridge. There was nothing for the left wing to do but work along as best it could.[111]

In spite of Longstreet's talent for understatement and his use of "work" for planning and executing operations, his description of the meeting (as well as that of several observers) and its outcome allows one to draw three conclu-sions: Bragg did not or did not want to comprehend the significance of his subordinate's astounding success; he would not listen to recommendations for exploiting the success of his left wing; and, for all apparent purposes, he had surrendered control of the battle, leaving a major force commander to his own resources. In other words, there would not be a general pursuit of the beaten Union right, no major move by Confederate forces to cut off the routed enemy, nor a reinforcement of the left wing to enable it to defeat the still-standing forces of the enemy.

THOMAS BECOMES THE "ROCK OF CHICKAMAUGA"

Throughout the Stones River and the Chickamauga campaigns Rosecrans had increasingly relied on the judgement and general character of Major Gen-eral George Henry Thomas, the commander of the XIV Corps and the general who could be considered the army's second-in-command, so much was the trust placed in him. Rosecrans' reliance on Thomas must have had its foun-dations in the opposing facets of their two natures. As Peter Cozzens has observed, "Where Rosecrans was impulsive and excitable, George H. Thomas was methodical and phlegmatic, where Rosecrans was voluble and moody, Thomas chose his words carefully and always seemed in good spirits."[112] Moreover, Thomas was a solid professional, a graduate of the West Point class of 1840 who had stayed in the regular army up through the start of the war, despite the fact that he was a native Virginian, one of the few who had chosen to stay with the Union. His rocklike character was matched by his physical appearance. "Pap" Thomas, as his troops called him, was a huge man, standing a solidly erect six feet, and weighing 200 pounds, with what a staff officer called a "leonine appearance." His solidity was accentuated by his broad shoulders, his square jaw, heavy brows, and piercing blue eyes. He was as honest and forthright as he was unassuming, having no overriding ambition or thirst for glory, even continuing to wear a colonel's eagle for some time after he had been promoted to brigadier general. He came as near to being loved by his troops as any Union general, not only from his frequent appearance among them, but more for the care he took for their welfare. This was the man on whom Rosecrans had relied to form the bulwark of the army's defense from the first day of the battle, and who was now having to shoulder the responsibility for not only holding the positions of his corps against heavy odds, but saving what could be rallied of the whole of the army. He did all that with the courage and tactical skill that earned him the title "Rock of Chickamauga."

As might be expected of a general of Thomas' capabilities, the command of the army could not have been thrust upon him as a surprise; on the contrary, he became increasingly aware of the collapse of the Union right through reports, encounters with subordinate commanders, and personal observation of what had happened. Accordingly, as he found his right flank being forced back at an ever increasing angle, he was taking measures to rally the scattered units of the divisions of Wood, Negley, and Van Cleve to bolster his right against the threat of Longstreet's impending attack. His main anchor on his extreme right was Brannan's division, on which he had to form the elements from the aforementioned divisions. At the same time he was striving to bolster his left and center—the latter being forced into an arc-shaped defensive posture—against the attacks of the divisions of Polk on Bragg's right wing (see Map 11.5).

As shown, the whole of Thomas' defensive line was eventually bent into a rough semicircle, facing, on the north and east, Forrest's cavalry and the attacking divisions of Polk, and on the south the divisions of Longstreet, which had become the greatest threat by midafternoon. Longstreet's attacks were thrown at Thomas' right (initially Brannan's division and a large part of Wood's) and that exposed flank. First there were attacks, led by Kershaw's division, which were repeatedly repulsed, then a series of attacks by Bushrod Johnson's and Hindman's divisions which came within a razor's edge of success, only to be beaten back by unexpected help which, in the nick of time, saved Thomas' force from being cut off and encircled. Major General Gordon

Map 11.5

Courtesy Martin L. Wilkerson.

Granger, commanding the reserve corps on the far north, heard and observed the battle raging to the south. Acting on his own, in a deservedly acclaimed show of initiative, he sent Brigadier General James Steedman southward on a forced march to arrive and deploy into line on Brannan's right, just in time to throw back the Confederate assault that would have smashed the exposed Union flank.

Longstreet's attacks continued through the late afternoon—Longstreet admitted later to no less than twenty-five attacks by various elements—until he had committed the last of his divisions, Preston's, in attacks that were also thrown back. They were repulsed by a grimly determined defense that was bolstered throughout by Thomas' show of personal leadership along the line. In the meantime, Garfield had made his now famous ride (one that would be referred to years later during his candidacy for the presidency) to arrive at Thomas' side by 3:35 P.M. "We have repulsed every attack so far," Thomas told him, "and we can hold our ground until the enemy can be kept from our rear."[113] Garfield wasted no time in writing a detailed report to Rosecrans, informing him of the masterful defense that Thomas' troops were making, even stating, "I think we may in the main retrieve our morning disaster," adding that there was a real need for the replenishment of ammunition, and dating the dispatch 3:45 P.M.

When the exhausted Rosecrans had read Garfield's report, he sent back a message to Thomas at 4:15:

Major-General Thomas:

Assume command of all the forces, and with Crittenden and McCook, take a strong position and assume a threatening attitude at Rossville. Send all the unorganized force to this place for re-organization. I will examine the ground here and make such dispositions for defense as the case may require and join you. Have sent ammunition and rations.

W. S. Rosecrans
Major-General[114]

Clearly this was not an order from a commander who would go forward and take control of forces that were still engaged with repulsing an enemy obviously determined to finish off his army. It *was* a directive from a commander who (1) has turned over command of his remaining combat power to his second-in-command and (2) has on his mind only preparations for defense on the morrow. As for Thomas, it was equally clear that he was fully occupied with "taking up a strong defense and assuming a threatening attitude."

At last, as late afternoon was turning into dusk, Thomas was able to withdraw his battered divisions from the east side of his perimeter, beginning with Reynolds on the south, followed progressively by the three divisions to the north, and finally the others from the south side of his line. It was a brilliantly conceived operation and well executed, especially with nearly exhausted troops in the face of an enemy determined on their destruction. It is to Thomas' enduring credit that he had saved the entire army and had followed that achievement by getting his divisions safely away by way of McFarland's Gap and Rossville.

Back in Chattanooga, Rosecrans had followed his orders to Thomas with another dispatch, this time a telegram to Washington:

> Chattanooga, Tenn., September 20, 1863—5 P.M.
>
> Maj. Gen. H. W. Halleck
> General-in-Chief:
>
> We have met with a serious disaster; extent not yet ascertained. The enemy overwhelmed us, drove our right, pierced our center, and scattered troops everywhere. Thomas, who had seven divisions, remained intact at last news. Granger, with two brigades had gone to support Thomas on the left. Every reserve was used when the men stampeded. Burnside will be notified of the state of things at once, and you will be informed. Troops from Charleston, Florida, Virginia, and all along the seaboard are found among the prisoners. It seems that every available man was thrown against us.
>
> W. S. Rosecrans
> Major-General, Commanding[115]

AFTERMATH

The rough and ever ready Nathan Bedford Forrest was in the saddle by dawn of the 21st, and by early morning had his troopers scouting within a mile of Rossville. On a spur of Missionary Ridge his troopers had caught four Union Signal Corps men literally up a tree in their improvised signal station. Forrest "borrowed" a pair of captured field glasses, and climbed the tree to see things for himself. At 9:00 A.M. when he came down, he sent a galloper to his wing commander with a report, asking Polk to forward it to Bragg:

> Gen'l We are in a mile of Rossville. Have been on the point of Missionary Ridge can see Chattanooga and everything around. The Enemy's trains are leaving going around the Point of Lookout Mountain.
>
> The prisoners captured report two pontoons thrown across for the purpose of retreating. I think they are evacuating as hard as they can go. They are cutting timber down to obstruct our passage. I think we ought to push forward as rapidly as possible.
>
> Respectfully etc. N. B. Forrest Brig Gen
> [To] Lt. Gen L. Polk
> Please forward to Gen Bragg[116]

Forrest waited in vain for a reply. When he realized that one wasn't coming, he sent a second dispatch directly to Bragg, urging immediate action, climaxing it with the assertion that Chattanooga could be taken with a brigade of infantry if the opportunity could be seized. After getting no reply to either message, Forrest rode back to remonstrate with Bragg in person. Despite Forrest's urging, Bragg still thought he had good reasons to hesitate before making what may have seemed to him an impetuous advance. His losses had been frightful, his troops were exhausted after the heaviest fighting most had ever seen, there were as yet no trains for Longstreet's troop supply, and all of the army's soldiers were about to go on half rations until the supply trains could catch up. In short, there would be no authorization for a pursuit of Rosecrans' forces. If the rest of the generals—and the army—had known of the decision at the time, they would have shared Forrest's disgust as he rode back to his command. All that was yet to come.

What followed the climactic events of 20 September has been summarized in the *West Point Atlas of American Wars*: "By the night of 21 September, Rosecrans had withdrawn into Chattanooga. He had succumbed to a defeatist attitude, accepted investment, and thus surrendered his ability to maneuver. His troops occupied and began to strengthen the fortifications left earlier by the Confederates; his cavalry was posted . . . to protect his line of supply . . . and to warn of Confederate attempts to cross the river. . . . By the same night Bragg had invested Chattanooga, posting the brigade of Brig. Gen. E. McIver Law in the valley to the southwest."[117]

By the next day, it was becoming evident to Bragg that he would have to choose between three courses of action, none of which must have seemed palatable to him. First, being in position to maneuver (in comparison to Rosecrans' unenviable situation), he could adapt a lesson learned from his opponent and outflank Rosecrans by crossing the Tennessee, thus cutting his communications and isolating his army. Second, he could move in force against his enemy's as yet incomplete defenses, storm the fortifications, and destroy Rosecrans' army or force it to surrender. Third, he could occupy the high ground which looked down on Chattanooga, besiege the Union army, and starve it into surrender. He decided on the third, thus leading to the siege of Chattanooga and its disastrous outcome for the Confederacy.

CHAPTER 12

The Two Perspectives of Chickamauga

One of the surest ways to turn an American student away from a love of history is for him to find in his textbook such passages as "In September of 1863, 66,000 Confederate troops under General Braxton Bragg defeated 58,000 Union troops under General William S. Rosecrans in the battle of Chickamauga." Certainly the facts are there, but to say that they leave the bored student unimpressed is an understatement. Even if he were forced to swallow this stale ort, he would never digest it. So it would be with us if we were left with merely finding out how close Bragg's army came to destroying Rosecrans' forces without discovering the "why" behind each commander's ability to control events.

From what we have seen in the early stages of the campaign, each army commander had a deduced mission to guide his planning and operations. "Deduced" because each was operating under general directives from his government telling the commander what was expected of him, but leaving the details of its execution to him. In Rosecrans' case, despite his recurring run-ins with the high command in Washington, it was understood that he was expected to clear the Confederates out of east Tennessee and open the South to invasion by way of Chattanooga. Bragg's mission evolved through several stages, beginning with the strategic concentration of forces to reinforce his army in the Chattanooga area to enable him to take the offensive against Union forces in the western theater. Unfortunately for Bragg, his offensive was preempted by Rosecrans, who took the initiative by crossing the Tennessee River and advancing in force with the evident intent of cutting Bragg's communications and capturing Chattanooga. Bragg, though forced temporarily on the strategic defensive, set an objective of first trying to attack and destroy widely separated forces of Rosecrans' army. When those efforts failed, he altered his mission by setting himself new objectives: to cut his opponent's vital link to Chatta-nooga by turning his northern flank, then destroying his army in the valley between the Chickamauga and Missionary Ridge.

Because both commanders' operations had to be redirected after 4 September (the day that Rosecrans began crossing the Tennessee), it suits our purpose to see how each commander proceeded to carry out his mission after that date. During the critical two weeks that followed, each had to reconsider his concept of operation, based mainly on how he evaluated his intelligence re-garding his enemy. To begin, each had the fault of overestimating his enemy's strength, though not to the heights of hyperbole that General George B. Mc-Clellan had raised to an art form. In Rosecrans' case, his intelligence capability was crippled by his thinly stretched cavalry screen, which was held at bay by Confederate cavalry that was superior in numbers and in quality. In Bragg's case it appears that he allowed his cavalry corps leaders, Forrest and Wheeler, too much latitude in securing the army's flanks, while not placing enough emphasis on gathering information on the movement of Union forces in the army's front—in the valley between the Chickamauga and Missionary Ridge. Then too, Bragg himself may have been at fault when he chose to downplay the significance of reports from Wheeler and Polk indicating that major enemy forces were moving on the Dry Valley Road.

In weighing the impact of each commander's evaluation of intelligence on his operations, significant changes emerge: a marked shift in each leader's concept of operation after the Union army had gotten across the Tennessee. We have already seen the impact on Rosecrans when he finally credited his intelligence with the fact that Bragg was no longer retreating in disarray to-ward Dalton and Atlanta, but was instead regrouping his forces to get between the Union army and Chattanooga and even attack one or more of its widely separated corps. The shock of this realization seems to have affected Rose-crans' state of mind—to the extent that he no longer thought of himself as the hunter, but the hunted.

In comparison to his opponent, Bragg's transition from a commander who was leading a forced retrograde to one who turned on his enemy and attacked him was progressive in nature, more of a sequence of responses to a devel-oping situation. Doubtless he was caught off guard by the success of Rose-crans' river crossing, which came suddenly and was unopposed by Bragg's unprepared forces. But when he was forced to give up Chattanooga, Bragg not only made an orderly withdrawal to regroup his forces, but also employed deceptive measures (like the programmed "deserters" who did a good job of misleading Rosecrans) that, for a time, caused his enemy to push his widely spread corps in "pursuit." Yet even while he was falling back and had tem-porarily deceived his enemy about his intentions, Bragg showed flashes of indecision before he made up his mind on the night of 9–10 September to attack Thomas' exposed force, Negley's division in McLemore's Cove. After that abortive attack, Bragg still sought to defeat his opponent in detail, this time on a larger scale, by attacking Crittenden's corps on the 13th. Though that attack also failed, Bragg deserves credit for his resolve to continue the offensive by committing his entire army to the all-out purpose of cutting off Rosecrans' army and destroying it. Thus Bragg had managed to make the transition from an outmaneuvered commander to one who could take the offensive when the situation presented the opportunity. Regardless of how the circumstances may have been forced on him—through his own shortcomings or the failures of some subordinates to carry out his plans—he showed that he could make the reversal of roles from hunted to hunter. That he failed to pursue the latter role to its final end has to be the subject of closer examination. It is obvious that the decision-making process had already been set in motion once each commander had revised his concept of operation. It should be borne in mind, however, that a Civil War army commander, like most commanders throughout history, had to make his decisions under two vastly different sets of circumstances. When developing (or changing) his concept of operation, he was allowed plenty of time for reflection and, if he wished it, consultation with staff and subordinate commanders. On the other hand, when he had to make *timely* decisions during a battle, his whole art of command was challenged, involving not only his professional skills but his whole intellect as well as his physical stamina—all having to respond at the same time under the stress of battle.

When considering Rosecrans' handling of the art, his personal character appears to intervene in a discernible way under both sets of circumstances. There can be no doubt regarding his skills as a strategist. He continued to display them from the time he outmaneuvered Bragg in the Tullahoma phase of the campaign to the subsequent phases when he crossed the Tennessee and forced Bragg to give up Chattanooga and withdraw into Georgia. Yet, as we have seen, his boldness as a strategist turned to caution when he decided that he must go on the tactical defensive because he could no longer bring his enemy to battle on his terms. Because of that pivotal decision all his actions as a tactician became reactions to his enemy's maneuvers. Whether the decision was caused by a failure of moral courage is debatable, but it is certain that a facet of his character—manifested by his changed *state of mind*—influenced his decision.

Whatever that characteristic may have been, it shows up even more markedly under the latter circumstances—Rosecrans' decisions made during the heat of battle. Throughout the most critical periods, when the battle was at its height on the 20th, he continued to demonstrate that he was in full control of events on his side. He was out and making a personal inspection of his lines at daybreak, visiting his commanders and their troops, riding past regiments in their battle positions (the 6th Ohio of his native state cheering him as he rode past), and making on-the-spot adjustments to ensure that his defensive lines were intact. Back in his headquarters, he made sure that he was following every development in the situation; he made decision after decision without hesitation, and, with one fateful exception, issued coherent and timely orders. He continued to show confidence in his conduct of affairs, and it showed when his forces continued to repulse one major attack after another. Then everything changed when Longstreet's breakthrough piled disaster upon disaster on the right of the Union line. It is easy to understand that the personal efforts of Rosecrans to quell the panic and rally his troops had to be useless in the face of the overwhelming flood of fugitives, but what happened after he and Garfield had time to dismount and catch breath is another matter. His decision to abandon the battle by riding off to Chattanooga, while sending Garfield to Thomas, was as damaging to his image as a commander as it was to the fate of his army. It showed the world, as Tucker has pointed out, "that Rosecrans had an erratic temperament incompatible with the high responsibilities of army leadership. His superior talents might carry him through nine times out of ten, but a great general cannot fail so utterly in the tenth emergency."[118] If "erratic temperament" seems too general a term, one cannot dismiss a failure of nerve, which calls to mind a maxim of Napoleon's that should have come up in the discussions in Mahan's Napoleon Club in Rosecrans' West Point days: "The first quality for a commander-in-chief is a cool head, which receives a correct impression of things. He should not allow himself to be confused by either good or bad news."[119] Much has been made of the effects on Rosecrans' demeanor in the hours after his disaster when he had retired to Chattanooga. "Helped from the saddle," "a stunned appearance," and the like are common among the descriptions of his reactions—all dramatizing the distress of a leader who has suffered a devastating blow of ill fortune. While one cannot fail to empathize with Rosecrans' plight, the cold logic of Napoleon's maxim deserves to be the primary consideration, as Tucker has pointed out. In any case—character flaws or Napoleonic maxims aside— the fact remains that Rosecrans made the decision that resulted in his leaving the field and relegating conduct of the battle to a subordinate.

In Braxton Bragg's case, there is a curious dichotomy between his ability to make vital decisions in a reflective, strategical sense and his capability under the stress of command in battle. This singular difference was manifested when he made the decision to concentrate his forces after the evacuation of Chattanooga and take the offensive with a new objective of cutting off Rosecrans' army and destroying it. While it has seemed fashionable to denigrate Bragg's abilities as a field commander, his percipience and flexibility of mind as a strategist should not be overlooked in this phase of the campaign.

When it came to making decisions in the midst of battle, the difference between Bragg's and Rosecrans' state of mind becomes evident in their reactions to critical turns in the battle: Bragg appeared to be unbending in his adherence to his original plans, while Rosecrans seemed to react continually to perceived changes. The latter didn't hesitate to make many changes in the deployment of his forces, constantly shifting divisions—even brigades—to meet what he perceived to be the demands of the tactical situation.

Conversely, once Bragg had made his tactical decisions and issued his orders he appeared to take on an aloofness to unfolding events. On more than one occasion, after consulting with a commander during an action, he would retire to his command post, where he sometimes ignored reports from subordinates or failed to act in response to them. As a result, he sometimes put off making a decision or failed to make one in time to change the course of events. No doubt, his reluctance to respond in several cases may have been influenced by personal animosity, particularly in the case of his dealings with Polk and Hill.

Finally, Bragg's failure to arrive at a workable decision at the crisis of the battle (from the Confederate viewpoint) was nearly as fateful as that of Rosecrans when he chose to retire from the field. In Bragg's case, there were at least *two* decision points which have already been related. The first was Longstreet's meeting with him at midafternoon of the 20th, when he had urged Bragg to "abandon the plan for battle by our right wing," reinforce Longstreet's left wing, and pursue the routed Union forces to their destruction. It will be recalled that Bragg then broke off the discussion, and, in Longstreet's words, "rode for his head-quarters at Reed's Bridge." Bragg's decision represented both his inflexible refusal to abandon his original plan as well as a rejection of any effective pursuit that would have destroyed not only the enemy army, but also any Union hopes of an early opening of the gateway to the heart of the Confederacy. Thus, it was surely one of the most fateful decisions ever made by a Confederate commander in the west. The second occasion, the rejection of Forrest's urging for a pursuit on the following day, only served to confirm Bragg's failure, thus losing the victory that his army had fought so hard to achieve—as well as dooming that army to the siege of Chattanooga and its subsequent defeat in the battles of Lookout Mountain and Missionary Ridge.

There were also notable differences in the way that the two commanders formulated and issued the orders that translated their decisions into actions. Bragg's orders tend to reveal shortcomings in this regard. At times, his written orders lacked clarity, at others they were incomplete, leaving their recipients to make their own interpretation or to request the next higher commander for clarification. It appears that seldom, if ever, did a subordinate commander go directly to Bragg with a question regarding an order; the dissension and distrust between Bragg and his generals had already closed the door to such open communication. As a consequence, if there were errors or omissions in their orders, the recipients either carried them out to the letter or failed to execute what the army commander had intended. In fairness to Bragg, the faulty wording or transmission of an order was not always due to a personal fault for two reasons: he lacked the communicative skills of a chief of staff who—like Napoleon's Berthier or Rosecrans' Garfield—could translate his dictated commands into written orders that would not be misunderstood. Moreover, Bragg's relations with his staff lacked the warm "family" rapport that would have allowed a continuing exchange of ideas and questions. In the latter regard, the lack of mutual confidence has been made clear in the recounting of Bragg's questioning his staff about his remaining in command and the staff's reply that he should indeed resign.

An opposite case seems to have ruled in Rosecrans' headquarters. The commander of the Army of the Cumberland had been fortunate indeed in finding Brigadier General James A. Garfield for his chief of staff. From the time of his selection, Garfield maintained a close, personal relationship with his fellow Ohioan, even accepting Rosecrans' invitation to share his quarters in camp and in the field. His chief treated Garfield more like a son or younger brother than a staff officer, and Garfield responded by honing his skills at converting Rosecrans' verbal directives into written orders that were models of clarity and conciseness. An example of his competence has been cited with regard to the command conference at army headquarters on the eve of the battle. Garfield took notes during his commander's briefing of his corps commanders, composed the notes into drafts of orders which he then read and circulated to all present. After questions had been resolved, he had the drafts rewritten into final orders which he handed to the commanders before they left the command post.

With such an efficient alter ego Rosecrans was able to concentrate fully on his own problems, but with one unfortunate drawback: while Bragg may have issued too few or incomplete orders, Rosecrans tended to issue too many. Even though Garfield could translate Rosecrans' thoughts into clear orders, he couldn't dog his chief's footsteps and convert every verbal order into writing. As a result, Rosecrans felt free to bombard his corps and division commanders with a succession of orders during his rounds of inspections and command visits. Though this practice didn't appear to result in confusion or mishap, it tended to make Rosecrans a little careless in the number of orders that he issued verbally in or outside his headquarters. It was this habit, unwittingly abetted by Garfield's efficiency, that could have led to issuing the fatal order which caused General Wood to take his division out of the line of battle, thus creating the gap through which Longstreet's divisions poured and routed the right of Rosecrans' army. It has already been recounted that Garfield was busy writing orders to Generals Sheridan and Davis at the time when Captain Kellogg was informing Rosecrans about the supposed gap in the line, and further that Rosecrans was too occupied to interrupt Garfield and have him write the order to General Wood. Instead Rosecrans directed Major Bond to write the order, which he did and then sent it out by courier *without Rosecrans having read it.*

After reviewing all the circumstances, it becomes clear that the responsibility for writing and sending the order rests ultimately where it should— with Rosecrans himself. When an army commander accepts a verbal report that a dangerous gap exists in his battle line, then fails to investigate the circumstances, and neglects to have his chief of staff write the corrective order, it is clear that the fault lies with the commander. No matter how otherwise occupied were the commander and chief of staff, in this instance it can hardly be questioned that Rosecrans should have given his full attention to the matter, first to determining the accuracy of the report, then to seeing that clearly worded orders were issued to ensure that timely and adequate measures were taken to correct the fault. There is no need to go into the details of how the commander (and/or his chief of staff) should have gone about taking the proper measures; it is sufficient to say that they were not taken—with the fatal results we have already observed.

We have also been able to observe that most critical function of the commander after issuing his orders, that of seeing to it that his orders are being executed as he intended. In Bragg's instance, two factors, both linked to his personal makeup, adversely affected his capability to supervise personally the execution of his orders. First, as we have seen, was his curious tendency to remain aloof from actual operations, once his commanders had been given their orders and their forces had been committed to battle. This characteristic was the subject raised in private huddles between Bragg's generals, and it unfortunately became all too evident at Chickamauga. The other factor, closely tied to the underlying cause of Bragg's aloofness, was the strained relationship of the commander with his senior generals, which underlay an attitude seeming to say, "All right, you've got your orders, I'll be watching to see what you do with them." This ill-starred characteristic was most apparent in the latitude that Bragg gave his two wing commanders in the execution of his battle plan at its most crucial stage. This was compounded when Bragg, apparently inflamed when he learned that the attacks intended to crush the Union left had failed, resorted to the ill-considered issuing of orders *directly* to several division commanders, thereby bypassing the command channels of both wing and corps commanders. As we have seen, the only thing that saved the Confederate army from this aberration was Longstreet's breakthrough of the Union right.

Rosecrans, on the other hand, didn't hesitate to exercise personal supervision of his operations whenever time and circumstances allowed. When command responsibilities demanded his presence at headquarters, he took care to select a location for his command post that was as close to his front line as possible, as evidenced by his being only some 600 yards behind Wood's division when the fatal order was issued. As for his relations with his subordinate commanders, Rosecrans had managed to maintain a good professional working relationship with them throughout the campaign. Although the flaring of his bad temper was common knowledge, it was also recognized that the offender who brought on a display of wrath usually deserved what followed. Yet Rosecrans' habitual cheerfulness, even a bluff heartiness on occasion, made him generally well liked, and tended to more than offset any fear of his short temper. His show of geniality, however, never extended to creating a warm Nelsonian "band of brothers" among his higher commanders. As much as his generals might have favored such a fellowship, any feeling in this regard was kept at bay by their being overawed by their chief's intellectual powers, which were never restrained in any meetings, public or private. Unfortunately for Rosecrans, any promise of rewarding command relations disappeared like smoke on the wind after he had revealed his despair and loss of control by retiring into Chattanooga.

He hadn't yet drained his cup of despair when he resigned himself to defending the city, for an even greater blow was not long in coming. In Washington, Secretary of War Stanton, who was anything but an admirer of Rosecrans, had made up his mind only three days after the battle that the Army of the Cumberland needed a new commander, and the sooner the better. He was alarmed by frantic telegrams from his assistant, Charles A. Dana, who had been with Rosecrans' staff during the campaign and he had Lincoln's ear; it was only a matter of days until the president would consent to relieving Rosecrans. By 30 September, Stanton had wired Dana, "All that the Army of the Cumberland can need will be a competent commander. The merit of General Thomas and the debt of gratitude the nation owes to his valor and skill is fully appreciated here and I wish you to tell him so. It is not my fault that he was not in chief command months ago."[120] Lincoln, who had been reflecting on the overall strategy and command problems in the west, had decided to combine the departments of the Cumberland, the Tennessee, and the Ohio under one new command, the Military Division of Mississippi, and place Grant in overall command. The president then left the crucial decision up to Grant: should Rosecrans remain in command or should he be relieved by Thomas? Grant chose Thomas.

On 19 October Grant's orders relieving Rosecrans and replacing him with Thomas were received in the headquarters of the Army of the Cumberland. That evening Rosecrans handed the orders to Thomas in a scene that must have been painful for both of them. After conferring late into the night with Thomas, Rosecrans departed early in the morning for assignment to the ignominious command of the Department of Missouri.

On the other side of Missionary Ridge, things were in no happier state in the headquarters of the Army of Tennessee. The wild jubilation that ignited the army's victory bonfires and sent the rebel yell ringing up the valleys was not long shared by the generals in higher command. Any exhilaration that might have accompanied their amazing success was quickly dampened by the word that Bragg had decided not to follow up their victory. That dampening was only the beginning of the troubles that were to beset the command. By late September, Bragg, taking action against what he considered egregious failures of command, had suspended Polk and Hindman from command and ordered them to Atlanta to await further orders. In the meantime the anti-Bragg faction was already at work to oust Bragg from command. In Cozzens' narration, "On 4 October, the corps commanders met secretly to consider an alternate commander for the army and to prepare a petition to Davis for

Bragg's removal. . . . The culmination was a long petition that carefully avoided any reference to Bragg's military failings, which would have been construed as mutinous, and argued instead for his removal on the sole ground that 'the condition of his health unfits him for the command of an army in the field.' "[121] Twelve generals signed the petition.

Whether Bragg knew of the meeting is not known, but it is certain that he was aware of the undercurrent of feeling against him, and on 5 October he telegraphed Davis, asking him to intercede personally in the matter. Davis, already torn between his friendship for Bragg and Polk, sent Colonel James Chesnut to investigate matters at Bragg's headquarters. Chesnut, alarmed at the high feelings running against the army commander, telegraphed Davis recommending that he come at once to settle matters.[122]

When Davis arrived at Bragg's headquarters on 9 October he had already decided on a way of settling the affair. After consulting with Bragg and rejecting his offer to resign his command, "Davis would call a council at which he, Bragg, and the four senior generals of the army—Longstreet, Hill, Buckner, and Cheatham—would be present. Then he would ask each general to express his opinion of Bragg. Apparently Davis reasoned that the general hostility to Bragg was greatly exaggerated and even if some of the generals had been engaging in loose talk here and there, they would surely profess loyalty to Bragg in his presence and the president's."[123] In spite of Davis' good intentions to clear the air and restore harmony, his plan exploded in his face. When Davis got to the point of the meeting and asked the senior general, Longstreet, for his opinion, the general gave a somewhat evasive reply. Davis asked for a straight opinion. He got one—and then three concurring sentiments—all of the opinion that Bragg should go. During the discussion that ensued, an embarrassed Davis managed to maintain his composure, while a stony-faced Bragg (one can imagine *his* embarrassment) sat it out in silence.

The upshot of the matter was Davis' decision, after later reflection, to retain Bragg in command. Actually the president had gotten himself into a dilemma and the only way out of it was to choose between Bragg and two unpleasant alternatives. He could in effect sack the recalcitrant generals—transferring or reassigning them in some tactful fashion—or he could replace Bragg then and there. But if he chose the latter course, he had no one whom he considered a suitable replacement. So, in his reasoning, he avoided the alternatives and retained Bragg. Wise or unwise, the decision was made, and the Army of Tennessee was left to face a clouded future.

In essence, what we have witnessed during the campaign and battle has been a contest between two leaders wherein each had to fashion his own art of command under conditions that were as trying as they were formidable. Each was a West Pointer who had left the regular army to make his own way in an unfamiliar, civilian world—and each had become successful in his own way. Granted that Bragg had had combat experience in the Mexican War and Rosecrans had not, the latter had to fight his way to the top in a highly competitive industrial field where only his will and personal resources counted. Then each had volunteered his services to the country he believed in, and each had proved himself in stages of command that eventually included the hardest test of all—higher command in battle. Finally, each commanded an army whose success or failure in a theater of war would determine the success or failure of a national strategy.

At this point it is worth pausing to reflect on the possibilities of the opposing commanders applying paradigms from Napoleonic warfare (Chapter 3) in their campaign. As recounted in Chapter 9, Rosecrans referred to "grand tactics" in the opening of his history of the campaign and showed promise of employing a *bataillon carré* system in the maneuver of his four corps in their approach to the crossing of the Tennessee and their advance to contact in the following phase. That he was either ignorant of the system's applicability or was unable to master its use was demonstrated by his haste to reassemble his army instead of letting a corps commander pin down Bragg's forces and subsequently maneuvering his other corps to concentrate and strike the enemy in one climactic battle. It is arguable that Rosecrans—even if fully cognizant of the worth of Napoleonic grand tactics in this case—could have decided not to adapt the system after considering that the compartmented, rugged terrain hindered the essential maneuvers or that he had not familiarized his corps commanders with the use of the system.

In Bragg's case, he should be credited with a Napoleonic perception of seizing the opportunity to take the offensive and destroy in detail a part of his enemy's forces while that enemy's major elements were widely separated. That he failed to act successfully on the perception (the twin failures to destroy Negley's division in McLemore's Cove and to overwhelm Crittenden's vulnerable divisions in the days following) may have been due in part to his vague orders or lack of personal supervision of operations; but it was certainly due in great part to the ineptness shown by Generals Hindman and Hill to act aggressively and carry out the mission assigned by their army commander.

The most singular aspect of an art of command that does emerge from what we have observed is the evidence that each commander may have deserved to win the battle and thus the campaign on his own merits—if one considers the merits *solely and impersonally on a professional basis*. Both Bragg and Rosecrans were competent strategists and both had developed a workable plan of battle. Though each had seen an aspect of his plans thwarted by the failure of a subordinate, each should have been able to overcome the frustration through his own resources. It is the question of each man's personal resources that then becomes crucial, and it is apparent that each failed in the ultimate test of command due to an unfortunate feature of those resources.

In Rosecrans' case, the unfortunate feature was his failure to keep his head when the disaster to his right wing threatened the ruin of his whole army. If he had kept a clear head and had gone to Thomas' side, he would have had every chance to take control of events by personally directing troop movements, reforming reserves, and generally directing the battle as he had before the disaster to his right. However, as we have seen, he surrendered control to Thomas and left the fate of the army in his hands. Rosecrans paid the price of his defeat when he was relieved of command.

In a very real sense Braxton Bragg lost his victory by his failure to pursue his enemy's broken forces, but in a deeper sense he was already on his way to losing it because of the mutual distrust that existed between him and his subordinates. The distrust was compounded by his abrasive nature—he simply could not get along with anyone who failed to measure up to his rigid standards—and his fragile health, which seemed to fail him at the time of his greatest need. The price that he paid was demonstrated by his disastrous defeat in the battles of Lookout Mountain and Missionary Ridge, which ended the siege of Chattanooga and opened the door to the Union invasion of the heartland of the Confederacy.

PART FOUR

NASHVILLE: THE LAST GREAT ADVENTURE

He who knows when he can fight and when he cannot will be victorious.

— Sun Tzu, *The Art of War*

CHAPTER 13

John B. Hood and Certain Differences in Confederate Strategy

It was a rainy Sunday on 25 September 1864 when Jefferson Davis' train pulled into the rickety station at Palmetto, Georgia, and the president left his railway car to review the honor guard awaiting him. The rain-soaked ranks of the 1st Tennessee Regiment presented arms, then grounded arms in the red Georgia mud to stand stolidly while the president addressed them. His remarks, intended to be morale raising despite the sodden scene, were brief and concluded, "Be of good cheer, for within a short while your faces will be turned homeward and your feet pressing the soil of Tennessee."[124] Though the Tennessee soldiers had responded with cheers and rebel yells there were intermingled shouts of "Johnston! Give us Johnston!," clear signals that many of the rank and file would have liked to have back their old commander of the Army of Tennessee in place of General John B. Hood, whose invitation had occasioned this visit of the president to army headquarters at Palmetto.

Davis' visit, however, was prompted by far more than a response to an army commander's invitation. This was the third time in the war that he had felt it necessary to leave Richmond for the western theater, and this trip was being made because he was already convinced that matters demanded his personal attention. In the back of his mind—ceaseless reminders that underlay all his present concerns like ocean currents demanding a ship captain's attention—were the events that had led up to the fall of Atlanta and its occupation by Sherman's Yankee armies. There were the seemingly endless retrograde movements when General Joseph E. Johnston had fallen back toward Atlanta before Sherman's overpowering advance, and though the Army of Tennessee had been skillfully maneuvered under Johnston's hand against heavy odds, the public eye had only seen what appeared to be needless retreat after retreat. In mid-July, after Davis had reluctantly replaced Johnston with Hood,

John B. Hood

the latter had undertaken an unrelenting series of aggressive maneuvers that had been skillfully parried by Sherman and which were highlighted by the bloody battles of Peachtree Creek, Atlanta, and Ezra Church—always with ill-afforded Confederate losses that exceeded those of the enemy. Then had come the final blow when Sherman had swung the bulk of his three armies in a great wheel south of Atlanta to cut Hood's communications, which had forced the evacuation of the city and allowed Sherman's forces to march in on the morning of 1 September. With these events behind him, Jefferson Davis needed no invitation to come to Georgia and see things for himself. In the first place he had a deep concern for the morale of the people: What effects had the fall of Atlanta had on the people, with Yankee armies trampling their land? What was the morale of the army after its terrible bloodlettings of the past weeks? And what about Hood's generals? Was the Army of Tennessee going to be plagued forever with dissension between its chief and his higher leaders? Yet with all these problems pressing on his visit, the president had an even more urgent matter that demanded his attention, as soon as he could meet privately with Hood. He would deal with the morale of the people and the army as he made his way on his tour—just as he had addressed the Tennessee troops when he got off his train at Palmetto—and he would confer, as he thought necessary, with the senior generals. What remained uppermost in his mind was the need to work out with Hood the strategy essential to driving the Union armies out of Georgia—as well as Alabama and Tennessee.

During the next two days, Davis would first dispose of the ill feeling that had arisen after Hood's last battles and the loss of Atlanta. Hardee was the principal dissident, since he had never considered Hood to be a better choice for army commander, and after lengthy consultations with him and the other generals, Davis nevertheless decided to retain Hood and place Hardee in command at Charleston. Though Hood had earlier offered his resignation, Davis had rejected it and went on to decide that Beauregard would be placed in overall command of both Hood's Army of Tennessee and Lieutenant General Richard Taylor's forces in Mississippi; thus, in effect Beauregard would be commanding the departments covering the Deep South. Hood would, of course, remain in command in the field, and with those matters settled Davis was ready to discuss strategy with Hood.

Earlier, in his dispatch to Davis concerning his visit, Hood had outlined a tentative plan for his army's employment against Sherman's forces. Basically, Hood had been and continued to be forceful in proposing that an offensive strategy was the only kind to employ against Sherman. To force his enemy to give up Atlanta and fight on Hood's terms or face being isolated in Georgia, Hood proposed the following offensive moves. First, he would seize the initiative by moving northward in the direction of Chattanooga, placing his forces in position to cut Sherman's communications, mainly his vital railroad line linking Atlanta to Nashville, Tennessee, the Union armies' base for the whole western theater (see Map 13.1). Then Sherman would be faced with the di-

Map 13.1

Courtesy Martin L. Wilkerson.

lemma of leaving Atlanta—as Hood believed he would—and either fighting
Hood or trying to open up a new supply line on the coast of the Atlantic or
the Gulf. If Sherman pursued Hood, the Confederate commander would withdraw into the rugged terrain in northern Georgia or Alabama where he could
force a battle on his own terms. Alternatively, if Sherman did move toward
either coast, Hood would follow and not only continue to sever his communications to the north, but also harass his enemy's rear and force him to turn
and do battle on the worst terms for him. Moreover, in Hood's own words, if
Sherman should "divide his army by sending off a portion to Tennessee . . . I
might be able to defeat the wing of the Federal Army, remaining in Georgia,
drive it from the country, regain our lost territory, reinspirit the troops, and
bring hope again to the hearts of our people."[125]

During their lengthy discussion, Davis not only approved in principle
Hood's strategic concept but added a touch of his own. "If Sherman did try
to drive Hood off his communications, as it was expected he would, Hood
should fall back on Gadsden, Alabama, whence he could draw supplies by rail
from the southwest. His own supply lines would thus be secure while, in that

position, he remained a continual threat to Sherman. Whatever happened, Hood was to follow Sherman wherever he went, north or south."[126] Hood was in complete agreement with the provision, so by this time the commander in chief and his commander of the Army of Tennessee had arrived at the Confederacy's overall strategic plan for regaining control of the war in the west. Though at this time the plan left open the question of Hood's further action should Sherman concentrate his main strength and march it toward Savannah (leaving other Union forces in his rear to deal with Hood), it was a bold concept, conceived under conditions where only bold actions could save the Deep South from the invader. As coming events would show, it was also the start of a national adventure from which there could be no turning back. Their plans confirmed, Davis took his leave, departing Palmetto on the late afternoon of 27 September.

Two days later Hood began his advance northward by starting his army of 40,000 across the Chattahoochee River, after sending orders to General Joseph Wheeler to rejoin the army with a mission of screening the army's advance and providing security against an enemy cavalry threat. By 1 October Hood had started his march toward his initial strategic objective, getting into position to cut Sherman's railroad link, the Georgia Central Railroad to Chattanooga. As his army moved toward its objective, Hood's cavalry was intercepted by Sherman's near Marietta, northwest of Atlanta. Apparently by now Sherman was aware of Hood's threat to his communications, but in reality Hood's enemy was far from sure of either Hood's capabilities or objectives. What ensued as this phase of the campaign took shape has been summarized as follows: "Actually for the next three weeks, Sherman had difficulty keeping abreast of Hood's movements. Hood moved rapidly, screened his marches well, and—by virtue of having the initiative—consistently baffled his adversary. Sherman, served poorly by his cavalry—which he had apparently neglected to train and mold to the desired pattern—trailed after Hood, seeking an opportunity to attack. But, in so doing, he never so dispersed his forces as to leave them exposed to the attack Hood's strategy envisioned."[127]

During those first three weeks of October, while Hood and Sherman played out their deadly game—like a bold toreador flaunting his scarlet cape to outmaneuver a wily and dangerous bull—Hood was becoming increasingly aware that time was running out for him in the strategy that he and Davis had agreed on. Although he was able, between 15 and 20 October, to carry out Davis' idea of withdrawing to Gadsden and drawing Sherman after him, Hood had begun to review the strategic picture and see that he had arrived not only at Gadsden but also at a critical decision point. In his review of the situation Hood had learned that Sherman had authorized General George H. Thomas (headquartered at Nashville) to assemble forces to reconstitute a strong army that would enable him to cover Sherman's rear while the latter turned his back on Hood's threat and started his main army toward Savannah—and a new supply base on the Atlantic coast. It was at this decision point that Hood apparently decided to exercise his own judgement and end his strategic game with Sherman. In effect, he was saying, Very well, let Sherman try to start his march (in actuality, Sherman was already wringing Grant's grudging consent to concentrate an army of 68,000 and begin his now famous march to the sea); if I move swiftly enough I can not only prevent Thomas from moving to unite with Sherman, I can defeat him (Thomas) before he can assemble his forces, which are still scattered all over Tennessee. But Hood's planning didn't end with defeating Thomas. As he saw it, when he had knocked Thomas out of the picture, he could move across northern Tennessee into Kentucky to recruit new forces to threaten Ohio. Then if Sherman were to abandon his march to Savannah and turn back to follow him, Hood could fight him in Kentucky. Even if he were defeated there, he could march his forces eastward through the Cumberland Gap to join Lee in Virginia. If John Bell Hood had his shortcomings—and his critics would say they were numerous—a lack of imagination was not among them. His strategic vision was "based upon many variables, few of which, as it developed, worked in his favor; but it also depended on how two Union generals reacted—the slow, dependable Thomas, and the fiery, brilliant Sherman."[128]

While at Gadsden Hood took time to get approval of his plan to move into Tennessee and deal with Thomas. Beauregard, in theater command since 28 September, met Hood at Gadsden, where he heard with some dismay of Hood's new plan, which appeared to him to be far more than a new strategic phase. To the Creole general, who was no stranger to creating grandiose schemes, Hood's "revised strategy" represented a complete departure from the plan that Davis and Hood had agreed on at Palmetto, the plan on which he had been briefed personally by the president when the latter had given him the overall command in the west. That strategy had envisioned Hood following Sherman, regardless of whether he marched north or south. What Hood was now proposing was actually a 180–degree turnabout, leaving Sherman free to operate in Georgia while Hood went north on his own. Apparently after some persuasive discussion, Beauregard gave his reluctant approval, after adding a condition of his own. He directed that the theater cavalry capability be employed in two widely separated efforts: Wheeler would be left in the area where he was now operating to observe Sherman; Forrest, who was then conducting raiding operations in western Tennessee, would come under Hood's command for the Army of Tennessee's advance to the north. When he parted company with Beauregard, Hood wasted no time in implementing his new strategy.

He began by moving toward Guntersville, Alabama, where he would have Forrest join him. As Hood was keenly aware, everything in his strategy depended on his army's rapid movements; not only had Davis and Beauregard made that a condition of their approval, but it was even more important that he must defeat Thomas before he and Sherman could unite against him. But nature, which has a way of upsetting all kinds of human endeavors, intervened in the form of flooded rivers which would delay the marches of Forrest's cavalry. When he learned of this development, Hood pushed on to the Tuscumbia–Florence area, where he would await Forrest while he gathered supplies to replenish his wagon trains for the advance northward. He arrived at Tuscumbia on 31 October, to be greeted with news which made it seem that fate had again turned her back on him. Forrest had continued to be held up by unfordable streams, and—equally disturbing—rainy weather and mired roads had combined with torn-up rail lines to delay the assembly of badly needed supplies, especially rations. The last item was particularly worrisome because Hood had planned to move his army into Tennessee even if his troops had to march on short rations, but with even shorter rations morale would become dangerously low. The upshot of these misfortunes was that Hood would have to wait at Tuscumbia until both Forrest and the supplies arrived— and lack of the latter was going to drag out the delay for the next three weeks. The question of how the combined pressure of the delay and the urgency for action would affect the impetuous and impatient Hood's implementation of his plans now becomes the focus of interest. What kind of man was this whose personal qualities would go so far to determine the conduct—and even the outcome—of the coming campaign?

Lieutenant General John Bell Hood, at age thirty-three brevetted full general to command the Army of Tennessee, had a meteoric rise to army command unsurpassed by any other general in the Confederate service. Yet there was little in his early life to indicate that he could aspire to high command, let alone become a general. He had been born into a middle-class family at Owingsville, Kentucky, like Bragg's one of moderate wealth but not of the plantation aristocracy. His father, John W. Hood, was a doctor, a general practictioner who also taught the making and use of prosthetics, and who wished son John to take up a similar profession. Young John, whose head was filled with romantic tales of Indian fighting and the Mexican War, only wanted to be a soldier. Over his father's objections he wangled an appointment to West Point from his uncle, Judge Richard French, the congressman from his district, and reported as a cadet in July 1849. His four years as a cadet became an increasingly hard grind for the would-be soldier. Always in the lowest quartile of his class, he had to struggle against two handicaps: his inadequate earlier schooling and his romantic inclinations, which leaned the other way from scholarship. The academy library's records show that, out of its 20,000 volumes, in four years Hood checked out only two books, Jane Porter's *Scottish Chiefs* and Sir Walter Scott's *Rob Roy*, a clear indication of his basic interests.[129] In general his fellow cadets considered him a "jolly good fellow" and for the most part one who shrugged off discipline to such an extent that in his last year he received 196 demerits out of the 200 that meant automatic dismissal. In fact, an escapade at Benny Haven's Tavern and subsequent AWOL brought down the final avalanche of demerits and an official reprimand from none other than the superintendent of the academy, Colonel Robert E.

Lee. In spite of that first painful encounter, which Lee handled with tact and compassion, Hood began a lifelong admiration of Lee which amounted to nothing less than hero worship.

Despite his demerits and low grades—especially in mathematics and engineering—he managed to graduate in the class of 1853, with a standing of forty-fourth in a class of fifty-two, and was commissioned a second lieutenant in the 4th Infantry Regiment. He served two years in the 4th in California before he "escaped" to an assignment in the 2nd Cavalry in Texas, a posting which an undistinguished shavetail could hardly have earned, but one which the ambitious Hood grasped as the opportunity that it represented. The officers of the 2nd Cavalry were handpicked (why Hood was among them remains a mystery): the regimental commander was Colonel Albert Sidney Johnston; Lieutenant Colonel Robert E. Lee was second-in-command; and George H. Thomas and William J. Hardee were majors. Hood's most vivid memories of his experiences in the 2nd would include his service under Lee, who acted as a mentor to the green lieutenant, though their association was never closer than that of a senior advisor to a junior officer. He would also remember the occasion which brought him a department commendation for gallantry and leadership in action. Hood led his troop against an Indian war party that outnumbered his little command by three to one. While he led the charge an arrow pierced his left hand, pinning it and his bridle rein to the saddle. Without hesitating, Hood broke off the arrow shaft, pulled out his hand, and continued to lead his men after they had withdrawn to reload their carbines. When the Indians galloped off in retreat, he rallied his troop and returned to garrison in triumph. It was highly indicative of the kind of leadership that was to characterize Hood's later career—dashing, recklessly brave in leading his troops with no regard for his own person.

In 1861, still a first lieutenant, he turned down the career plum of an assignment as cavalry instructor at West Point, and in April resigned to offer his services to the Confederacy. He rose rapidly from a mere first lieutenant, being commissioned a brigadier general in March 1862 to take command of the "Texas Brigade" in Lee's Army of Northern Virginia. He led his brigade to gain fame by breaking the Union line at Gaines' Mill in the third day of the Seven Days Battles. He went on to gain even greater reputation at Second Manassas and again at Sharpsburg. Because of his gallant conduct and leadership in the Maryland campaign, even Stonewall Jackson didn't hesitate to recommend his promotion to major general, which was confirmed on 11 October 1862, after which he was assigned to command a division in Longstreet's corps.

On the second day at Gettysburg, while leading his division in an attack up the Emmitsburg Road, he was badly wounded in his left arm, and had to be taken from the field. While convalescing at Richmond, Hood engaged in what Steven Woodworth has called "an unfortunate campaign of his own" with the objective of winning "Buck" Preston, Sally Buchanan Preston, a southern belle from an aristrocratic South Carolina family. Hood was smitten with the flirtatious Buck, who saw only what has been described as " 'a tall, rawboned country-looking man who looked like a raw backwoodsman dressed up in an ill-fitting uniform and who had a long face, a long tawny beard, a large nose, and eyes with the sad expression of a hound dog, in spite of his being one of the most celebrated division commanders in Lee's famous army."[130] Though he was, then and later, to continue his pursuit of Buck, it was without the success he had gained on the battlefield; eventually she turned down his proposal of marriage.

When he rejoined the army he was, as we have seen, destined to lead the attack of Longstreet's wing at Chickamauga, where, at the head of his successful attack, he took an even more serious wound, this time a minié ball that shattered his right leg at the thigh. The leg had to be amputated on the field, leaving him with a stump only a few inches long. Though he made a full recovery—in Richmond there were at first false reports of his death—he was doomed to being strapped in the saddle in the field, with an aide following and carrying his crutches. During his recovery he was promoted to lieutenant general to date from the day of his wounding at Chickamauga. A few days later he joined Joseph E. Johnston's Army of Tennessee as a new corps commander. The assignment and his service under Johnston during the Atlanta campaign were to bring on two conditions that would profoundly affect his performance in the field. The first was physical; his disabled arm and his missing leg assured that "he would always be impaired in moving about the battlefield to control and direct his troops. He might tire more quickly, and if so his judgment might often be clouded by fatigue as well as pain from his old wounds."[131] The other effect was psychological in nature, stemming directly from his service as Johnston's subordinate. Knowing only the offensive in war, he had to serve under a chief who was committed to a campaign based on retrograde and defensive operations. "Under Joe Johnston, every time the Confederates halted, they got out their spades and axes and constructed pits, trenches, and other earthworks. . . . Hood deplored this practice because he thought it impaired the morale and fighting spirit of the men. . . . from the moment he took command of the Army of Tennessee, Hood determined that his army was going to have to go on the offensive if it ever hoped to defeat the bluecoats and their overwhelming numbers, and he was resolute that his men must learn to get out from behind their breastworks and go on the attack, even if it killed them."[132] Finally, as recounted, Jefferson Davis, prompted by the public's outcry and his own distrust of Johnston, relieved him of command and replaced him with Hood on 17 July 1864. In spite of some inner misgivings, Davis entrusted Hood with the command, mainly because he had become convinced that Hood's combat experience and style of leadership would assure that he would take the offensive.

By the time that Hood had begun to implement his own strategy and had led his army to its delayed stay at Tuscumbia, he had become more and more

Figure 13.1
Hood's Army of Tennessee

Courtesy Martin L. Wilkerson.

aware of the deficiencies of the poor logistical system he had inherited from Johnston, and his ineptitude with logistics did little to ready the army for its next move. To make matters worse, the command structure of his army was no longer functioning as a well-ordered system, in part due to the mutual mistrust that had begun to grow between Hood and his senior commanders. Though he was not hated as Bragg had been—he could still be the "gallant Hood" to the army at large—some of the old uncertainties and qualms that had once permeated the army's leadership seemed to come back to haunt its new commander. Not only was he haunted by those uncertainties, but he also had to worry about the rickety railroads, the heavy rains that had continued to hinder movement, the looming threat of the concentration of Thomas' forces, and the absence of Forrest's cavalry. Because he feared intervention with his new operations, Hood continued to avoid Beauregard—and the threat he posed to Hood's freedom of action—by ignoring his superior, even to the point of moving his command post across the Tennessee River when Beauregard was about to make a visit to Tuscumbia. Finally, however, a great burden was lifted from Hood's mind by the arrival of Forrest on 18 November. The next day Hood issued his orders for his army to cross the Tennessee.

The army's effective strength came to about 38,000, comprised of about 30,000 infantry and 8,000 cavalry. Its major components were three infantry corps (see Figure 13.1), commanded respectively by Lieutenant General Stephen D. Lee, Lieutenant General Alexander P. Stewart, and Major General Benjamin F. Cheatham; the cavalry corps was commanded by Major General Nathan B. Forrest. The army's morale, in opposition to Hood's misgivings, was generally good—the bands played and the men of Lee's corps cheered as they led the march across the pontoon bridge over the Tennessee River— and being the veterans they were, the troops were ready to prove themselves against a new enemy.

Their commander already had plans to cut off a major force of that new enemy just as fast as their marches would move them to accomplish that end. Hood planned to cut off the Union forces at Pulaski from Thomas (at Nashville) by capturing the crossings of the Duck River at Columbia (see Map 13.2). To do so, his three infantry corps, preceded by Forrest's cavalry, would move over parallel routes on an axis of advance west of the Nashville and Decatur Railroad. Forrest, with his usual aggressiveness, would cover the advance, driving before him the enemy's cavalry screen, and push on to seize the Duck River crossings before Union forces could escape. It was a good plan, and it should have worked as intended if the cavalry and the other three corps could have moved rapidly enough to keep the enemy off balance. Unfortunately for the Confederates the capricious, late autumn weather played havoc with the troops and the roads. Cold rains interchanged with snow and sleet to make the dirt roads switch from frozen ruts to quagmires, at times holding back infantry marches to less than ten miles a day. Amazingly, despite all the adversities, Hood did achieve a degree of surprise: his enemies had thought that he would be scarcely able to move at all. But Forrest was doing a superb job of using superior numbers to drive back Hatch's Union cavalry while screening Hood's advance, and by 22 November, Stewart's corps had reached Lawrenceburg, sixteen miles west of Pulaski.

In the meantime, however, Schofield, the Union commander, taking heed of Thomas' warning about the threat to his right and becoming suddenly aware of that threat's progress on the 22nd, rushed two divisions to Columbia. Their lead elements arrived on the 24th, in the nick of time to prevent the aggressive Forrest from seizing the bridges over the Duck River. By 27 November, Hood was confronting Schofield just south of Columbia. Schofield, fearful that Hood could turn him out of his precarious position with the river at his back, withdrew across the river during the night of 27–28 November. Schofield had ample reason to be concerned; though he had for the moment escaped Hood, the latter had readied a new plan to cut him off. This time Hood had planned a turning movement to the east by crossing Cheatham's and Stewart's corps at Davis' Ford while leaving Lee's corps to attack Schofield and lead him to believe that he was dealing with the whole Confederate army. Schofield, however, had learned from Wilson (the new and skillful Union cavalry commander) early on 29 November of the Confederate large-scale movements threatening his withdrawal route, and had dispatched two divisions to secure Spring Hill and cover the withdrawal of his remaining forces from Columbia.

Map 13.2

Courtesy Martin L. Wilkerson.

What followed was typical of many of Hood's operations as an army commander—brilliant conception and faulty execution, this time leading to what
has been called the "Spring Hill affair," which "became perhaps the most
controversial of the nonfighting events of the entire war."[133] At about noon
of the 29th Schofield started the rest of his forces and wagon trains toward
Spring Hill, where they might have been intercepted by Cheatham, whose
lead elements arrived near Spring Hill by 3:00 P.M., in time to attack Wagner's
Union division covering the withdrawal. What resulted instead was a series
of confused events—misunderstandings caused by faulty or even undelivered
orders as well as plain old sluggishness—led off by Cheatham's half-hearted,
piecemeal attacks. The latter failed utterly to halt the enemy's march along
the Columbia–Franklin Turnpike, slow as it was moving at the pace of wagon
trains. In his official report Hood asserted,

Major-General Cheatham was ordered to attack the enemy at once vigorously and get
possession of this pike, and, although these orders were frequently and earnestly
repeated, he made but a feeble and partial attack, failing to reach the point indicated.
Had my instructions been carried out there is no doubt that we should have possessed
ourselves of this road. Stewart's corps and Johnson's division [of Lee's corps] were
arriving upon the field to support the attack. Though the golden opportunity had passed
with daylight, I did not at dark abandon the hope of dealing the enemy a heavy blow.[134]

Hood went on in his later account of Spring Hill to relate that, once night
had fallen, he had received reports that the enemy was marching along the
turnpike unmolested, though "almost under the light of the campfires of the
main body of the [Confederate] army." And continuing in his official report
to sum up his frustration, he would claim, "Thus was lost a great opportunity
of striking the enemy [the blow] for which we had labored so long—the
greatest this campaign had offered, and one of the greatest during the war."
Even if Hood can be suspected, in both his official and unofficial accounts, of
stating a one-sided case, he must bear the command responsibility for the
failure at Spring Hill. In fairness, it should be recognized that personal supervision of his widely separated forces had to be constrained by his physical
handicap: after a day of being strapped in the saddle while having to endure
the pain from the stump of his missing leg, he no doubt would collapse with
a fatigue that would prevent him from making night rounds to check on matters in person.

However, even if one can set aside the controversy over the Spring Hill
affair, it is still clear that the failures there led directly to the battle of Franklin
on the following day. Schofield, taking every advantage of his good fortune,
hurried his troops and trains up the Columbia Pike to Franklin. There he
hastily entrenched a perimeter around the south side of Franklin, with his
flanks secured on the Harpeth River (see Map 13.3). Beginning early on the
same morning of the 30th, Hood followed, pushing his troops relentlessly up

Map 13.3

Courtesy Martin L. Wilkerson.

the pike: Stewart's corps in the lead, followed by Cheatham, with Lee farther
to the rear. When Hood arrived to find an entrenched enemy awaiting him,
he hastily deployed Stewart's corps, then Cheatham's on its left, and began
preparing an all-out attack on the entrenched enemy. He chose to ignore
Forrest's recommendation for a turning movement as well as the fact that two
of Lee's divisions wouldn't be available for some time.

Whether Hood was still burning from the humiliating debacle at Spring
Hill or was overcome with a passion to destroy the enemy this time before
he could again escape is still conjectural. What is certain, however, is that
Hood launched a series of frontal attacks at 3:30 P.M. with his two corps (plus
French's division), resolved to overrun the enemy positions with main force.
His corps and division commanders, still smarting from Hood's rancor after
Spring Hill, were fully determined to acquit themselves and their soldiers like
the brave fighters they were: "Though logic dictated against a frontal assault,
they vowed to demonstrate that their troops could storm fortifications as
bravely as any."[135]

Again and again the Confederate ranks were thrown against the entrenchments, only to suffer one bloody repulse after another. Only once did they succeed in penetrating the Union lines when they broke and drove back Wagner's division (deployed in front of the lines as a covering force), making a gap in the enemy line, but that was rapidly closed by a desperate Union counterattack. By 4:00 P.M. Lee had arrived and was ordered to continue the attack with Johnson's division of his corps. This augmentation failed to redeem the repulses of the other attacks. The fierce fighting—unexcelled by any other in the war—went on for five hours, even though sunset on this late autumn day was at 5:15 P.M. Finally, darkness and crippling losses caused even Hood to reconsider, though his only action by 9:00 P.M. was to order late-arriving artillery into positions from which it could fire a preparation in the early morning, presumably to support a renewed attack by the other two divisions of Lee's corps which he had not committed to the attack. But when the frightful toll of casualties began to be totaled at army headquarters, even the reluctant Hood was forced to call an end to a battle that should never have been fought.

The losses were frightening: Schofield's came to 2,326 out of 22,000 troops actually engaged, but Hood's exceeded his enemy's by three times, amounting to 6,252 out of 30,000 infantry, a loss of 21 percent. And the Confederate total included twelve generals and fifty-four regimental commanders, a grim reminder of the commitment of Southern leadership to the senseless slaughter. Yet, incredibly, when Hood learned that the Union forces were evacuating Franklin that night, crossing the Harpeth on newly repaired bridges, he was determined to pursue at first light. He was only deterred by the realization that his army was in complete disarray from its losses and the confusion resulting from night attacks as well as the grim fact that the troops were nearing exhaustion. Nevertheless Hood managed to reorganize and start his army toward Nashville on the morning of 1 December: Lee's corps in advance, followed by Stewart's, and then by Cheatham's. At about 2:00 P.M. of the next day, the Confederate lead elements arrived before Nashville, where Hood saw for himself the extensive entrenchments behind which Thomas had assembled a formidable force. Hood deployed his forces and started them preparing their own entrenchments. Since there has been much discussion about Hood's reasons for his moving to Nashville, followed by contention over his grounds for entrenching before Nashville and "challenging" Thomas to battle, it could prove helpful to our purpose to consider Hood's own rationale for his decisions:

I remained with an effective force of only twenty-three thousand and fifty-three. I was therefore aware of our inability to attack the Federals in their new stronghold with any hope of success, although Schofield's troops had abandoned the field at Franklin, leaving their dead and wounded in our possession, and had hastened with considerable alarm into their fortifications [at Nashville]. . . . I knew equally well in the absence of the prestige of complete victory, I could not venture with my small force into Kentucky, without first receiving reinforcements. . . . Thus, unless strengthened by these long-looked-for reinforcements, the only remaining chance of success in the campaign, at this juncture, was to take position, entrench around Nashville, and await Thomas's attack which, if handsomely repulsed, might afford us an opportunity to follow up our advantage on the spot, and enter the city on the heels of the enemy. . . . In truth, our Army was in that condition which rendered it more judicious the men should face a decisive issue rather than retreat—in other words, rather than renounce the honor of their cause, without having made a last and manful effort to lift up the sinking fortunes of the Confederacy.[136]

If one discounts the wishful thinking about reinforcements—with the Confederacy nearing its death throes, only a being higher in station than Jefferson Davis could have provided Hood with the forces he had envisioned for carrying out the threat of invading Kentucky and Ohio—one can still appreciate Hood's dilemma and his reasoning to deal with it, however unrealistic that reasoning may now appear. Whatever his other reasons, it is a certainty that Hood, when he positioned his army to confront Thomas, fully intended to make "a last and manful effort to lift up the sinking fortunes of the Confederacy."

CHAPTER 14

The "Rock of Chickamauga" Prepares a New Kind of Battle

It will be recalled that after Hood had worked out a strategy with Jefferson Davis at Palmetto back in September, General Sherman was understandably uncooperative with the aims of the Confederate president and his commander of the Army of Tennessee. Among Sherman's uncooperative measures was his regard for his vulnerable communications which stretched all the way back to Major General George H. Thomas' base at Nashville. Although he was eager to gain Grant's approval for his projected "march to the sea," Sherman was keenly aware that, in marching an army to Savannah, he would have to be assured—and that meant first assuring Grant—that Hood would not be left free to threaten either Sherman's communications or an invasion of Kentucky. And that is why Sherman, on 26 October, sent Stanley's IV Corps of three divisions to reinforce Thomas, while directing him to take all other measures necessary to unite his forces into one army in order to deal decisively with Hood. Four days later Sherman, wishing to reinforce Thomas with everything he could spare, dispatched Schofield's XXIII Corps of two divisions to Thomas. Then, after receiving Grant's approval on 2 November, Sherman left Atlanta on the 12th with an army of 62,000 and started his march to the sea.

In Tennessee, Thomas had meanwhile entrusted a provisional force, composed of IV Corps and XXIII Corps (a total of five divisions with a strength of about 32,000), to the command of Major General John M. Schofield to deal with Hood's advance toward Nashville. As we have seen, Schofield succeeded in eluding Hood's turning movements at Columbia and Spring Hill, then fought a successful defensive battle at Franklin, one that proved disastrous to both Hood's plans and his army. In spite of his successful defense, Schofield was forced to leave his dead and wounded on the field—a blow to the morale of any force and its commander—but redeemed himself, at least in part, by

George H. Thomas

safely withdrawing the whole of his command and uniting it under Thomas' command at Nashville on 1 December. Schofield's force had been preceded on the same day by Major General Andrew J. Smith's XVI Corps, which had come up the Cumberland River by steamer from Missouri. That evening another reinforcement reached Nashville, the provisional detachment, District of the Etowah, under Major General James B. Steedman, consisting of a provisional division and two brigades of black soldiers.

With all those reinforcements pouring into Nashville one might have thought that Thomas would make immediate preparations to organize his new command and sortie forth to overwhelm Hood before he could make any further forays around Tennessee. In fact, no such offensive operation was about to be undertaken in the near future—not until the Union army commander was good and ready. Thomas had indeed been doing everything in the Nashville area to build up a force to defend his strategic base at the city—organizing the Post of Nashville into provisional units made up of cooks, clerks, and quartermaster employees—to carry out Grant's telegraphed instructions: "Arm and put into the trenches your quartermaster employes citizens, &c." What he was not hurrying to do, however, was to implement the other part of Grant's advisory, "With your citizen employes armed you can move out of Nashville with all your army and force the enemy to retire or fight upon ground of your own choosing."

What ensued instead was reminiscent of Rosecrans' preparations for his Tullahoma and Chickamauga campaigns, when Thomas had been a corps commander under him. It was not that Rosecrans' genius for logistical and topographic detail had rubbed off on Thomas (though he was a stickler for details in some respects). Rather, there were at least three areas of concern that must have remained uppermost in his mind. The first was an innate part of his style of command: even though he might seem a "plodder" in getting ready, he was going to make sure that every step was being taken to assure that he had all available combat power at hand when he faced Hood in an all-out battle. The second, a corollary of the first, was organizing his forces for combat while they continued to strengthen the entrenchments they would occupy before he moved against Hood. The third concern was that Major General James H. Wilson's cavalry corps must have the mounts and equipment it needed to contend with Forrest. Wilson, recently reassigned from the east, was a brilliant and energetic cavalry commander with a reputation to match, and Thomas' concern for his command was evident in his telegraphed report to Halleck: "After General Schofield's fight of yesterday [30 November], feeling that the enemy very far outnumbered him in infantry and cavalry, I determined to retire [him] to the fortifications around Nashville, until General Wilson can get his cavalry equipped. He had but one-fourth the number of the enemy, and consequently is no match for him."[137]

Thomas' telegram had a far greater impact in Washington than its stolid sender could have envisioned. It set off a chain reaction resulting in the same kind of pressure that Washington had applied to Rosecrans, a volley of dispatches intended to get the recipient moving at once, in keeping with what served as the national strategy at the time. Halleck had shown the telegram to Lincoln and Stanton, and on 2 December the latter telegraphed Grant as follows: "The President feels solicitous about the disposition of General Thomas to lay in fortifications for an indefinite period 'until Wilson gets equipments.' This looks like the McClellan and Rosecrans strategy of do nothing and let the rebels raid the country. The President wishes you to consider the matter."[138] Grant did consider the matter in a telegram to Thomas that, Grantlike, came right to the point: "If Hood is permitted to remain quietly about Nashville, you will lose all the road back to Chattanooga and possibly have to abandon the line of the Tennessee. Should he attack you it is all well, but if he does not you should attack him before he fortifies."[139]

Grant, at the time concerned with both national strategy and the operations of the Army of the Potomac in the east, naturally shared Lincoln's and Stanton's worries about Hood's threat to Ohio, especially at a time when Congress was about to convene. The specter of Hood's breaking loose and terrorizing loyal citizens at the very time when the administration's war aims were about to be realized also haunted Grant. This caused him to pressure Thomas relentlessly to leave his provisional force of "casuals" to man the Nashville fortifications while he took his army of three corps to the field to eliminate the threat of Hood once and for all. Thus, the barrage of Grant's telegraphic advisories, counsels, and instructions fell upon Thomas at the time when he was busied with what he considered vital preparations for his operations. As a result we again have to witness the spectacle of faraway strategists badgering the man on the ground to get moving, while the man on the ground is facing at first hand a host of obstacles invisible to his remote superiors. And like the case of Rosecrans versus Washington, the interchange of telegrams reached a climax with a peremptory order. On 6 December Grant telegraphed Thomas, "Attack Hood at once, and wait no longer for a remount of your cavalry. There is great danger of delay resulting in a campaign back to the Ohio River."[140] Thomas replied, like the good soldier he was, that he would attack Hood as ordered, but added that "I believe it will be hazardous with the small force of cavalry now at my service." Yet, even with Grant's order hanging over his head, Thomas' conscience was pressing him even more to deal with the obstacles at hand and postpone launching his offensive for at least three or four days, until 9 or 10 December.

In appreciating Thomas' situation, it is essential to realize that the pressure from his superiors was no less than that exerted by his own conscience. To understand his dilemma it would be helpful, indeed necessary, to gain an insight into the background of his character. George Henry Thomas was born and bred a Virginian every bit as much as Robert E. Lee and Stonewall Jackson, though later he was to decide that his loyalty to his state was overridden by a greater loyalty. He was born in 1816 and raised in southeastern Virginia, in the heart of slave country, where, at age fifteen, he and his family were caught up in Nat Turner's rebellion, and once with his widowed mother and two sisters he had to flee their home and hide in the woods until they were safe. He got his early education at Southampton Academy, and began serving his uncle as a law clerk. Thomas had no taste for the law, and when his uncle could get him an appointment to West Point, he jumped at the opportunity. He reported as a cadet in 1836, just shy of his twentieth birthday, and therefore about two years older than the average plebe. Compared to most of his classmates his appearance was that of a grown man, standing five feet, ten inches tall, muscular and well built, with a flair for good horsemanship. Fellow cadets saw him as a handsome fellow who, according to Cadet William Starke Rosecrans, "bore a remarkable resemblance to Stuart's portrait of Washington. Dignified, self-possessed, and steady in manner, Thomas became known to the cadets as 'Old Tom' and 'George Washington.' "[141] He shared a room with twenty-one-year-old Stewart Van Vliet and red-haired "Cump" Sherman. It turned out that Van Vliet and Thomas became model cadets, keeping themselves, their equipment, and their room in perfect regulation order, and garnering only the minimum of demerits. The nervous, jumpy Sherman was slipshod in dress and conduct, accumulating 109 demerits in his plebe year. In contrast, Van Vliet got only 10 and Thomas 22. After a year Sherman had had his fill of his two model roommates and moved to other quarters. Thomas went on to become a good though not outstanding student, graduating twelfth out of the forty-two members of the 1840 class, while Sherman ranked sixth. Among the other cadets Thomas knew during his four years were those with names like Grant, Rosecrans, Buell, and Hooker; others to become famous for other reasons bore names like Bragg, Bushrod Johnson, William J. Hardee, and Daniel H. Hill.

His first assignment after graduation was to the 3rd Artillery Regiment, then serving in Florida in the Second Seminole War. Among his messmates were Braxton Bragg and Cump Sherman. Like his comrades, Thomas saw little combat action and eventually began a series of assignments in the artillery that would last for the next fifteen years. Like Bragg and Sherman he saw service in the Mexican War under Zachary Taylor, starting out as a first lieutenant in Bragg's battery of the 3rd Artillery. He received two brevet promotions, mainly for gallantry, to captain at Monterrey, then to major for "gallant and meritorious service" under fire at Buena Vista. During that action, Thomas continued to direct the fire of an isolated section of Captain Bragg's battery, holding off repeated Mexican infantry attacks until, as Captain Sherman recalled, "I joined Lieutenant Thomas, who had been constantly engaged during the forenoon in the preservation of that important position, and whom I found closely engaged with the enemy, and too, in a very advanced position . . . Lieutenant Thomas more than sustained the reputation he has long enjoyed in his regiment as an accurate and scientific artillerist."[142] That part of the battle where Thomas was so "closely engaged" has been described as being so violent that among "the roar of musketry loud and continuous; it was impossible above the general clamor and din, to distinguish the report of any single gun. . . . The whole air vibrated with the rushing current of balls." After the many similarly dramatic histories of the artillery's part in the battle, Thomas' personal account stands out as starkly characteristic: "The Battle of Buena Vista was fought on the 22 Feb. '47 and I was under fire from 6 o.c. A.M. until 4 P.M."[143]

After the war his service included a three-year tour as an artillery and cavalry instructor at West Point from 1851 to 1854, during which he met and married Frances Kellogg, described by his fellow instructors as a "noble woman, good natured and congenial." During his honeymoon, the bridegroom received notice of his promotion to his regular rank of captain. A later assignment in 1855 was to the newly organized 2nd Cavalry, where Thomas was delighted to find himself not only among fellow horsemen, but also one of the regiment's new majors. His new colonel was Albert Sidney Johnston, the regiment's lieutenant colonel was Robert E. Lee, and among the lieutenants was one John B. Hood. The regiment's service in Texas was taken up with protecting settlers from Indian raids and generally keeping peace on the frontier. On one of his peacekeeping missions, Major Thomas led a detachment against a not so peaceful party of Indian warriors, and during the encounter the major took two Indian arrows, one in the chest and another on the chin, neither of which proved to be serious wounds.

Beginning in November 1860 Thomas was allowed twelve months' leave, most of which he spent with his wife in the east, until he had to make the most heart-wrenching decision of his life. Like Lee and Jackson, Thomas was faced with the choice of going with his native state of Virginia into the Confederacy or keeping his commission in the U.S. Army. Unlike his famous fellow Virginians, Thomas chose to honor the oath of allegiance he had taken when he had accepted his commission upon his graduation from West Point. He confirmed his decision by declining the offer of Governor Letcher to become the chief of ordnance of Virginia's newly forming state forces. This formal break with his state must have seemed a simple act compared to the agony that he had to endure when his family turned against him for his decision. It was considered the act of a traitor, and his sisters never spoke to him or otherwise communicated with him for the rest of their lives.

In spite of his personal troubles and the suspicion that hung over him when critics in the Union army referred to him as "that Virginian," Thomas rose rapidly in rank as the war progressed. He commanded a brigade in the Shenandoah during the first Bull Run campaign, being made a brigadier general of volunteers in August 1861. In November he assumed command of a division in the Army of the Ohio. In January 1862 he led a small force of 4,000 to attack a comparable force of Confederates and win the battle of Mill Springs, the "most severe setback suffered by the South up to that time." He then saw action at Shiloh under Buell, followed by his serving as Buell's second-in-command in the Perryville operations, which resulted in driving Bragg out of Kentucky. Having been promoted major general of volunteers in 1862, he protested serving under Rosecrans when the latter was appointed army commander to replace Buell, on the grounds that he was senior to Rosecrans. However, when the president antedated Rosecrans' commission to give him seniority, Thomas served him loyally, as we have seen, as commander of XIV Corps during the Chickamauga campaign. We witnessed him becoming a national hero on the second day of the battle, when he saved the Army of the Cumberland from disaster and earned the title "Rock of Chickamauga," which has distinguished him to this day. It will be recalled too that he replaced Rosecrans as army commander in the month following the battle. Upon receipt of Grant's directive that Chattanooga be held "at all hazards," Thomas' reply that "we will hold the town till we starve" was carried out almost literally, his army holding out against Bragg's siege until relieved in November 1863, after which Grant got ready to assume the offensive. Then in the battles at Chattanooga, Thomas' command played a major role in defeating Bragg's army when it was overrun on Lookout Mountain and Missionary Ridge.

Beginning in May 1864, Thomas' Army of the Cumberland, consisting of nine infantry and three cavalry divisions, fought under Sherman in his Atlanta campaign, taking an offensive role throughout all the major operations. It was Thomas' army that successfully beat back Hood's counterstroke at Peachtree Creek on 20 July. Later Thomas took the surrender of Atlanta and marched his troops into the city on 1 September. Then, as recounted, when Sherman had gotten Grant's assent for his march to the sea, it was Thomas who was made responsible for the safeguarding of Sherman's communications, a mission which included defeating Hood wherever he might take the offensive. Now, at Nashville, Thomas was being reminded of the irony of the position in which he had been placed by Sherman and Grant—ironic because neither of those two superiors had been there on the ground with him to appreciate the problems of assembling, equipping, and organizing a makeshift army of disparate elements into a force that could overnight destroy its enemy in one engagement. Yet, as one is assured from his background, the rocklike Thomas was the man for the job, despite all the pressure applied by Grant and the War Department. The summing up of his character by Thomas Robson Hay gives one an insight into the man who would, in his own way and time, move to attack his enemy:

Thomas was a man of reserved power, of poise and self-control; a somewhat cold and impassive man, usually little subject to human passions and infirmities. In spite of this make-up he was human in every sense of the word. He had ambition, but few men seem to be freer from its subtle influence. . . . A gentle voice and manner, quick high temper, unconquerable courage, inflexible will, delicate sensitiveness, and a commanding sense of duty, harmonized into a well-rounded character. He was a man of few words and was by no means a rapid thinker or a brilliant conversationalist, but his mind was always vigorous, alert, quick to perceive, to decide, to act. . . . He was a man of deep religious convictions and his wonderful hold upon the confidence and affection of his army was due to the fact that all realized that to him everyone was always a man and a soldier. . . . In spite of his apparent indifference to personal preference and advancement Thomas was human enough to write [before the battle of Nashville]: "This will be the only opportunity I shall have to distinguish myself and not to be able to avail myself of it is too bad."[144]

To Thomas' imminent peril, that opportunity was about to slip away. By 8 December Grant, exasperated by pressure from Stanton, was about to replace Thomas, as he indicated in a telegram to Halleck on that date: "If Thomas has not struck yet, he ought to be ordered to hand over the command to Schofield. There is no better man to repel an attack than Thomas, but I fear he is too cautious to ever take the initiative." Fortunately for Thomas, the order to relieve him was never sent; it was set aside in the press of events and the continued exchange of telegrams between all concerned. Then on 9 December an act of nature intervened, and Thomas telegraphed both Grant and Halleck, "A terrible storm of freezing rain has come on since daylight, which will render an attack impossible until it breaks." When Halleck received the message, he wired Grant informing him that it had been thought better to hold up the orders relieving Thomas—unless Grant wished them to be sent. Grant replied to the effect that the orders should be suspended "until it is seen whether he will do anything." On the following day Thomas was indeed starting to do something.

One of Thomas' well-known command methods was his practice of listening to the recommendations of his staff and commanders, then making his decisions in private and sticking to them once they had been announced. On 10 December, however, Thomas called a command conference at his quarters at the St. Cloud Hotel and reversed his usual procedure: instead of asking for his corps commanders' recommendations, he announced a decision, then asked for their opinions on it. In effect, he told them about Grant's peremptory order to attack and his decision "that obedience was impracticable" at the time due to the ice-covered ground. Each corps commander (see Figure 14.1) was then asked to give his views on the matter. His generals unanimously upheld his decision. "Then, after listening to all they had to say, he handed to each of them his Special Field Orders No. 342, outlining precisely what each of the bodies of troops were expected to do."[145]

Three days later there were clear signs that the ice had begun to melt, and orders were issued to unit commanders for their men to be equipped for action—haversacks filled with three days' rations, and each infantryman carrying sixty rounds of ammunition. At 3:00 P.M. on 14 December Thomas called a final command conference at his headquarters, where he went over his

Figure 14.1
Organization of Thomas' Army

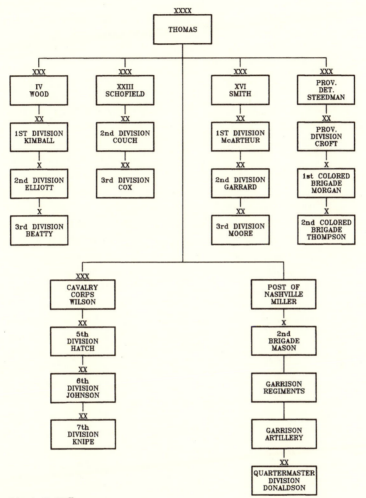

previously issued battle plan in detail. The attack was set for the next morning; reveille would be sounded for all troops at 4:00 A.M. The Rock of Chickamauga was about to become a missile that would shatter forever the last hopes of the Confederacy in the west.

CHAPTER 15

The Battle of Nashville

Hood's Army of Tennessee was ready for battle and it was not ready for battle. In one sense it was ready, not with the dash and spirit with which it had started its march from Florence, but with an urge for any kind of action after the weeks spent suffering behind the frozen breastworks in the pseudo-siege of Nashville. The poorly equipped Confederate soldiers had shivered for the past two weeks, exposed to cold rains, sleet, and snow; a great many were without blankets, warm clothing, and even shoes. "Thousands of Hood's men remained barefooted as the sleet and snow pelted down on their bare heads and froze their threadbare, ragged clothing."[146] Small wonder that the men were ready for any change that would take their minds off their present woes. In another sense, the Confederates were not ready for an attack in the pre-dawn hours of the morning of 15 December, when their sentries heard the strange echoes of Yankee bugles sounding reveille in the pitch-black darkness. The sentries, however, were more concerned with keeping their feet out of the clinging mud that had accumulated since the frozen ground had begun to thaw over the past two days.

TERRAIN AND WEATHER

When daylight broke, Thomas was already riding toward the spot he had selected for a command observation post, a high knoll in the salient in the entrenchments between the Hillsboro Pike on the west and the Granny White Turnpike to the east (see Map 15.1). He and his staff had to pick their way carefully through the dense fog that had covered the ground since daybreak. It was a chilly, late autumn day that would remain dry after the fog lifted, which would occur by midmorning. When the fog did clear, the army com-

Map 15.1

Courtesy Martin L. Wilkerson.

mander was able to take advantage of the panoramic view that his O.P. afforded. When he looked south toward his enemy's entrenchments, he could see, about a mile to his left (to the east), the valley of Brown's Creek and two miles to the southwest was another valley, that of Richland Creek. The two creeks originated within about a mile of each other in the Brentwood Hills, directly to the south at a distance of about four miles from the town of Nashville. Both creeks flowed into the Cumberland River on opposite sides of the town. The ground was mostly hilly farmland broken by numerous ridges and knolls which tended to rise from 200 to 300 feet above the level of the river. In general, the terrain was open, affording room for maneuver and good fields of fire except for scattered stands of timber. As would be expected in late autumn, the fields were bare, but the ground surface had turned muddy due to the thawing from the ice storm.

Thomas could also observe much of the five-mile-long series of breastworks that made up the Confederate line, starting from the Nashville and Chattanooga Railroad on the east, extending westward in a long, concave curve all the way to the Hillsboro Pike. At that point the line made a sharp right-angle turn to the south, forming a salient with its west side running along the pike, taking advantage of the stone wall alongside the road. On the opposite side of the pike Hood had erected a series of three detached redoubts, supplemented by two more on hilltops, also west of the pike. He had also outposted the front of his line with covering elements extending from the Hillsboro Pike eastward along the crest of Montgomery Hill, then angling back to connect with the center of his main line.

THOMAS' PLAN AND THE LAUNCHING OF HIS ATTACK

Thomas' plan and its execution were once referred to as a "rather old-fashioned battle." If that were true, Nashville could be so categorized along with Cannae and Leuthen—simple but remarkable. Thomas' concept of the operation was to make a secondary, feinting attack against Hood's right while the main and heavily weighted attack would make an envelopment of the Confederate left with the dual purpose of rolling back and destroying Hood's forces while cutting his army's communications to the south. To accomplish this, the main attack was made by two corps, Smith's XVI Corps on the right and Wood's IV Corps on Smith's left. Initially, Smith was assisted on his right by Hatch's cavalry division from Wilson's cavalry corps. Hatch's mission was not the simple cavalry role of covering Smith's (and the army's) right flank. His troopers fought dismounted, using their seven-shot repeating rifles, thus adding a tremendous dimension of firepower to the attack. Steedman's provisional detachment (actually amounting to an army corps with the equivalent of two divisions) made the secondary attack. Schofield's XXIII Corps was initially in general reserve, with the mission of following the main attack, being prepared for commitment to the attack on order. Wilson's cavalry corps (minus

Hatch's division) was prepared initially to support the main attack while detaching one division to protect the army's right and rear in the direction of the Charlotte Pike, this division also being prepared to support the main attack on order. When Smith's XVI Corps and Wood's IV Corps had left their entrenchments to move to the attack, General Donaldson's force of quartermaster troops and armed civilians would move in and occupy the entrenchments.

By first light, around 6:00 A.M., all of Thomas' attacking forces were on the move, though their movements were slowed considerably by the dense fog and muddy ground. Despite the obstacles of ground and weather, Steedman was able to launch his attack by 8:00 A.M. and managed to keep Cheatham's Confederate corps fully occupied for the next several hours. In the meantime, Wood and Smith had advanced their corps, making a gigantic wheel pivoting on Wood's IV Corps in order to bring Smith's XVI Corps parallel to and advancing on the Confederate left along the Hillsboro Pike. While Smith was completing his maneuver, Beatty's division of Wood's corps assaulted and carried the Confederate positions on Montgomery Hill. By noon, Smith's XVI Corps, powerfully assisted by Hatch's division, had stormed and overrun the redoubts west of the Hillsboro Pike and had advanced to the pike itself.

At about 1:00 P.M. Thomas, seeing that the battle had reached a critical phase, issued three sets of orders: Wood to continue his attack beyond Montgomery Hill and break through the salient in Hood's line held by Stewart's corps; Schofield to come into action on Smith's right to continue the main attack in that area; Wilson to commit the rest of his cavalry corps, and, along with Hatch's division, to shift southward and get around the enemy left to seal off the Granny White Turnpike. By 1:30 P.M. Stewart's corps, which had held the left of the Confederate line, was being battered by the repeated assaults of the combined combat power of Wood, Smith, Schofield, and Wilson. Finally, after Smith's troops had carried the stone wall that had made up the Confederate defenses along the Hillsboro Pike and Wood's attacking units had broken through the salient to their front, the Confederate left began to collapse. By late afternoon the broken elements of Stewart's corps were streaming to the southeast toward the Granny White Turnpike, and before nightfall Hood's forces had been driven back a full two miles south of their entrenchments. Although almost routed, Hood's shattered forces were saved by approaching nightfall. Thomas' forces—elated by success but frustrated by disorganized and intermixed attacking units in the falling darkness—had to hold up their attack until they could get reorganized to continue the attack the next morning.

HOOD'S REACTIONS TO THOMAS' ATTACKS

Of all the problems that beset Hood on the first day of battle one of his greatest was caused by a miscalculation of his own. Nine days before he was attacked by Thomas, he had detached a force of 6,500 under Forrest to take

Murfreesboro, twenty-five miles to the east of Nashville. The reasoning behind Hood's action is still indeterminate; in his official report he says only that

I had sent Major-General Forrest, with the greatest part of his cavalry and Bate's division of infantry, to Murfreesboro, to ascertain if it was possible to take the place. After a careful examination and a reconnaissance in force. . . . it was determined that nothing could be accomplished by assault, Bate's division was then withdrawn [back to Nashville], *leaving Forrest with Jackson's and Buford's divisions of cavalry in observation* [italics added].[147]

That last phrase has been emphasized because it shows clearly that Hood, by sending Forrest so far away, had, as the military cliché goes, deprived himself of his eyes. Although Chalmers' division of Forrest's cavalry corps had remained under Hood's direct command, the sad fact was that the invaluable Forrest was not present in person with his corps to direct and coordinate the intelligence effort of the army before Nashville. One of the immediate consequences of Forrest's absence was that in the early morning hours of 15 December, Chalmers found himself being overwhelmed by Wilson's cavalry corps as it maneuvered to cover the Union infantry forces while they advanced in their great wheeling movement to attack the Confederate left. Even more important than Chalmers' inability to cope with Wilson was the lack of early warning that should have alerted Hood to all the masses of enemy forces maneuvering to threaten his left, even allowing for the fact that the early morning fog had obscured much of the Union movements.

Another factor that added to Hood's problems was that Steedman's secondary attack—Thomas' feint—did succeed in deceiving him into thinking that it was actually the Union main attack. Thus, Thomas had succeeded in attaining a degree of tactical surprise; that is, his feint had struck his enemy at an unexpected time and place, causing Hood to react too late to counter effectively the real main attack. Due to Steedman's efforts, Cheatham's corps on the Confederate right was fully occupied until noon in repulsing a series of Union assaults. This development—plus the lack of early warning, the morning fog, and the delays that held up the initial Union movements—kept Hood's attention fixed on his right. The distraction resulted in a fatal tactical assessment: Hood was delayed in detaching urgently needed forces from Cheatham to reinforce Stewart's corps at a crisis in his defense against Thomas' main attack.

A contributing factor to Hood's delayed reactions was his being out of touch with his corps commanders during the critical phases of the battle. He had located his command post at a farmhouse, at least four miles from the salient in Stewart's line, the same distance from Cheatham on the right, and a good six miles from Chalmers' cavalry command covering the left. These distances in combination with the factors already mentioned were bound to thwart

Hood's personal contact with his commanders at the times when most needed by both.

When Hood was able to exercise personal control of his forces at the center of events, it was too late to do anything but reorganize them to continue the action on the morrow. For Hood, the hard-charging fighter, any other course of action at this stage was unthinkable. He had gone through the last stages of his campaign with no other purpose than to bring Thomas to battle, to force his enemy to leave his Nashville defenses and attack him. Thomas had done just that, and the consequences were anything but what Hood had planned. To Hood's mind, half a battle had been fought, and now there was nothing left to do but get every last veteran of the Army of Tennessee into the line of battle and ready to recoup what had been lost—and turn an unfortunate series of events into a victory that would at least allow a change of campaign objectives.

Accordingly, he was directing his energies to making new deployments—and throwing up hasty fieldworks—for the coming day. He moved Cheatham's relatively intact corps to replace Stewart's on the left of his new and shortened line, about two miles south of his original defenses (see Map 15.2). To make place for Cheatham and to take some of the pressure off Stewart's battered divisions, Hood shifted that corps to the center, then deployed S. D. Lee's corps to the right of the new line. Both flanks were refused, (i.e., turned back) in order to contend with any enemy attempt to make a new envelopment. Chalmers' cavalry was deployed to screen the army's left rear.

THE SECOND DAY: UNION ATTACKS OVERWHELM CONFEDERATE RESISTANCE

By the night of 15–16 December, Thomas believed that his troops would be able to finish the job of crushing Hood's forces the next morning. That was to prove an overly optimistic assessment. The muddy ground and the necessity to ready all forces to launch them into a renewed attack were to put a brake on Thomas' plans for much of the morning of the 16th. Moreover, the muddy ground slowed the movement of horse-drawn artillery to the firing positions from which it was to fire the preparation for the renewed attacks. And, as events were to prove, Thomas' artillery was to play a central role in the battle of the 16th.

Thomas had rightly concluded it unnecessary to change his basic concept of the operation, to maintain the main attack to envelop the enemy left while throwing the remainder of his combat power in converging attacks against his right and center. Moreover, he was well aware that Hood's original line of five miles of entrenchments had now shrunk to three miles of a thrown-together defensive line that could be broken at weak places. Accordingly, when viewed from east to west, Thomas' five major commands would continue their attacks: Steedman and Wood against the enemy right, Smith against its

Map 15.2

Courtesy Martin L. Wilkerson.

center, Schofield against the Confederate left, and Wilson's cavalry to drive off the enemy cavalry and cut off the last available Confederate route of withdrawal, the Franklin Pike.

By 9:00 A.M. the Union artillery had commenced firing its preparation, which was to continue throughout the next two hours. Its heaviest fire was directed against the curve of the Confederate line on its left and in a lesser degree against the enemy right on and around Peach Orchard Hill. Beginning at 10:00 A.M. Steedman's leading brigades were launched against the enemy right. This series of secondary attacks was repulsed, mainly by Clayton's division of Lee's corps. By early afternoon, Wood's corps had joined in the attack against Lee's corps, but his attacks also failed to drive the Confederate right from its improvised entrenchments. On the Confederate left, however, the strength of Thomas' main attack—now being made by Smith's XVI Corps from the north and Schofield's XXIII Corps from the west—was converging on the curving salient held by Cheatham's corps. The initial phase of that massive attack was preceded by an artillery preparation that reached the climax of its effectiveness when the Union batteries opposite Stewart's Confederates were able to wedge themselves into firing positions from which they could almost enfilade Cheatham's corps from the east. By 3:30 P.M. they had so neutralized the firepower of Cheatham's defending infantry that it could no longer withstand the massed force of the assaulting waves of Union infantry, which then broke through and overran the regiments defending the salient forming the bulwark of the Confederate left. Cheatham's corps, attacked from front and flank, was shattered into fragments that broke and fled to the rear. While Smith's and Schofield's forces were being launched into their attacks against Hood's left, Wilson had dismounted the greater part of his cavalry corps and sent its horses to the rear—too far to the rear, as it turned out—while his troopers attacked their enemy with the firepower of their repeating rifles. After 4:00 P.M. the remnants of both Cheatham's and Stewart's corps were pouring rearward, and only Lee had managed to hold together the divisions of his corps and make a somewhat orderly withdrawal while saving the rest of Hood's army from complete dissolution. Thomas Lawrence Connelly in his history of the Army of Tennessee has described Lee's actions: "Only Lee's corps retained any organization. Stunned to see the army evaporating before his eyes, Lee skillfully pulled back his troops to the Overton Hills. While a young drummer beat the long roll, Lee held firm until his entire corps could be put in retreat. Still the end had come so swiftly that sixteen of Lee's guns had been captured before the artillery horses could be brought up from the rear."[148] Nevertheless, before nightfall the battle of Nashville was over and Hood's Army of Tennessee had suffered the worst defeat in its history.

AFTERMATH

In spite of the magnitude of the disaster, Hood managed to salvage what remained of his army. It was saved mainly by nightfall and the difficulties that

Wilson failed to overcome in reassembling his cavalry corps into a compact force that might have made possible an overpowering Napoleonic cavalry pursuit that would have destroyed the enemy when his demoralized forces were most vulnerable. It could be said, in defense of Wilson's failure, that three things combined to thwart his capability to organize an immediate pursuit. First, in deploying his dismounted units to maximize their firepower, they were so dispersed that a great deal of time had to be sacrificed in reassembling them. Second, precious time was lost in bringing up the troopers' horses, which had been held in areas much too far to the rear. Third, both of the foregoing difficulties were multiplied by the early coming of the late autumn darkness, which was accompanied by a heavy rain. On the following morning, 17 December, Wilson did take up the pursuit, but was slowed by the mud and the rearguard actions of the remains of Chalmers' cavalry supported by infantry elements. Thomas also sent Wood to follow and support Wilson, yet those combined forces were further checked by the arrival of Forrest and his cavalry when he joined Hood at Columbia on the 18th. With Forrest covering his retreat for the next week, Hood managed to get the remainder of his broken forces to the Tennessee River, where they made the saddest of crossings on Christmas Day. The Union pursuit ended effectively at the banks of the Tennessee.

The remnants of Hood's army reached Tupelo, Mississippi, on 10 January, and on the 14th Beauregard arrived to "learn the stunning truth. Hood had only about fifteen thousand infantrymen remaining with the army. Of these, fewer than half were still equipped or considered effective. A large part of the army's artillery had been captured, abandoned, or destroyed. Some thirteen thousand small arms were missing, and wagon transportation had been annihilated on the long march."[149] Beauregard also found that, for the few thousand "effectives" left, there was no food, still no winter clothing, and only a few blankets. But by far the most demoralizing fact of all for the Confederate cause in the west was that the Army of Tennessee no longer existed as a fighting force. And its commander, the greatest fighter of them all, realized that he too was no longer an effective fighting force. On 13 January, the day before Beauregard's arrival, Hood had written to his president requesting that he be relieved from command. Jefferson Davis accepted the request.

CHAPTER 16

Why Thomas Won More than a Victory

Of all the effects of the art of command on the Tennessee campaign none could have had more impact than Hood's interpretation of the strategic mission that he had proposed to Jefferson Davis and which Davis had accepted— subject to a mutual understanding. In the discussion that took place between the two at Palmetto, Georgia, on 25 September, Davis had approved Hood's proposals and added the condition that Hood, if threatened by Sherman's turning back to drive Hood off his communications, would withdraw into northern Alabama and continue to threaten those communications. Even more important, an extension of Davis' condition was the understanding between the two that *whatever happened, Hood was to follow Sherman wherever he went, north or south.*

Yet it became evident, at a critical turn in his strategical sparring with Sherman, that Hood chose to put a different interpretation on his mission; in the jargon of modern-day journalists, he put his own spin on it. In so doing, he won the reluctant approval of Beauregard, his theater commander, for his invasion of Tennessee. Hood's new interpretation—as revealed by Beauregard's dismay when Hood first disclosed it to him—was no less than an abandonment of the mission of following Sherman (while cutting his communications) in exchange for approval to turn his back on Sherman and venture into Tennessee with a new objective of defeating Thomas' "scattered forces." Moreover, the extended objective of invading Kentucky and threatening Ohio—and if overpowered there by the forces of Sherman and Thomas—to march to join Lee in Virginia, was not simply an alternative course of action. It was in reality an operational and logistical fantasy that depended on the tacit cooperation of Union strategists who would permit their enemy to range at will across border states, while he depended upon undisturbed communications that were hard enough to sustain in his own territory.

The effects of the revised mission became increasingly manifest as Hood moved northward after he had crossed the Tennessee River. At first he attained a degree of strategic surprise as his forces moved rapidly under conditions of weather and terrain that his enemies thought too adverse for mobile warfare. He was able to exploit his new strategy to outmaneuver his enemies, but failed at Columbia and again at Spring Hill to entrap Schofield's force, in part due to the inadequacy of his command supervision of operations and his flawed relationships with his major force commanders. Then, apparently obsessed with an urgency to attain his strategic aims and disgusted with the performance of several commanders, he threw away a great part of his operational capability in the battle of Franklin when he persisted in squandering the combat power of his army by a series of frontal attacks that wasted thousands of brave men—bloody repulses that were bound to fail in the face of defensive firepower that could doom even the efforts of the most gallant of attackers. In spite of Franklin he seems to have lost none of his offensive spirit, which drove him to confront Thomas at Nashville, where he entrenched his forces—reduced, by his own accounting, from 32,000 to 23,000 effectives—in a siege that persisted in name only. In the meantime Thomas was using valuable time to build up and prepare his forces to take the offensive. During the "siege" Hood's command intellect seems to have been submerged in a sort of dream world where reality gave way to the *idée fixe* that once Thomas emerged from his field fortifications, he could be defeated and his base captured.

In contrast to Hood's interpretation of his mission, Thomas seems to have been so firmly grounded in the meaning of his that he often appeared at odds with his superiors in executing it. His adherence to the letter of his mission might have appeared to superiors like Grant or Sherman as sluggishness or obstinacy. In reality, his methodical procedures were only the outward signs of his determination to carry out his mission as he saw it—and it was characteristic of him that he never undertook an assignment until he was sure that he could see it through. This seeming conflict between substance and appearance was never more evident than in Thomas' situation at Nashville when, for two weeks, he was subjected to a constant, telegraphed needling from an impatient Grant whose patience wore thinner by the day. To provide balance to the picture, the record shows that Grant perceived Thomas as an indomitable commander in the defense but one who couldn't be counted on to take the offensive on his own initiative. That Grant was wrong in his presumption regarding Thomas' offensive spirit was clearly shown by Thomas' planning and execution of a battle that was won entirely by a series of hard-pushed attacks. Yet Grant's anxiety to get things moving at Nashville is understandable when viewed from the perspective of a national strategy that placed an overriding importance on getting the western theater cleared of any obstacles which could hinder Sherman's ending the war in the Deep South. Hence Grant's tendency to minimize Thomas' logistical and organizational problems, while the man on the ground doggedly persisted in completing the preparations that would in his mind assure staking everything on one final battle. Those differences were rendered meaningless by Thomas' victory and its elimination of any further threat to Union strategic aims in the west.

After each commander had evaluated his mission it followed that the next step in conceiving operational plans would depend upon his evaluation of his enemy's capabilities to oppose those plans. In Hood's case it is evident that his strategic intelligence estimate of Thomas' disposition of forces was flawed even before he started his army across the Tennessee River. One of his basic assumptions in the revised strategy he had proposed to Beauregard in order to gain his approval of an advance into Tennessee was that he could defeat Thomas' "scattered forces" before his enemy could concentrate a superiority of force against him. As it turned out, instead of scattered forces Hood was opposed by Schofield's two corps, which actually amounted to an army with a strength of some 32,000. And Schofield's force, as it proved, was fully capable of conducting a series of delaying actions against the Army of Tennessee's 38,000 until the entire Union force withdrew into the Nashville entrenchments. There is no need to dwell on the far-reaching effects of that flawed element in Hood's strategy; what happened to his army at Nashville and the aftermath speak for themselves. There was, however, also a breakdown in Hood's combat intelligence capability that contributed to his failure to react effectively to Thomas' attacks. His error in dispatching Forrest to Murfreesboro and the consequences of Forrest's absence could be seen in the crippling effects on Hood's lack of intelligence of his enemy's impending attacks. Moreover, the other results can only be imagined in the possible effects that Forrest and his cavalry corps might have had in upsetting the role of Wilson's cavalry in Thomas' main attack against Hood's left flank at Nashville.

As for Thomas' intelligence estimates, he suffered more from an inadequacy of the collection of intelligence than from his evaluation of it. There is ample evidence to show that, as an old cavalry officer, he was acutely aware of the weakness of his cavalry arm, both in its quality and quantity when compared to its counterpart; hence he was equally aware of the resulting weaknesses in the intelligence that was provided him. That awareness was clearly demonstrated in his telegram to Grant on 1 December, when he expressed his anxiety for the time needed to get Wilson's cavalry equipped (read horses, forage, and accoutrements) because the strength of his command was only one-fourth of that of his enemy. But Thomas' inadequacy in the collection of intelligence shouldn't excuse his inclination to exercise that shortcoming so common among many Union commanders—overestimating the enemy's strength at critical times during an operation. Overestimating, in such cases, meaning not "safesiding," but unrealistic exaggerations. For example, following the arrival of Hood's forces before Nashville Thomas estimated their strength at over 50,000 despite the facts that the Army of Tennessee could not have mustered those numbers at the start of the campaign and it had suffered severe losses in its disastrous attacks at Franklin. Yet, as we have seen, Hood at Nashville was bemoaning the fact that his army's strength had fallen to less than half that number. Fortunately for Thomas his planning for battle was not adversely affected by his overestimate of his enemy's numbers, *and* perhaps he was doubly fortunate in knowing his enemy's dispositions, since they were tied to field fortifications.

Once each of the two commanders had evaluated the intelligence available to him he had to realize his objectives before he could conceive an operational plan. Martin Van Creveld in his penetrating study of command has made an insightful observation in this regard: "The objectives selected must be both desirable and feasible, two requirements that are not always compatible. The alternative ways of action presented to the commander and his staff, should be real, not just subterfuges presented as a matter of form. (As Moltke remarked to his aides, the enemy always seemed to have three alternatives open to him and he usually chose the fourth.)."[150] Since history has borne out the soundness of Van Creveld's observations, our evidence indicates that Hood could have profited from observing the two requirements for objectives when he was planning his campaign. The evidence shows, however, that he chose to select two campaign objectives that appeared highly desirable but which proved to be anything but feasible. The discussion of Hood's mission in the opening of this chapter has already pointed out the infeasibility of both. First, instead of defeating Thomas' supposedly scattered forces in detail, Hood was confronted from the start by Schofield's concentrated corps, which fought successful delaying actions all the way to Nashville. Second, extending the campaign into Kentucky—based on the assumption that Thomas' forces could be defeated and eliminated as obstacles—would have become, even under the assumed conditions, an operational and logistical nightmare. Regrettably for Hood, an unsound selection of objectives did not end with the above choices. When he entrenched his army to confront Thomas at Nashville, Hood was counting on Thomas to attack him in his entrenchments; and he believed that during the ensuing battle he would defeat the Union army and capture Nashville. Even if a historian could set aside, for the moment, the record of the Confederate disaster, it would still be clear that Hood had decided on an infeasible objective. How could an army of some 23,000, suffering under wintry, icy rains without winter clothing, defeat an enemy of more than twice its numbers—a warmly clothed and well-fed enemy secure behind prepared fortifications and whose numbers were being reinforced almost day by day? How could Hood himself propose to defeat an enemy who could employ his superior strength to strike at will on the Confederate front or flanks? These were questions that Hood could have asked before he entrenched and awaited Thomas' attack. Instead he let his ambition overcome his reason when he decided, in his words, that it was "more judicious that the men face a decisive issue rather than retreat . . . without having made a last and manful effort to lift up the sinking fortunes of the Confederacy." These were more like the words of a King Arthur on the eve of his last battle than those of a general planning the commitment of a nineteenth-century army to a critical phase of a campaign.

The objectives that Thomas decided on when he conceived his campaign to deal with Hood were practicable as well as logically set in terms of time. He chose to provide Schofield with a two-corps force of 32,000 to delay Hood's northward advance while he, Thomas, organized his mixed bag of Nashville garrison and incoming reinforcements into a cohesive force that could build field fortifications while they were being organized for combat. Those two interdependent objectives, when set as goals within the same time frame, could buy Thomas the time he so urgently needed—time wherein he could realize a third and final objective: to organize a powerful striking force that he could employ to maneuver against and defeat Hood's army in its defensive positions. As events have shown, the three main objectives were not only attainable but further formed the bases for plans that worked when put into execution.

A final consideration that follows from Thomas' decisions regarding objectives could well be the most important of all to our interest, centered as it is on the maturation of a Civil War commander's art of command. In this case the focus is on Thomas' planning and conduct of the battle itself. His planning is noteworthy not only for its thoroughness but for the fact that he continued to bring his major force commanders in on the planning stages, both to heed their questions and ideas and to ensure their complete understanding of the operational plan and thus their full cooperation in its execution. Yet even the significance of these important factors fades when another conclusion emerges from the execution of Thomas' battle plan: Nashville was the only Civil War battle which assumed and foreshadowed the character of a battle of the First World War, over a half century later. Attacking units moved into attack positions under cover of darkness and fog. An artillery preparation preceded the launching of both main and secondary attacks. At prearranged times, waves of assaulting infantry left their trenches to slog their way through mud to throw themselves against defending infantrymen in their trenches. Massed units of the main attack succeeded in making a breakthrough through a critical point in an enemy salient. The breakthrough was quickly exploited by attacking units from a corps which had been held in reserve. The army commander remained in control of events throughout the two days of the battle, receiving timely reports from major force commanders, making decisions and issuing appropriate orders when the situation warranted.

It may be argued that the foregoing picture lacks the hardware that characterized the First World War battlefield—the magazine rifle, machine gun, indirect-firing artillery, electronic communications—but that is simply a part of the rationale of the theorists who contend that the materiel of the American Civil War was the determinant of the "modern battlefield." The essential meaning of Nashville remains—it was the *thought* behind Thomas' art of command that determined the form and meaning of the battle. Yet even setting aside the nature of the battlefield, there remains a far more important feature of the battle that resulted from Thomas' forethought. Two scholars and military historians have jointly reached a conclusion in this regard: "Thomas came close to fighting the battle of annihilation which had for so long existed in the minds of the public, politicians, and journalists."[151] That Thomas only "came close" was due, as we have seen, to the fact that his cavalry could not be reorganized in time to deliver a Napoleonic *coup de grace* at the critical time when most of Hood's army was shattered and in full flight. The fact remains, however, that Nashville was the only Civil War battle where the objective of annihilation was made possible by the victor's deliberate intent being carried through to its end.

PART FIVE

REFLECTIONS

Generalship in war would be the easiest of arts to practice—if only
the general could get his opponents to cooperate.

—W. J. Wood

Chapter 17

Reflections

The story goes that when Alexander the Great had subjugated the Greek states to Macedonian rule he took time to walk the streets of Athens and see at first hand the center of Greek culture and resistance to the conqueror. In his tour he came upon the philosopher Diogenes, sunning himself as he sat on the ground outside the barrel that formed his only abode. As he towered over the seated philosopher, Alexander asked Diogenes if there was anything he could do for him. Diogenes replied, "You can take your shadow out of my sun." Alexander stood aside.

The goal of this writing has been to keep the art of command exposed to the sunlight of common sense while taking it out of the shadow of what Clausewitz called "the very opposite of practice, and not infrequently the laughing stock of men whose military competence is beyond dispute." What he was referring to was a display of erudition and an accompanying misuse of historical examples by critics who purported to analyze military leaders and campaigns, critics who had neither a background of experience nor a foundation of practical knowledge. What Clausewitz disdained most about such analysts was that they failed to measure up to his standards of critical analysis: "The influence of critical truths on practical life is always exerted more through critical analysis than through doctrine. . . . [and critical analysis should include] the tracing of effects back to their causes. This is *critical analysis proper*."[152]

What this exploration of a military art has sought to do throughout has not been to lead up to Clausewitz as the be-all and end-all of its aims, rather it has tried to show that each observed commander did not—could not—rely on military doctrine to create and develop his own individual methods of command. During our explorations each commander was observed as he planned and carried out a campaign and fought its climactic battle—observed always from the viewpoint of the commander *as he saw things at the time*. In this way it was hoped that the observer could see practical experience forming the skills that developed into an art. Further steps allowed the explorer–observer to witness opposing commanders confronting each other on the battlefield, where each sought to defeat his opponent by controlling the course of events. Finally, the observations concluded with a critical review of the actions of the opposing commanders after they had put their art into practice.

In addition it may be recalled that (near the end of Chapter 4) methods of command were referred to as comprising a "highly personalized art." While that description aptly fits our purpose, another useful way of putting it would be to say that the sum total of a commander's methods amounted to his style of command. Taken in review, there can be little doubt that each of the observed commanders developed his own style of command.

Stonewall Jackson's style was as undeniably idiosyncratic as the *image* of the man that has become so crystallized in the popular mind. Historians, particularly military historians, have carried the characterization a step further by projecting the picture of a military genius who made brilliant plans which he refused to reveal to subordinates who had to put them into execution. Unfortunately for the purposes of this work, the enigma has become so firmly rooted that nothing can be gained from trying to analyze its substance. What can be done, however, is to recognize two salient points. In the first place, it is apparent that Jackson's chief reason for his secretiveness was to gain that most important of all tactical advantages—surprise. To his mind, keeping his plans wholly to himself meant keeping them secure from friend as well as foe. Secondly, and an unfortunate consequence, was that the withholding of his concepts and plans from his subordinates had harmful effects on his command relationships. Picture, if you will, the frustration of one of Jackson's division or brigade commanders, a dedicated officer who was expected to continue to demonstrate aggressiveness in leading his command in an offensive operation while left in ignorance of the objective of his mission—if indeed he knew the substance of the mission. Historians have commented on the number of Jackson's senior commanders facing court-martial charges while in the midst of a campaign. What should really be a cause of wonder is that those leaders continued to serve competently while under such duress. Actually, almost all of them performed superbly in carrying out their chief's—to their minds—shadowy plans.

To give balance to the picture of Jackson as a force commander, however, it would be unfair in the extreme to overlook the brilliance of his personal leadership in action. And it was in action that his charismatic influence was most felt by the soldiers and junior officers who did the fighting. Once his forces were committed to battle, Jackson never failed to make his presence known on the field, whether seen giving an order to a brigade or regimental commander to advance to the attack, personally rallying battle-shattered regiments—as shown so clearly at Cedar Mountain—or simply riding in front of regimental lines before they were committed to action. In every case he was invariably greeted by resounding cheers from the ranks. But what is so remarkable about Jackson's command performance was that the charisma of his personal leadership was complemented by his insight and vision in the fields of both strategy and tactics. He not only could grasp the meaning of the overall strategic situation, but saw clearly the part his mission would play in the conduct of a campaign. His strategic vision did not end with his forming a concept of operation; it was automatically transformed into aggressive action whose aim was the commitment of his forces to battle once he had his enemy "dancing to his own tune" and brought to bay on Jackson's terms.

Nathaniel Banks, on the other hand, presents an enigma of a different kind. Here one sees a prominent and powerful politician transformed overnight into a major general (the highest rank in the Union army at the time) who was expected to lead thousands of men into battle. Banks was not simply a fish out of water, he was a fish that was supposed to survive and flourish in its new environment. If one feels wonder at Lincoln's appointment of political figures to high military positions—desperately grasping at straws in the throes of a national crisis?—there must be cause for more wonder when one tries to picture Banks trying to adapt to a role that was as foreign to him as would have been his leading Jules Verne's expedition to the center of the earth. It seems that the enigma that Banks presented to his inner military world, his staff and senior commanders, was largely of his own making. A man driven by ambition who had reached for and attained the highest political offices in the land was not about to appear anything less than a winner in his new role. The key words in his struggle to adapt were "appear" and "role." This new office was a role that had to be played out—as essential to success as the public role he had played so often—and appearance was as essential to the role as was proper dress in a proper world. And appearance came as naturally to him as breathing; his features verged on the handsome, his carriage was erect and poised, and his voice was as strong as it was resonant.

That was the outward shell of the enigma. The inner part was where his difficulty lay. He was keenly aware of his lack of military experience and education, and though he worked manfully at the manuals, like most of the amateur officers of the time, he would always remain inwardly aware of his lack of a solid pedestal for the statue he showed to the world. It was this sense of professional inadequacy that must have gnawed at him as he strove to formulate plans, make decisions, and issue orders, once he had to take the field and assume command of forces as large as an army corps. It was, moreover, that same inner sense that prompted him in tight situations to take chances when he might have been more cautious, and to assume a boldness that seemed to arise from a moral courage that he did not really possess, the moral courage that should be an inherent part of the makeup of a commander confident of his skills. It is probable that it was this inner prompting at Cedar Mountain that led him to cross that thin line that separates boldness from rashness. Yet though he lacked the basic qualities that make a successful commander—successful in terms of winning battles—Banks showed qualities that would have been redeeming had he not been shoved into operational commands where he was obviously out of his element. He had undoubted physical courage which he demonstrated on numerous occasions, and he showed coolness under fire, which did him credit on the battlefield. He might have proved a capable leader at the regimental or brigade level, but he was clearly unqualified for higher-level command, where a mastery of strategy and tactics was essential. It was evident that taking care of his men held a high priority in his exercise of command, and he displayed management skills that marked him as a competent administrator and logistician. Had he been appointed quartermaster general of the army or placed in charge of providing, say, transportation for the forces in the field, in all probability he would have done an outstanding job. Instead he found himself cast in a role where eventually, as demonstrated by his disastrous Red River campaign in 1864, he was relieved of high-level command in the field.

William Starke Rosecrans was no enigma to his staff and senior commanders. He was, if anything, recognized as a leader who always had the time to take them into his confidence when forming an operation plan or in reviewing the orders that would put a plan into execution. He was not only known as a brilliant operational planner but was equally perceived as a commander who had logistical details at his fingertips and who would follow up to see that the required supplies were made available when and where needed and that troop movements were made according to plan. In addition, not only was he skilled at analyzing strategical and tactical situations and formulating plans to carry out his conclusions, his staff and commanders knew it was certain that Rosecrans would personally supervise matters to see that his orders were being carried out. He wanted his every order, whether in camp or on campaign, clearly understood and executed accordingly, or woe betide the officer who failed—and on whose unhappy head the army commander's wrath would fall.

On another side of the picture, the record is clear that Rosecrans was a leader who possessed both physical and moral courage. He showed the former throughout the course of battles like Iuka, Corinth, and Stones River, where his presence on the battlefield could turn setbacks into victories. It was his moral courage—and not obstinacy—that allowed him to resist the heavy, continued pressures from Washington when he was trying to complete his preparations for both the Tullahoma and Chickamauga phases of his last campaign.

Finally, no command portrait would be complete if it lacked recognition of the two aspects of Rosecrans' character that influenced his effectiveness as an army commander. First, there is the continuing evidence that he was a product of West Point whom the faculty and staff could point to with pride. His engineer's mind—honed to a razor's edge by instruction and the growth of that part of his intellect—enabled him to analyze and solve operational and logistical problems at the highest level. Moreover, that keenness of intellect led to a grasp of strategy (developed mainly through his own studies and efforts) that was unsurpassed by any other Union army commander. Second, and in spite of his brilliance as a strategist and all the accompanying attributes that made up his art, there remained character flaws that contributed to his downfall at Chickamauga. His uncontrolled temper, which prompted his dressing-down a division commander in front of his staff—engendering a smoldering resentment that led to the misconstruing of a key order—was one failing. Of greater import, however, was his loss of nerve at the most critical turn of the battle, when he was so shaken by the ruin of the right wing of his army that he left the field, sending his chief of staff—instead of going in person—to ascertain what was happening to the remainder of his army. Though there were undoubtedly psychological factors that shaped such a decision in Rosecrans' mind, this writer is not qualified to analyze their nature or their causes. What we do know is that the decision was made, a command lost, and a career ruined.

Braxton Bragg's methods of command could, at times, be as puzzling as the personality of the man behind them. Here was a professional soldier who had spent his youth and his adult life in the company of his military and social peers, in the army and on the "outside," but who simply didn't get along with people. While it was true that he could be amiable, even charming, with a few close friends, he held everyone else to a strict set of standards that he seems to have erected all on his own. The standards were an integral part of the nature of this complicated man whose character continues to baffle historians who have had to deal with its effects on the history of the war. Following his graduation from West Point his early military career was marked with run-ins with fellow officers and superiors, especially the latter, who failed to measure up to Bragg's ideals. These standards included the maintenance of discipline, which remained a priority for Bragg throughout his later career; he was one of the few Southern commanders who could establish and maintain discipline in large forces, even though he may have stirred up animosity in the ranks in so doing. In his prewar career, however, his rigid set of ideals and his sometimes peculiar enforcement of them were usually overlooked by his messmates, who only half understood them or wrote them off as simply Bragg's way of doing things. He was respected for his professional capabilities, and few were surprised when he became a national hero (however briefly) for his conduct at Buena Vista and brevet promotions during the Mexican War. But in his career as an army commander, our principal concern, his command effectiveness was marred by both physical and professional shortcomings. In the former, an analysis by a historian has concluded that "Bragg's [health] was appalling. Migraine headaches, dyspepsia, boils, and rheumatism headed the list of his complaints and infirmities. He proved particularly vulnerable to illness during periods of stress, indicating that much of his frailness may have been psychosomatic. . . . Psychosomatic illnesses are very real and debilitating, often brought on by difficult, intolerable, or frightening situations, of which Bragg faced many during the war years."[153] Indeed, many of the "frightening situations" with which Bragg had to deal during his Perryville, Stones River, and Chickamauga campaigns were brought on by his failure to inspirit—or even control—dissident corps and division commanders, several of whom were not only disloyal but plotted for his removal from command. Grady McWhiney, one of the most insightful of Bragg's biographers and analysts, has summed up the shortcomings on the professional side of Bragg's character:

Handicapped by poor health, he had no real taste for combat. . . . Nor did he have the ability to inspire confidence in his subordinates. Notoriously inept at getting along with people he disliked, he simply could not win the loyalty of his chief lieutenants. He lacked what has been called the common touch. By training and by preference a regular army man, contemptuous of volunteers and a democratic military establishment, he was unsuited to lead an army of individualistic citizen-soldiers. A mediocre tactician, he seemed unaware of the technological changes that had outdated pre-war assault tactics and strengthened the advantages of defensive combat.[154]

While one can accept that part of the last sentence regarding Bragg's failure to adapt to "technological changes" (such as the firepower of the rifle in the defense), it might be unfair to dub him a mediocre tactician. His weakness in switching from the strategical to the tactical role was not due to mediocrity, rather to four closely related factors, the first of which stemmed from his distrust of his senior subordinates to carry out the details of his operation plan. The second was his general pessimism regarding the capabilities of his soldiers and officers. The third—a weak point which may well have escaped Bragg's own attention—was his tendency sometimes to rely on verbal orders and at others to lack clarity in specifying what he wanted done in a written order. The fourth factor was an occasional inclination to remain aloof from a phase of combat, causing him at times to lose touch with reality.

On the positive side, the conclusion regarding the overlooked possibility of assigning Banks to an administrative role in the Union forces might well apply to Bragg's case. Jefferson Davis failed to recognize the value of taking advantage of Bragg's capabilities as a strategist and organizer by placing him in a high office such as chief of staff of the armies early in the war. Instead, Davis kept him in field command until he had, in McWhiney's words, "made a major contribution to Confederate defeat." That he made such a contribution was in great part due to his command failure to exploit his victory at Chickamauga, a victory he failed—or refused—to acknowledge at the time due to a retreat from reality.

John Bell Hood was a name rarely referred to in the South without the appellation "the gallant Hood" being used. The reason was simple enough: the title was as widely known as it had been fairly earned on a half dozen battlefields. Moreover, he had not only earned his reputation as a fighter, but in the process had gained the all-out admiration of his men, who would have—and did—follow him anywhere. Douglas Southall Freeman, in prefacing his references to Hood's leadership in three upcoming battles in 1862, had this to say: "He is now a division commander whose soldiers are, man for man, the best combat troops in the Army [of Northern Virginia]. . . . As the fighting quality of his troops is, in a measure, of his making, he appears to have a brilliant future."[155] As we know, Hood did fulfill that promise of a brilliant future, reaching its zenith as a battlefield leader that afternoon of the second day at Chickamauga, just after he had led his three divisions in the headlong attack that had wrecked Rosecrans' army and gained Hood his promotion to lieutenant general—and cost him his right leg from a bullet wound. It was a disabling wound—his second, following the crippling of his left arm at Gettysburg—that would have sent an ordinary man into an honorable retirement. Not Hood. As soon as he could walk with crutches and manage on horseback while strapped in the saddle, he was back in command of troops, this time as a corps commander.

And therein lies an all-important difference in the levels of command he achieved in a rise to rank and fame unsurpassed on either side in the war. He loved battle because he was a born fighter; he knew it and his men knew it. It seemed only natural that he came to be regarded as the best combat commander that could be relied on to lead a brigade or a division in an all-out attack. But once placed in command of an army he had reached a pinnacle where he could not maintain his balance, in his case a precarious balance between personal leadership and the essential qualities of a successful army commander: a mastery of strategy and tactics coupled with a firm grasp of logistics, administration, and command relations. When Davis wrote to Robert E. Lee asking his opinion of replacing Joseph Johnston with Hood, Lee replied to the president with his usual blend of clarity and tact: "Hood is a bold fighter. I am doubtful as to other qualities necessary."

Hood did possess strategic vision, but the brilliance of his planning was not combined with a commonsense view of the possible. In practice he could make far-reaching plans, but he lacked the patience and the intellectual discipline to tie up all the loose ends, to fit the means to the end. In essence, he was long on vision, but short on executing a strategic plan. There were other limiting factors. One was his distaste for logistics, which is understandable when one takes into account his restless nature in combination with his lifelong admiration for the physical feats of the heroes of legend and story. Another was his relations with his senior commanders, which may have been hampered by his physical inability to get everywhere he wanted to go on horseback. This was due, of course, to his having to be strapped in the saddle, which must have caused him to endure constant pain when he had to make his presence felt on the field or to make personal contact with his commanders. This physical limitation, by lessening his ability to communicate on a personal basis, may have contributed to his tendency to attribute some of his failures on campaign to his subordinates, such as Cheatham's delays and aborted attack at Spring Hill. Yet, in retracing Hood's all too human shortcomings, it seems almost unfair to look back on this cavalier, who represented the South's finest martial ideals, as a military failure, but the hard fact remains that one must share the common conclusion of historians: he was simply out of his depth as an army commander.

If one were seeking a contrast to Hood, both in personality and character of command, one would have to create a fictional character—if George Henry Thomas had not already existed. Where Hood may have been dashing and "seeking the bubble reputation even in the cannon's mouth," Thomas was quiet, reserved, and untouched by ambition even to the point of continuing to wear a colonel's eagle on his shoulder after he had been promoted to brigadier general. Where Hood may have conceived brilliant strategic goals, Thomas would methodically set a series of objectives that would lead step-by-step to the accomplishment of his mission. And where Hood was seeking fame in battle, Thomas had it thrust upon him when he became the "Rock of Chickamauga." There is an irony in the title itself. Before that battle and throughout his military career, both in peace and war, Thomas was known as a rock of a man who was as solid and steadfast as he appeared: six feet tall, weighing 200 pounds, and, as a war correspondent aptly described him, "hewn out of a large square block of the best-tempered material that men are made of, not scrimped anywhere, and square everywhere—square face, square shoulders, square step; blue eyes with depths in them . . . and the whole giving the idea of massive solidity, of the right kind of man to tie to."[156] He had always drawn comment as being exactly the man he appeared. Yet, though rock-solid in appearance and seemingly as reserved in manner, behind that solid shell was a mind whose keenness was enhanced by a calm way of reasoning and a tenacity of purpose that could be mistaken for inflexibility—a mistake once shared by Grant and Halleck, to their later chagrin. His command methods were as systematic as those of Rosecrans (this is not to be misconstrued as meaning that Thomas was a "pupil" of the latter) in that he took his major commanders into his confidence, both in his planning process and in the review of draft operation orders before they were issued. Perhaps the most pertinent observation that could be made about Thomas' command abilities would be that he *grew* in command. His record shows that he not only learned from personal experience, but must have put to use that centuries-old but little-tested advice of Polybius: "Whereas there are for all men two ways of improvement, to wit by one's own disasters or those of others, the former is the more vivid, the latter is the less harmful." Thomas undoubtedly had the opportunity to observe plenty of disasters on both sides during his progress up the ladder of command—from brigade to division to corps to army—and it is certain that he learned, not simply the hard way, but by increasingly developing confidence in his powers until he could demonstrate at Nashville that he had gained mastery of his own art at the highest operational level of command.

In summing up the essential nature of those six cases one cannot overlook their diversity, both in the character of each commander and the way in which it affected his style of command. There is, despite their diversity, a common thread that runs through them: *each had to create and develop his own methods of command*. None had the advantage of progressive schools of instruction or a systematic grounding in a doctrine expressly fitted to a high level of command over forces made up of thousands of civilian soldiers. Yet the responsibility was there, and each accepted it and did what he could with what he had. What each had to do—however well or badly managed—was to fashion his natural abilities in a practical way to accomplish what amounted to, in today's terms, his own on-the-job training. The outstanding feature in each case was its pragmatism. That pragmatism was not only exhibited in action during a campaign or a battle, but was reflected, in at least two ways, in how the commanders came to perceive the impracticality of trying to apply the tenets of the manuals or the presumptions of the theorists to solving their ever present problems.

In the first place, the commanders on both sides were only too well aware of the effectiveness of the rifle in the hands of defending infantry. They knew that they were being forced to employ the formations of linear tactics in attack and defense, simply because they were the only tools they had at hand. Under the pressure of time and existing conditions they couldn't afford the luxury of sitting back and visualizing—and experimenting with—tactical theories to solve their problems. As a consequence, they were forced to rely on the limited tactics that were available, particularly maneuver in the offense—for example, an envelopment, a turning movement, or weighting a main effort at a critical point—or face the inevitable toll of casualties from frontal attacks. That some commanders succeeded and some failed is to state the obvious; what is not so obvious is a realization that on the "right" occasion they made a tactical system work that was already proving inoperable. That the acknowledged masters of Civil War command could also misapply the system has been demonstrated conclusively when one considers the cases of Grant at Cold Harbor, Sherman at Kennesaw Mountain, and Lee on the third day at Gettysburg.

Secondly, and unfortunately for the commanders in question and their counterparts, they weren't able to avail themselves of the practical paradigms of Napoleonic warfare. Even the generals who had studied, or tried to study, Napoleon's grand tactics or the battlefield tactics of his generals found that they were unable to apply the exemplary models due to the pressure of time and prevailing conditions. This meant that their subordinates could not be trained for their roles, nor did the troops have either the training or combat experience to fight Napoleonic-style battles. While both sides had adopted a semblance of the *corps d'armée* to their use, the corps commanders had neither the indoctrination nor the experience to operate independently under a

grand tactical system like Napoleon's *bataillon carré*, where they were expected to engage a numerically superior enemy force or to maneuver to come
to the timely support of another corps. Moreover, the cavalry in both the
Union and Confederate armies, while becoming skilled in reconnaissance and
security as well as raiding on a grand scale, was neither organized nor trained
to operate en masse on the battlefield in conjunction with infantry and artillery. By the same token, the infantry and artillery were neither trained nor
expected to operate as a combined arms team with the cavalry. That was the
main reason why Civil War commanders lacked the capability to follow up a
success on the battlefield with a massive cavalry pursuit to exploit it.

Granted that Civil War commanders had, in spite of all the obstacles, developed a pragmatic art, what does that mean to an observer standing in the
doorway to the twenty-first century? In what way can that art mean anything
to us? The questions are best addressed in terms of two related periods of
time: the first would be the period extending from the end of the Civil War
to the present; the second would lie in the near future, conceivably extending
through the early decades of the twenty-first century. In either case the base-
line or starting point for an answer is based on the conclusion reached from
the foregoing cases—test cases if you will—*that they have left the legacy of a
pragmatic art*. If the conclusion is a valid one, the evidence for its validity
should be found in the first period.

The evidence, unsurprisingly, lies in the wartime careers of American commanders whose character and operations have withstood the test of history.
The first that comes to mind is that of Pershing in the First World War. Raised
almost overnight into command of the first American Expeditionary Force to
operate with allied armies far beyond American shores, Pershing had neither
the indoctrination nor the experience to arm himself for such an unprecedented mission, let alone one which had to be accomplished under the scrutiny of the Western world. Yet without a trained staff, an appropriately
organized headquarters, or experienced subordinate commanders and staffs
he set about overcoming a host of obstacles with only his own character and
common sense to guide him—and accomplished his mission to win the ac-
claim of his country.

Others readily present themselves throughout the global operations of the
Second World War. At the highest command level, Eisenhower and MacAr-
thur proved unquestionably their abilities to handle the task and successfully
complete their missions. At the highest operational levels the names of such
figures as Bradley, Stilwell, Patton, and Mark Clark stand out in our military
history as commanders who stood to profit from a legacy of pragmatism, leaders who were not only on their own but also knew that they could not afford
to fail in their times of trial. There are, of course, many other commanders in
the various theaters of war who deserve recognition, but whose accomplishments are beyond the scope of this exploration. There is, however, another
source of evidence that a pragmatic legacy did extend throughout the officer

corps in the period through the Second World War to the present. That was a universal tendency—one might say almost a second nature—of commanders in particular and senior officers in general to scoff at dependence upon "following the book," that is, an unquestioning acceptance of doctrine as exemplified by the field manuals and service school instruction. Why? Because such dependence showed a lack of professionalism, a lack of initiative as well as the absence of grounding in practical experience. The scoffing came from hard-nosed professionals whom Clausewitz would have considered "men whose military competence is beyond dispute," and who usually expressed their scorn in guidance to staffs or subordinate commanders.

The second period, that of the near future is, of course, open to all sorts of conjecture and speculation. Rather than indulge in useless presumptions it might prove more useful (and realistic) to look at a legacy of command as a challenge in a world where our country's leadership is needed but must be dealt with in pragmatic terms: how can the United States project global strategies and still make them affordable in economic and social terms? The answers are unquestionably beyond the scope of this work, but that military leadership of the highest quality will be a top priority is equally beyond question. In a world where the armored division will be as obsolete as the flintlock, where warfare between aircraft carrier groups will be as outdated as battleship engagements, and where the B-2 bomber will be as useless as the B-17 and B-29, an art of command will be as urgently in demand as the funds required to support the strategies of the future. The base on which that art must rest is a vital part of that challenge of the future.

Notes

1. John R. Elting, "Jomini, Disciple of Napoleon?" *Military Affairs* 28 (Spring 1964), 17–26.

2. U.S. Army Field Manual 100–5, *Fighting Future Wars*, 6–2, First Brassey's Edition 1994.

3. J. F. C. Fuller, *A Military History of the Western World*, 3 vols., Vol. II (New York, 1955), 527.

4. M. I. Finley, *Ancient History: Evidence and Models* (New York, 1986), 104.

5. Bell Irvin Wiley, *The Life of Billy Yank, the Common Soldier of the Union* (Louisiana State University Press, 1978), 54.

6. Ulysses Grant, cited in John Keegan, *The Mask of Command*, 188.

7. Stephen Crane, *The Red Badge of Courage* (New York, 1944), 35–46.

8. John Keegan, *The Face of Battle* (New York, 1976), 54.

9. Hans Delbrück, Letter of 19 August 1870, Gravelotte, "Hans Delbrück in Briefen," cited in Arden Bucholz, *Hans Delbrück and the German Military Establishment: War Images in Conflict* (University of Iowa Press, 1985), 23.

10. U.S. Department of the Army Technical Report 1–191, *Art and Requirements of Command (ARC)* by Joel N. Bloom, Adele N. Farber, et al. (prepared by the Franklin Institute Research Laboratories for the Office of the Director of Special Studies, Office of the Chief of Staff, Department of the Army, Contract No. DA 49–092–ARO-154, April 1967).

11. From the Introduction by Len Deighton (page 1) to Simon Goodenough's *Tactical Genius in Battle* (Oxford, England: Phaidon Press, 1979).

12. *The Military Maxims of Napoleon*, translated from the French by Lieutenant General Sir George C. D'Aguilar (New York, 1988).

13. Carl von Clausewitz, *On War*, edited and translated by Michael Howard and Peter Paret (Princeton University Press, 1976), 141.

14. Roger Beaumont, "Command Method: A Gap In Military Historiography," *Naval War College Review* (Winter 1979), 72.

15. Charles Royster, *The Destructive War: William Tecumseh Sherman, Stonewall Jackson and the Americans* (New York, 1991), 68.

16. Stephen Vincent Benet, *John Brown's Body* (New York: The Heritage Press, 1948), 228–230.

17. Royster, 47.

18. Official Records (O.R.): *The War of the Rebellion: A Compilation of the Official Records of the Union and Confederate Armies*, Series I, Vol. XII, Part II (Washington, 1885), 181.

19. O.R.: I, XII, II, 435.

20. Fred Harvey Harrington, *Fighting Politician: Major General N. P. Banks* (reprinted by permission of University of Pennsylvania Press, 1970; originally published American Historical Association, 1948), 63.

21. Edward J. Stackpole, *From Cedar Mountain to Antietam* (Harrisburg, PA, 1993), 31–32.

22. George H. Gordon, *Brook Farm to Cedar Mountain, in the War of the Great Rebellion, 1861–62* (Boston, 1883), 277.

23. O.R.: I, XII, III, 474.

24. Letter from Pope to Banks, 14 July 1862, cited in Harrington, 81.

25. Letter of 8 August 1862, cited in Harrington, 81.

26. Cited in Harrington, 81; O.R.: I, XII, II, 25–27 and 133–135.

27. Gordon, 282.

28. Cited in Harrington, 81–82.

29. Colonel G. L. Andrews, "The Battle of Cedar Mountain," in Massachusetts Military Historical Society, *Papers of the Military Historical Society of Massachusetts*, Vol. II: *The Virginia Campaign of 1862 under General Pope* (reprinted Wilmington, NC, 1898; originally published 1895), 416.

30. Stackpole, 63–64.

31. Andrews, 423–424.

32. Robert K. Krick, *Stonewall Jackson at Cedar Mountain* (University of North Carolina Press, 1990), 189.

33. Krick, 203–204.

34. Cited in Krick, 205.

35. Douglas Southall Freeman, *Lee's Lieutenants: A Study in Command*, 3 vols., Vol. II (New York, 1942), 37–38.

36. Stackpole, 70.

37. Freeman, II, 41.

38. Gordon, 305–308.

39. Freeman, II, 26 and note 53.

40. Andrews, 439.

41. Freeman, II, 46.

42. G. F. R. Henderson, *Stonewall Jackson and the American Civil War*, 2 vols., Vol. I (Secaucus, NJ, 1987), 58.

43. Freeman, II, 2 and note 6.

44. William S. Rosecrans, "The Campaign for Chattanooga," *Century Magazine* (May 1887), 129–130.

45. *The West Point Atlas of American Wars, 1689–1900*, Vol. I, edited by Vincent J. Esposito (New York, 1959), 108.

46. Rosecrans, 130.

47. Ibid., 131.

48. William M. Lamers, *The Edge of Glory: A Biography of General William S. Rosecrans, U.S.A.* (New York, 1961), 5–6.

49. James L. Morrison, Jr., "Educating the Civil War Generals: West Point, 1833–1861," *Military Affairs* (September 1974), 108–111.

50. Ibid., 109.

51. Lamers, 15.

52. Ibid., 13.

53. Glenn Tucker, *Chickamauga: Bloody Battle in the West* (Indianapolis, 1961), 35.

54. Lamers, 15.

55. Tucker, 40.

56. Ibid., 38–39.

57. As cited in Cozzens, *This Terrible Sound: The Battle of Chickamauga* (University of Illinois Press, 1992), 24.

58. Rosecrans, 129.

59. Cited in Herman Hattaway and Archer Jones, *How the North Won: A Military History of the Civil War* (University of Illinois Press, 1983), 444.

60. Rosecrans, 132.

61. Ibid.

62. Hattaway and Jones, *How the North Won*, 279.

63. Ibid., 444.

64. Shelby Foote, *The Civil War, a Narrative (Fredericksburg to Meridian)* (New York, 1958), 171.

65. Ibid., 172.

66. Don C. Seitz, *Braxton Bragg: General of the Confederacy* (Columbia, SC, 1924), 2–3.

67. Grady McWhiney, *Braxton Bragg and Confederate Defeat*, Vol. I: *Field Command*, (Columbia University Press, 1969), 82.

68. Ibid., Bragg to Sherman, March 1, 1848, cited in note 21, p. 88.

69. Seitz, *Braxton Bragg*, 15.

70. Steven E. Woodworth, *Jefferson Davis and His Generals* (University Press of Kansas, 1990), 94 (citing McWhiney, 202–203).

71. Archer Jones, *Civil War Command and Strategy: The Process of Victory and Defeat* (New York, 1992), 92.

72. *Battles and Leaders of the Civil War* (Secaucus, N.J.) III, 13.

73. Edward Hagerman, *The American Civil War and the Origins Of Modern Warfare: Ideas, Organization, and Field Command* (Indiana University Press, 1988), 178.

74. W. J. Wood, *Leaders and Battles: The Art of Military Leadership* (Noveto, CA, 1994), 272.

75. Judith Lee Hallock, *Braxton Bragg and Confederate Defeat*, Vol. 2, (University of Alabama Press, 1991), 271.

76. McWhiney, 28.

77. Arthur J. L. Fremantle, *Three Months in the Southern States* (London, Edinburgh, 1863), 145–146.

78. Tucker, 66.

79. Ibid., 67.

80. Thomas Lawrence Connelly, *Autumn of Glory: The Army of Tennessee, 1862–1865*, (Louisiana State University Press, 1971), 188.

81. O.R., I, XXX, II, 24, 27, 31–32.

82. Cozzens, 92.

83. Tucker, 123.

84. Cozzens, 111.

85. Connelly, 197.

86. Cozzens, 116.

87. Connelly, 201.

88. Ibid., 199.

89. Ibid., 202.

90. Tucker, 140.

91. O.R., I, XXX, I, 57.

92. General James Longstreet, *From Manassas to Appomattox* (reprint, New York, 1992), 438.

93. Cozzens, 302.

94. Ibid., 300.

95. Lamers, 334.

96. Cozzens, 295; based on O.R., I, XXX, I, 69.

97. Tucker, 198–199.

98. Foote, 719.

99. Tucker, 219.

100. Ibid., 206–207.

101. Connelly, 223.

102. O.R., I, XXX, I, 58–59.

103. John B. Turchin, *Chickamauga* (Chicago, 1888), 112.

104. Tucker, 251–259; Cozzens, 360–367; Turchin, 112–115.

105. Foote, 738.

106. Ibid.

107. Longstreet, 448–449.

108. O.R., I, XXX, I, 60.

109. Rosecrans, 134.

110. As cited in Tucker, 314, based on Alfred Lacey Hough, *Soldier in the West: The Civil War Letters of Alfred Lacey Hough* (University of Pennsylvania Press, 1957), note 151.

111. Longstreet, 452.

112. Cozzens, 9.

113. Cited in Cozzens, 469.

114. O.R., I, XXX, I, 140.

115. O.R., I, XXX, I, 142–143.

116. Cited in Tucker, 381.

117. *West Point Atlas of American Wars*, I, Map [page] 115.

118. Tucker, 389.

119. Lanza, Conrad H., *Napoleon and Modern War: His Military Maxims* (Harrisburg, PA, 1949), Maxim 73, p. 96.

120. Cited in Cozzens, 523.

121. Ibid., 531.

122. Ibid.

123. Steven E. Woodworth, *Jefferson Davis and His Generals: The Failure of Confederate Command in the West* (University Press of Kansas, 1990), 241.

124. Ibid., 291.

125. John B. Hood, *Advance and Retreat* (Indiana University Press, 1959), 254.

126. Woodworth, 292.

127. *West Point Atlas of American Wars*, I, 149.

128. Ibid., 150.

129. Richard M. McMurry, *John Bell Hood and the War for Southern Independence* (University Press of Kentucky, 1982), 8.

130. Woodworth, 268.

131. Ibid., 271.

132. Winston Groom, *Shrouds of Glory: From Atlanta to Nashville: The Last Great Campaign of the Civil War* (New York, 1995), 48–49.

133. Hattaway and Jones, 646.

134. O.R., I, XLV, I, 652.

135. *West Point Atlas of American Wars*, I, 152.

136. Hood, *Advance and Retreat*, 299–300.

137. Cited in Hattaway and Jones, 649.

138. Cited in Stanley F. Horn, *The Decisive Battle of Nashville* (Louisiana State University Press, 1956), 45 (from O.R., I, XLV, II, 3, 15–16).

139. Ibid., 45.

140. Ibid., 48.

141. Freeman Cleaves, *Rock of Chickamauga: The Life of General George H. Thomas* (University of Oklahoma Press, 1948), 9.

142. Thomas B. Van Horne, *The Life of Major-General George H. Thomas* (New York, 1882), 6.

143. Cleaves, 42.

144. Thomas Robson Hay, *Hood's Tennessee Campaign* (New York, 1929), 32–33.

145. Horn, 62.

146. Ibid., 44.

147. O.R., I, XLV, I, 654.

148. Connelly, 512.

149. Ibid., 513.

150. Martin Van Creveld, *Command in War* (Harvard University Press, 1985), 8.

151. Hattaway and Jones, 653–654.

152. Clausewitz, 169 and 156.

153. Hallock, *Braxton Bragg and Confederate Defeat*, II, 270.

154. Grady McWhiney, *Braxton Bragg and Confederate Defeat*, I, 390.

155. Freeman, II, xxviii-xxx.

156. Cited in Cleaves, 179.

Selected Bibliography

THE ART OF WAR: HISTORY, THEORY, COMMAND

Alger, John I. *The Quest for Victory: The History of the Principles of War*. Westport, CT, 1982.

ARC: Art and Requirements of Command. Department of the Army Technical Report 1–191. 4 Vols. Joel N. Bloom, Adele M. Farber, et al. The Franklin Institute Research Laboratories, 1967. Prepared for the Office of the Director of Special Studies, Office of the Chief of Staff, Department of the Army (Contract No. DA 49–092–ARO-154).

Ardant Du Picq, Charles J. J. J. *Battle Studies*. Harrisburg, PA, 1946.

Balck, Wilhelm. *Development of Tactics—World War*. Ft. Leavenworth, KS, 1922.

Bassford, Christopher. *Clausewitz in English: The Reception of Clausewitz in Britain and America, 1815–1945*. New York, 1994.

Beaumont, Roger A. "Command Method: A Gap in Military Historiography." *Naval War College Review* (Winter 1979), 61–74.

Becke, A. F. *An Introduction to the History of Tactics, 1740–1905*. London, 1909.

Blumenson, Martin, and Stokesbury, James L. *Masters of the Art of Command*. New York, 1975.

Bradley, Omar N. *A Soldier's Story*. New York, 1951.

Brinton, Crane; Craig, Gordon A.; and Gilbert, Felix. "Jomini." In Edward Mead Earle (ed.), *Makers of Modern Strategy: Military Thought from Machiavelli to Hitler*, 77–92. Princeton University Press, 1943.

Bucholz, Arden. *Hans Delbrück and the German Military Establishment: War Images in Conflict*. University of Iowa Press, 1985.

Burne, Alfred H. *The Art of War on Land*. Harrisburg, PA, 1947.

Camon, H. *La Guerre Napoléonienne: Les Systèmes d'Opérations, Théorie et Technique*. Paris, 1907.

————. *Quand et Comment Napoléon a Conçu Son Système de Bataille*. Paris, 1935.

————. *Quand et Comment Napoléon a Conçu Son Système de Manoeuvre*. Paris, 1931.

Chandler, David G. *The Campaigns of Napoleon*. New York, 1966.

————. *Dictionary of the Napoleonic Wars*. New York, 1979.

————. *On the Napoleonic Wars: Collected Essays*. Mechanicsburg, PA, 1994.

Clark, Mark W. *Calculated Risk*. New York, 1950.

Clausewitz, Carl von. *On War*. Edited and translated by Michael Howard and Peter Paret. Princeton University Press, 1976.

Colin, Jean L. A. *La Tactique et la Discipline dans les Armées de la Révolution (Correspondance du Général Schauenbourg)*. Paris, 1902.

————. *The Transformations of War*. London, 1912.

D'Aguilar, George C. *The Military Maxims of Napoleon*. New York, 1988.

Delbrück, Hans. *History of the Art of War: Within the Framework of Political History*. 4 vols. Translated by Colonel Walter J. Renfroe, Jr. Westport, CT, 1985.

Dixon, Norman. *On the Psychology of Military Incompetence*. London, 1976.

Dupuy, R. Ernest, and Dupuy, Trevor N. *The Encyclopedia of Military History—from 3500 B.C. to the Present*. New York, 1986.

Dupuy, Trevor N. *The Evolution of Weapons and Warfare*. New York, 1980.

————. *A Genius for War: The German Army and General Staff, 1807–1945*. Englewood Cliffs, NJ, 1977.

Earle, Edward Mead (ed.). *Makers of Modern Strategy: Military Thought from Machiavelli to Hitler*. Princeton University Press, 1943.

Eisenhower, Dwight D. *Crusade in Europe*. New York, 1948.

Elting, John R. "Jomini: Disciple of Napoleon?" *Military Affairs* 28 (Spring 1964), 17–26.

————. *Swords around a Throne: Napoleon's Grande Armée*. New York, 1988.

Erfurth, Waldemar. *Surprise*. Harrisburg, PA, 1943.

Finley, M. I. *Ancient History: Evidence and Models*. New York, 1986.

Fuller, J. F. C. *The Conduct of War, 1789–1961*. Rutgers University Press, 1961.

————. *Generalship: Its Diseases and Their Cure: A Study of the Personal Factors in Command*. Harrisburg, PA, 1936.

————. *A Military History of the Western World*. 3 vols. Vol. II. New York, 1955.

Gabriel, Richard A., and Savage, Paul L. *Crisis in Command: Mismanagement in the Army*. New York, 1978.

Gies, Joseph. *Crisis 1918: The Leading Actions, Strategies, and Events in the German Gamble for Total Victory on the Western Front*. New York, 1974.

Goerlitz, Walter. *History of the German General Staff, 1657–1945*. New York, 1953.

Griffith, Paddy. *Forward into Battle: Fighting Tactics from Waterloo to the Near Future*. Novato, CA, 1992.

Gudmundsson, Bruce I. *Storm Troop Tactics: Innovation in the German Army, 1914–1918*. New York, 1989.

Hays, Samuel H., and Thomas, William N. *Taking Command: The Art and Science of Military Leadership*. Harrisburg, PA, 1967.

Hittle, J. D. *Jomini and His Summary of the Art of War*. Harrisburg, PA, 1947.

————. *The Military Staff: Its History and Development*. Harrisburg, PA, 1949.

Hooker, Richard D., Jr. (ed.). *Maneuver Warfare: An Anthology*. Novato, CA, 1993.

Howard, Michael. "Jomini and the Classical Tradition in Military Thought." In Michael

Howard (ed.), *The Theory and Practice of War*, 3–20. Indiana University Press, 1965.

————. *The Franco–Prussian War*. New York, 1962.

————. "Men against Fire: The Doctrine of the Offensive in 1914." In Peter Paret with Gordon A. Craig and Felix Gilbert (eds.), *Makers of Modern Strategy from Machiavelli to the Nuclear Age*, 510–526. Princeton University Press, 1986.

Jomini, Antoine Henri. *The Art of War*. Translated by G. H. Mendell and W. P. Craighill. Philadelphia, 1862.

Jones, Archer. *The Art of War in the Western World*. University of Illinois Press, 1987.

Keegan, John. *The Face of Battle*. New York, 1976.

————. *The Mask of Command*. New York, 1987.

Lanza, Conrad H. *Napoleon and Modern War: His Military Maxims*. Harrisburg, PA, 1949.

Leckie, Robert. *The Wars of America*. New York, 1981.

Liddell Hart, B. H. *The Ghost of Napoleon*. Yale University Press, 1934.

————. *Strategy*. New York, 1957.

Lloyd, E. M. *A Review of the History of Infantry*. London, 1908.

Lossow, Walter von. "Mission-Type Tactics versus Order-Type Tactics." *Military Review* (June 1977), 87–91.

MacMunn, George. *Leadership through the Ages*. Freeport, NY, 1935.

Maude, F. N. *The Jena Campaign 1806*. New York, 1909.

McNeill, William H. *The Pursuit of Power*. University of Chicago Press, 1982.

Millet, Allan R., and Maslowski, Peter. *For the Common Defense: A Military History of the United States of America*. New York, 1984.

Moltke, Helmuth von. *Moltke on the Art of War: Selected Writings*. Edited by Daniel J. Hughes. Novato, CA, 1993.

————. *Strategy: Its Theory and Application: The Wars for German Unification, 1866– 1871*. Westport, CT, 1971.

Morison, Samuel Eliot. *The Oxford History of the American People*. Oxford University Press, 1965.

Murray, Williamson; Macgregor, Knox; and Bernstein, Alvin (eds.). *The Making of Strategy: Rulers, States, and War*. Cambridge University Press, 1994.

O'Connor, Raymond G. *American Defense Policy in Perspective: From Colonial Times to the Present*. New York, 1965.

Paret, Peter. "Napoleon and the Revolution in War." In Peter Paret with Gordon A. Craig and Felix Gilbert (eds.), *Makers of Modern Strategy from Machiavelli to the Nuclear Age*, 123–142. Princeton University Press, 1986.

Paret, Peter, with Craig, Gordon A., and Gilbert, Felix (eds.). *Makers of Modern Strategy from Machiavelli to the Nuclear Age*. Princeton University Press, 1986.

Patton, George S., Jr. *War As I Knew It*. Boston, 1947.

Quimby, Robert S. *The Background of Napoleonic Warfare*. Columbia University Press, 1957.

Rommel, Erwin. *Attacks*. Vienna, VA, 1979.

Roots of Strategy, Book 3:3 Military Classics: von Leeb's "Defense"; von Freytag-Loringhoven's "The Power of Personality in War": Erfurth's *"Surprise."* Harrisburg, PA, 1991.

Ross, Steven. *From Flintlock to Rifle: Infantry Tactics, 1740–1866*. Cranbury, NJ, 1979.

Rothenberg, Gunther E. *The Art of Warfare in the Age of Napoleon*. London, 1977.

Senger und Etterlin, Frido von. *Neither Fear nor Hope*. Novato, CA, 1989.

Shapiro, David. *Neurotic Styles*. New York, 1965.

Shy, John. "Jomini." In Peter Paret with Gordon A. Craig and Felix Gilbert (eds.), *Makers of Modern Strategy from Machiavelli to the Nuclear Age*, 143–185. Princeton University Press, 1986.

Tuchman, Barbara W. *Stilwell and the American Experience in China, 1911–45*. New York, 1971.

United States Army. *Field Manual, FM 100–5*. 1986.

United States War Department, Military Intelligence Service, Special Series No. 8, *German Tactical Doctrine*. 1942.

———. *Regulations for the Army of the United States, 1857*. New York, 1857.

Van Creveld, Martin. *Command in War*. Harvard University Press, 1985.

———. *Supplying War: Logistics from Wallenstein to Patton*. Cambridge University Press, 1977.

———. *Technology and War—From 2000 B.C. to the Present*. New York, 1989.

Veaudry, Wallace F., and Campbell, John G. "A New Look at Leadership Evaluation." *Army* (February 1974), 23–26.

Weigley, Russell F. *The Age of Battles: The Quest for Decisive Warfare from Breitenfeld to Waterloo*. Indiana University Press, 1991.

———. "American Strategy from Its Beginnings through the First World War." Peter Paret with Gordon A. Craig and Felix Gilbert (eds.), *Makers of Modern Strategy from Machiavelli to the Nuclear Age*, 408–443. Princeton University Press, 1986.

———. *History of the United States Army*. Indiana University Press, 1984.

———. *Towards an American Army: Military Thought from Washington to Marshall*. Columbia University Press, 1962.

Wilkinson, Spencer. *The Brain of an Army: A Popular Account of the German General Staff*. London, 1890.

Williams, T. Harry. *Americans at War: The Development of the American Military System*. Louisiana State University Press, 1962.

Wood, William J. "Forgotten Sword." *Military Affairs* XXXIV, No. 3 (October 1970), 77–82.

Woods, David L. *A History of Tactical Communication Techniques*. Orlando, FL, 1965.

Wylie, J. C. *Military Strategy: A General Theory of Power Control*. Rutgers University Press, 1967.

AMERICAN CIVIL WAR: CAMPAIGNS, BATTLES, COMMANDERS

Adams, Michael C. C. *Our Masters the Rebels: A Speculation on Union Military Failure in the East, 1861–1865*. Harvard University Press, 1978.

Aimone, Alan C., and Barbara. *A User's Guide to the Official Records of the American Civil War*. Shippensburg, PA, 1993.

Alexander, Bevin. *How Great Generals Win*. New York, 1993.

Ambrose, Stephen E. *Halleck: Lincoln's Chief of Staff*. Louisiana State University Press, 1962.

Anderson, Archer. "The Campaign and Battle of Chickamauga." *Virginia Pamphlets* 52 (1881), 1–38. Charlottesville, VA.

Annals of the Army of the Cumberland. Philadelphia, 1864.

Bean, W. G. *Stonewall's Man: Sandie Pendleton*. University of North Carolina Press, 1959.

Benet, Stephen Vincent. *John Brown's Body*. New York, 1948.

Bennison, R. T. "General Braxton Bragg." *The Field Artillery Journal* (November–December, 1931), 601–611. Fort Sill, OK.

Beringer, Richard E.; Hattaway, Herman; Jones, Archer; and Still, William N., Jr. *Why the South Lost the Civil War*. University of Georgia Press, 1986.

Black, Robert C. III. *The Railroads of the Confederacy*. University of North Carolina Press, 1952.

Blackford, Charles M. III (ed.). *Letters from Lee's Army*. New York, 1947.

Boatner, Mark M. III. *The Civil War Dictionary*. New York, 1959.

Boswell, James Keith. "The Diary of a Confederate Staff Officer." *Civil War Times Illustrated* (April 1976).

Bowers, John. *Chickamauga and Chattanooga: The Battles That Doomed the Confederacy*. New York, 1994.

———. "The Rock of Chickamauga." *MHQ: The Quarterly Journal of Military History* 3 (Winter 1991), 50–59.

Bragg, Braxton. "General Braxton Bragg's Report of the Battle of Chickamauga." *Our Living and Our Dead: Official Organ, N.C. Branch, Southern Historical Society* I (1875). Raleigh, NC.

Cain, Marvin R. "A Face of Battle Needed: An Assessment of Motives and Men in Civil War Historiography." *Civil War History* 28 (1982), 5–27.

Caldwell, Robert Granville. *James A. Garfield: Party Chieftain*. New York, 1931.

Casey, Silas. *Infantry Tactics for the Instruction, Exercise and Manoeuvers of the Soldier, a Company, Line of Skirmishers, Battalion, Brigade, or Corps d'Armée*. 3 vols. New York, 1862.

Chambers, Lenoir. *Stonewall Jackson*. 2 vols. New York, 1959.

Cist, Henry M. *The Army in the Civil War*. Vol. III: *The Army of the Cumberland*. New York, 1883–1885.

Cleaves, Freeman. *Rock of Chickamauga: The Life of General George H. Thomas*. University of Oklahoma Press, 1948.

Cleburne, Patrick. "General Cleburne's Report of the Battle of Chickamauga." In *The Land We Love*, 249–254. Charlotte, NC, 1866.

Clopton, J. J. *The True Stonewall Jackson*. Baltimore, 1913.

Commager, Henry Steele. *The Blue and the Gray: The Story of the Civil War As Told by Participants*. 2 vols. New York, 1950.

Connelly, Thomas Lawrence. *Autumn of Glory: The Army of Tennessee, 1862–1865*. Louisiana State University Press, 1971.

———. *Civil War Tennessee: Battles and Leaders*. University of Tennessee Press, 1979.

Connelly, Thomas Lawrence, and Jones, Archer. *The Politics of Command: Factions and Ideas in Confederate Strategy*. Louisiana State University Press, 1973.

Cooke, Philip St. George. *Cavalry Tactics: or Regulations for the Instruction, Formations and Movements of the Cavalry of the Army and Volunteers of the United States*. 2 vols. Philadelphia, 1862.

Cozzens, Peter. *This Terrible Sound*. University of Illinois Press, 1992.

Crabb, Alfred Leland. "Twilight of the Nashville Gods." *Tennessee Historical Quarterly* 15 (December 1956), 291–305.

Crane, Stephen. *The Red Badge of Courage*. New York, 1944.

Crow, Vernon H. "Confederate Indecision and Delay: The Empty Victory of Chickamauga." *The Kepi* (February–March 1984), 16–21.

Dabney, R. L. *Life and Campaigns of Lieut.-Gen. Thomas J. Jackson*. New York, 1866.

Dana, Charles A. *Recollections of the Civil War*. New York, 1898.

Davis, William C. *Rebels & Yankees: The Commanders of the Civil War*. New York,
1990.

———. *Rebels & Yankees: The Fighting Men of the Civil War*. New York, 1989.

Dictionary of American Biography. Edited by Allan Johnson and Dumas Malone. New
York, 1931–1932.

Dolton, George E. "Points of Dispute regarding Chickamauga." In *Blue and Gray*, Vol.
II, 402–405, 1893.

Douglas, Henry Kyd. *I Rode with Stonewall*. University of North Carolina Press, 1940.

Dowdey, Clifford. *The Land They Fought For*. Garden City, NY, 1955.

——— (ed.). *The Wartime Papers of R. E. Lee*. New York, 1961.

Downey, Fairfax. *Storming of the Gateway: Chattanooga, 1863*. New York, 1960.

Dupuy, R. Ernest, and Dupuy, Trevor N. *Brave Men and Great Captains*. Fairfax, VA,
1984.

Durham, Walter T. *Nashville: The Occupied City*. Nashville, 1985.

———. *Reluctant Partners: Nashville and the Union, July 1, 1863 to June 30, 1865*.
Nashville, n.d.

Dyer, John P. *The Gallant Hood*. Indianapolis, New York, 1950.

Eckenrode, H. J. and Conrad, Bryan. *James Longstreet: Lee's War Horse*. University
of North Carolina Press, 1936.

Ellsworth, Eliot, Jr. *West Point in the Confederacy*. New York, 1941.

English, John Alan. "Confederate Field Communications." M.A. thesis, Duke University, 1964.

Farwell, Byron. *Stonewall: A Biography of General Thomas J. Jackson*. New York, 1992.

Fieberger, G. J. *Campaigns of the American Civil War*. West Point, NY, 1914.

Fisk, Wilbur. *Hard Marching Every Day: The Civil War Letters of Private Wilbur Fisk*.
University Press of Kansas, 1992.

Foote, Shelby. *The Civil War: A Narrative*. 3 vols. New York, 1974.

Freeman, Douglas Southall (ed.). *A Calendar of Confederate Papers: With a Bibliog-
raphy of Some Confederate Publications*. Richmond, 1908.

———. *Lee's Lieutenants: A Study in Command*. 3 vols. New York, 1942.

Fremantle, Arthur, J. L. *Three Months in the Southern States*. Edinburgh, London,
1863.

French, Samuel G. *Two Wars: An Autobiography of Gen. Samuel G. French*. Nashville,
1901.

Fuller, Claude E. *The Rifled Musket*. Harrisburg, PA, 1958.

Gibbon, John. *The Artillerist's Manual*. New York, 1860.

Gibbs, Shirley M. "Lee's Command Procedures." M.A. thesis, Duke University, 1962.

Gilmore, James R. "*Garfield's Ride at Chickamauga*." *McClure's Magazine* 5, (1895),
357–360.

Gittings, John G. *Personal Recollections of Stonewall Jackson*. Cincinnati, 1899.

Glatthaar, Joseph T. *Partners in Command: The Relationship between Leaders in the
Civil War*. New York, 1991.

Gordon, George H. *Brook Farm to Cedar Mountain, in the War of the Great Rebellion, 1861–62*. Boston, 1883.

Gracie, Archibald. *The Truth about Chickamauga*. Boston, 1911.

Grant, U. S. *Personal Memoirs of U. S. Grant*. New York, 1895.

Griess, Thomas E. "Dennis Hart Mahan: West Point Professor and Advocate of Military Professionalism, 1830–1871." Ph.D. dissertation, Duke University, 1968.

Griffith, Paddy. *Rally Once Again: Battle Tactics of the American Civil War*. Ramsbury, Wiltshire, England, 1989.

Groom, Winston. *Shrouds of Glory: From Atlanta to Nashville: The Last Great Campaign of the Civil War*. New York, 1995.

Hagerman, Edward. *The American Civil War and the Origins of Modern Warfare: Ideas, Organization, and Field Command*. Indiana University Press, 1988.

Hagerman, Edward. "From Jomini to Dennis Hart Mahan: The Evolution of Trench Warfare and the American Civil War." In John T. Hubbell (ed.), *Battles Lost and Won: Essays from Civil War History*. Westport, CT, 1975.

Halleck, H. Wager. *Elements of Military Art and Science, or Course of Instruction in Strategy, Fortification, Tactics of Battles, etc*. New York, 1846.

Hallock, Judith Lee. *Braxton Bragg and Confederate Defeat*. Vol. II. University of Alabama Press, 1991.

Hardee, W. J. *Rifle and Light Infantry Tactics for the Exercise and Manoeuvers of Troops When Acting as Light Infantry or Riflemen*. Memphis, 1861.

Harrington, Fred Harvey. *Fighting Politician: Major General N. P. Banks*. Reprinted by permission of University of Pennsylvania Press, 1970. (Originally published by American Historical Association, 1948.)

Harsh, Joseph L. "Battlesword and Rapier: Clausewitz, Jomini, and the American Civil War." *Military Affairs* 38 (1974), 133–138.

Hattaway, Herman, and Jones, Archer. *How the North Won: A Military History of the Civil War*. University of Illinois Press, 1983.

Hay, Thomas Robson. "Braxton Bragg and the Southern Confederacy." *Georgia Historical Quarterly* IX, No. 4 (December 1925). Savannah, GA, 1925.

———. "The Davis–Hood–Johnston Controversy of 1864." *Mississippi Valley Historical Review* XI (1924), 54–84.

———. *Hood's Tennessee Campaign*. New York, 1929.

Helniak, Roman J., and Hewitt, Lawrence L. (eds.). *The Confederate High Command & Related Topics*. Shippensburg, PA, 1990.

Henderson, G. F. R. *Stonewall Jackson and the American Civil War*. 2 vols. Secaucus, NJ, 1987.

Hennessy, John J. *Return to Bull Run: The Campaign and Battle of Second Manassas*. New York, 1993.

Hicks, Roger W., and Schultz, Frances E. (eds.). *Battlefields of the Civil War*. Topsfield, MA, 1989.

Hill, D. H. "Gen'l D. H. Hill's Report of the Battle of Chickamauga." In *Our Living and Our Dead: Official Organ, N.C. Branch, Southern Historical Society*. Vol. I. Raleigh, NC, 1875.

Hood, John B. *Advance and Retreat*. Indiana University Press, 1959.

Horn, Stanley F. *The Army of Tennessee*. University of Oklahoma Press, 1952.

———. *The Decisive Battle of Nashville*. Louisiana State University Press, 1956.

Hotchkiss, Jedediah. *Make Me a Map of the Valley: The Civil War Journal of Stonewall Jackson's Topographer*. Southern Methodist University Press, 1973.

Hough, Alfred Lacey. *Soldier in the West: The Civil War Letters of Alfred Lacey Hough*. University of Pennsylvania Press, 1957.

Hubbell, John T. (ed.). *Battles Lost and Won: Essays from Civil War History*. Westport, CT, 1975.

Hurst, Jack. *Nathan Bedford Forrest: A Biography*. New York, 1993.

Jamieson, Perry David. "The Development of Civil War Tactics." Ph.D. dissertation, Wayne State University, 1979.

Johnson, Richard W. *Memoir of Maj.-Gen. George H. Thomas*. Philadelphia, 1881.

Johnston, Joseph E. *Narrative of Military Operations*. New York, 1874.

Jones, Archer. *Civil War Command and Strategy: The Process of Victory and Defeat*. New York, 1992.

———. "Jomini and the Strategy of the American Civil War, A Reinterpretation." *Military Affairs* 34 (1970), 127–131.

Kennedy, Frances H. (ed.). *Civil War Battlefield Guide*. Boston, 1990.

Korn, Jerry. *The Fight for Chattanooga*. Alexandria, 1985.

Krick, Robert K. *Stonewall Jackson at Cedar Mountain*. University of North Carolina Press, 1990.

Lamers, William M. *The Edge of Glory: A Biography of General William S. Rosecrans, U.S.A.* New York, 1961.

Linderman, Gerald F. *Embattled Courage: The Experience of Combat in the American Civil War*. New York, 1987.

Livermore, Thomas L. *Numbers and Losses in the Civil War in America*. Boston and New York, 1900.

Longstreet, James. *From Manassas to Appomattox*. (Reprint). New York, 1992.

Luvaas, Jay. *The Military Legacy of the Civil War: The European Inheritance*. University of Chicago Press, 1959.

Mahan, Dennis Hart. *Advanced-Guard, Out-Post, and Detachment Service of Troops, with the Essential Principles of Strategy and Grand Tactics for the Use of Officers of the Militia and Volunteers*. New York, 1847; and 2nd edition, 1863.

———. *A Complete Treatise on Field Fortification*. New York, 1836.

Marshall, Albert O. *Army Life; From a Soldier's Journal, 1861–64*. Joliet, IL, 1884.

Marshall, David J. "The Confederate Army's Signal Corps." In Max L. Marshall (ed.), *The Story of the U.S. Army Signal Corps*. New York, 1965.

Marshall, Max L. (ed.). *The Story of the U.S. Army Signal Corps*. New York, 1965.

Martin, W. T. "A Defense of General Bragg at Chickamauga." *Southern Historical Society Papers* XI (1883).

Massachusetts Military Historical Society. *Papers of the Military Historical Society of Massachusetts*. Vol. II: *The Virginia Campaign of 1862 under General Pope*. (Original, 1895). Reprint, Wilmington, NC, 1898.

McClellan, George B. *Regulations and Instructions for the Field Service of the U.S. Cavalry in Time of War*. Philadelphia, 1861.

McKinney, Francis F. *Education in Violence: The Life of George H. Thomas and the History of the Army of the Cumberland*. Wayne State University Press, 1961.

McMurry, Richard M. *John Bell Hood and the War for Southern Independence*. University Press of Kentucky, 1982.

——. *Two Great Rebel Armies: An Essay in Confederate Military History.* University of North Carolina Press, 1989.

McPherson, James M. (ed.). *The Atlas of the Civil War.* New York, 1994.

—— (ed.). *Battle Chronicles of the Civil War 1864.* New York, 1989.

McWhiney, Grady. *Braxton Bragg and Confederate Defeat.* Vol. I: *Field Command.* Columbia University Press, 1969.

——. "Who Whipped Whom? Confederate Defeat Reexamined." In John T. Hubbell (ed.), *Battles Lost and Won: Essays from Civil War History,* 261–282. Westport, CT, 1975.

McWhiney, Grady, and Jamieson, Perry D. *Attack and Die: Civil War Military Tactics and the Southern Heritage.* University of Alabama Press, 1982.

Military Analysis of the Civil War (An Anthology by the Editors of "Military Affairs"). Millwood, NY, 1977.

Moore, John G. "Mobility and Strategy in the Civil War." *Military Affairs* 64 (1960), 68–77.

Morrison, James L., Jr. *The Best School in the World: West Point, the Pre–Civil War Years, 1833–1866.* Kent State University Press, 1986.

——. "Educating the Civil War Generals: West Point, 1833–1861." *Military Affairs* (September 1974), 108–111.

Moseley, Thomas Vernon. "Evolution of the American Civil War Infantry Tactics." Ph.D. dissertation, University of North Carolina, 1967.

Munden, Kenneth, and Beers, Henry Putney. *The Union: A Guide to Federal Archives Relating to the Civil War.* Washington, DC, 1986.

Naisawald, L. Van Loan. *Grape and Canister: The Story of the Field Artillery of the Army of the Potomac, 1861–1865.* Oxford University Press, 1960.

Nesmith, Vardell Edwards, Jr. "The Quiet Paradigm Change: Evolution of the Field Artillery Doctrine of the United States, 1861–1905." Ph.D. dissertation, Duke University, 1977.

O'Connor, Richard. *Hood: Cavalier General.* New York, 1949.

——. *Thomas: Rock of Chickamauga.* New York, 1948.

Official Records (O.R.): *The War of the Rebellion: A Compilation of the Official Records of the Union and Confederate Armies.* 128 vols. Washington, DC, 1885.

Piatt, Donn. *General George H. Thomas: A Critical Biography.* Cincinnati, 1893.

Pohl, James W. "The Influence of Antoine Henri de Jomini on Winfield Scott's Campaign in the Mexican War." *Southwestern Historical Quarterly* 77 (1973), 85–110.

Pratt, Fletcher. *Eleven Generals: Studies in American Command.* New York, 1949.

——. *Ordeal by Fire.* New York, 1935.

——. *Stanton: Lincoln's Secretary of War.* Westport, CT, 1970.

Rogers, J. L. *The Civil War Battles of Chickamauga and Chattanooga.* Chattanooga, TN, 1942.

Ropes, John Codman. *The Army in the Civil War.* Vol. IV: *The Army under Pope.* New York, 1885.

——. *The Story of the Civil War.* Part II: *The Campaigns of 1862.* 3 vols. New York, 1898.

Rosecrans, William S. "The Campaign for Chattanooga." *Century Magazine* (May 1887), 130–135.

Royster, Charles. *The Destructive War: William Tecumseh Sherman, Stonewall Jackson and the Americans*. New York, 1991.

Scaife, William R. *Hood's Campaign for Tennessee*. Atlanta, 1986.

Schutz, Wallace J., and Trenerry, Walter N. *Abandoned by Lincoln: A Military Biography of General John Pope*. University of Illinois Press, 1990.

Seitz, Don C. *Braxton Bragg: General of the Confederacy*. Columbia, SC, 1924.

Selby, John. *Stonewall Jackson as Military Commander*. Princeton, NJ, 1968.

Sherman, William T. *Memoirs of General William T. Sherman*. Vol. II. New York, 1875.

Smith, John C. *The Right of the Federal Army at Chickamauga*. Chicago, 1894.

Smith, Page. *Ordeal by Fire*. 5 vols. Vol. V. New York, 1982.

Sorrel, G. Moxley. *Recollections of a Confederate Staff Officer*. ed. Bell Irvine Wiley. Jackson, TN, 1958.

Stackpole, Edward J. *From Cedar Mountain to Antietam*. Harrisburg, PA, 1993.

———. "Generalship in the Civil War." *Military Affairs* (Summer 1960), 57–67.

Steele, Matthew Forney. *American Campaigns*. 2 vols. Washington, DC, 1951.

Stephens, Michael W. "Learning from Civil War Battles." *Marine Corps Gazette* (June 1988), 27–29.

Stevenson, Paul. *War Gaming in History: The American Civil War*. New York, 1990.

Stout, L. H. *Reminiscences of General Braxton Bragg*. Hattiesburg, MS, 1942.

Sword, Wiley. *Embrace an Angry Wind: The Confederacy's Last Hurrah: Spring Hill, Franklin and Nashville*. New York, 1992.

Taggart, Joseph. *Biographical Sketches of the Eminent American Patriots*. Kansas City, MO, 1907.

Tanner, Robert G. *Stonewall in the Valley: Thomas J. "Stonewall" Jackson's Shenandoah Valley Campaign, Spring 1862*. Garden City, NY, 1976.

Thompson, George Raynor. "Civil War Signals." *Military Affairs* 18 (1954), 188–201.

Tucker, Glenn. *Chickamauga: Bloody Battle in the West*. Indianapolis, 1961.

Turchin, John B. *Chickamauga*. Chicago, 1888.

Turner, George Richard. *Victory Rode the Rails: The Strategic Place of the Railroads in the Civil War*. Indianapolis, 1953.

Vandiver, Frank E. *Mighty Stonewall*. New York, 1957.

———. *Rebel Brass: The Confederate Command System*. Louisiana State University Press, 1956.

Van Horne, Thomas B. *History of the Army of the Cumberland*. 2 vols. Vol. II. Cincinnati, 1875.

———. *The Life of Major-General George H. Thomas*. New York, 1882.

Wade, Arthur P. "Roads to the Top—An Analysis of General-Officer Selection in the United States Army, 1789–1898." *Military Affairs* (December 1976), 157–163.

Wagner, Arthur L. "Hasty Intrenchments in the War of Secession." In *Papers of the Military Historical Society of Massachusetts*, Vol. XIII, 129–153. Boston, 1913, 1895–1914.

Warner, Ezra J. *Generals in Blue: Lives of the Union Commanders*. Louisiana State University Press, 1964.

———. *Generals in Gray: Lives of the Confederate Commanders*. Louisiana State University Press, 1959.

Wert, Jeffry. *General James Longstreet, the Confederacy's Most Controversial Soldier— A Biography*. New York, 1993.

West Point Atlas of American Wars, 1689–1900. Vol. I. Edited by Vincent J. Esposito. New York, 1959.

Westrate, E. V. *Those Fatal Generals.* Port Washington, NY, 1936.

Wheeler, Richard. *We Knew Stonewall Jackson.* New York, 1977.

Williams, Kenneth P. *Lincoln Finds a General: A Military Study of the Civil War.* 5 vols. Vol. V. New York, 1959.

Williams, T. Harry (ed.). *Military Analysis of the Civil War: An Anthology by the Editors of Military Affairs.* Millwood, NY, 1977.

———. "The Military Leadership of North and South." In David Herbert Donald (ed.), *Why the North Won the Civil War.* Louisiana State University Press, 1960.

———. "The Return of Jomini—Some Thoughts on Recent Civil War Writing." *Military Affairs* 39 (December 1975), 204–206.

Wilson, James Harrison. *Under the Old Flag.* 2 vols. Vol. II. Westport, CT, 1971.

Wise, Jennings Cropper. *The Long Arm of Lee: The History of the Artillery of the Army of Northern Virginia.* Oxford University Press, 1959.

Woodward, C. Vann (ed.). *Mary Chesnut's Civil War.* Yale University Press, 1981.

Woodworth, Steven E. *Jefferson Davis and His Generals: The Failure of Confederate Command in the West.* University Press of Kansas, 1990.

Wyeth, John Allan. *That Devil Forrest: Life of General Nathan Bedford Forrest.* Louisiana State University Press, 1959.

Index

About the Author

W. J. WOOD is a retired U.S. Army lieutenant colonel whose background includes not only professional authorship but also combat experience in World War II and the Korean War, a decade spent in professional war gaming for weapons systems analysis at the Army Materiel Command, and a lifetime study of military history. The combination of these qualifications has made him well-suited to study the art of command. He is the author of *Leaders and Battles* (1984) and *Battles of the Revolutionary War* (1990).